Preface

This is a book about knowing that you have choices—about life-and-death decisions.

Most of us tend to think about death in the abstract, as something that is far removed, distant, and inconceivable, something that happens to other people, not to us. Even until a few decades ago, we did not talk openly about death. It was not until Elisabeth Kübler-Ross, the psychiatrist who counseled thousands of dying patients, wrote her book in 1969 that death came out of the closet and reached the consciousness of millions of people.

Yet the circumstances in which we die have changed dramatically in the last twenty years. I personally became acutely aware of this phenomenon while counseling hundreds of patients and families in the throes of terminal illness and while serving on a bioethics committee of a hospital. During that time, I learned not only that people die in new ways in hospitals, but also that dying can become an ordeal for patients and families who are not well informed about choices. The choices I mean are those about whether to extend life and prolong the dying process.

I remember the case of Mrs. J., who had just turned eighty-six and had been rushed to the hospital by ambulance. There she lay in the intensive-care unit, heavily sedated and semiconscious. She was hooked up to twenty wires and tubes that pumped oxygen, medicines, and chemical nutrients into her and drained out urine, secretions, and used air. She lay underneath an array of machines and monitors covering an entire wall. Several screens of green digital readouts displayed the innermost secrets of her poorly functioning body. A team of green-clothed technicians and nurses swarmed around the room, occasionally glancing at her, some staring at the screens with great intensity.

I heard of her case in the ethics committee when her family objected to further treatment. She had already waged a valiant battle against breast cancer, having received radiation therapy and having enjoyed five more years of life. Now, she was succumbing to pneumonia and septic shock, was on the edge of coma, and was totally unaware of her new destiny in the grinding wheels of medical technology.

"All she wanted was a quiet and peaceful death," said her daughter to the hospital ethics committee. The committee members listened with interest, some asking whether Mrs. J. had left a living will.

"No, I don't think she even knew about that sort of thing. All she wanted was to die quietly at home. Please, can't you leave her alone and let her rest without interfering with her wishes? I know that's what she wanted, and I would feel terrible if she knew what we were doing to her."

It was heart-wrenching to watch the devoted daughter pleading for her mother as if we were judges in a court. I felt compassion for the family caught in a web of hospital regulations, legal statutes, and medical zeal. I couldn't help thinking to myself, "But who are we to sit here, discussing this woman's choice and her mother's desperate plight? Are we slaves to our machines, or are we in charge of our technology? When will our laws catch up with the new emotional and social demands created by the high technology surrounding us?"

Modern technology is a wonderful thing. It can extend life for many people who years ago would have died much sooner. But for others, it can prolong the dying process to the point of absurdity or tragedy. Among the advances, we list cardiac pacemakers; cardiac bypass operations; heart, kidney, liver, and bone marrow transplants; and kidney dialysis—to name just a few. Nowadays in hospitals, there are ways of keeping people alive almost indefinitely with the help of respirators, artificial feeding, and other life-support measures, whether people are conscious or not.

But is this what people really want? Life at any cost, regardless of its quality, plus the pain and the suffering of all those involved?

It is only when one deals with real-life situations that dying takes on a meaningful dimension. An increasingly aware public is asking new questions: Can we expect the truth from our doctors? Can we retain control and make our own decisions about life-and-death situations? Do we have a choice about withholding or withdrawing treatment in certain circumstances? Do we have the right to expect a gentle and good death? Can we hope for a painless death? Can we avoid the humiliation that comes with a total deterioration of the body and the person? Who will help make a final choice if we lose control? These are just a few of the questions that are being asked increasingly in the complicated world we now live in.

In this book, I plan to provide you with enough information about life-sustaining treatments in the end stage of life to enable you to make informed decisions for yourself and for your family. It is my conviction that life-and-death decisions must be different for everyone, but that appropriate decisions can be made only with sufficient information. That means knowing about the latest developments in medical care, the legal and ethical issues, and current thinking within the nursing and medical professions.

The ultimate goal is to promote further dialogue on the issues surrounding life-sustaining measures, including a discussion of new ways to achieve a death that is painless and that allows for dignity.

This book deals with the ethical problems concerning only competent and incompetent adults. It does not include any discussion about children, as they are a major topic in themselves.

The book can be read start to end, or specific chapters can be consulted on subjects of particular and immediate interest. Spanning eleven chapters, an appendix, and a glossary, the book intends to address systematically topics of interest to both professionals and the general public.

Chapter 1 discusses the major problems of dying in today's society, using case material that illustrates different individual choices. Accompanying a discussion of the changing definition of death is an introduction to the types of death anxiety that people most often experience.

Chapter 2 acquaints you with the questions that you should ask yourself when you are well and before you meet with your doctor. It gives you examples of what to expect during encounters between patient and doctor when the end is near.

Chapter 3 delves into the dilemmas that face the medical profession when dealing with terminally ill patients. It also identifies some of the questions that you should be thinking about before meeting with your doctor. It discusses the importance of knowing what your doctor's philosophy is about the treatment of terminal illness and how to bring up the subject.

Chapter 4 deals with the difficult choices and tough decisions one has to consider in today's world of advanced technology. It examines death and dying as a matter of individual freedom and reviews the various options available in the hospital. It reviews the option of choosing death in special cases, citing two extreme examples of difficult decision making.

Chapter 5 underscores having one's own philosophy of death and dying. It shows how a sense of control over and acceptance of life's end stage can relieve your natural fear of death and your uncertainty about the dying experience. It talks about how you can retain a sense of pride and confidence, a feeling of dignity and control, and how these can lead to inner peace and acceptance.

Chapter 6 outlines the steps to be taken in initiating a dialogue with family members on the topics of treatment options and of dying and death. It explores the problem of unfinished business with the dying person and ways to let go and part on good terms. It discusses the unique problems of families dealing with AIDS.

Chapter 7 highlights U.S. landmark law cases that illustrate the major conflicts between the medical profession, the legal system, and families. It reports on prototypical cases of individuals caught in the plight of brain death or persistent vegetative states.

Chapter 8 focuses on the right-to-die movement and the controversial issues raised by various interest groups. It discusses the question of euthanasia, how it is viewed in the United States, and how it is practiced in Holland.

Chapter 9 reviews the history of the hospice movement in the United States and its philosophy of treatment and care. It debates the issues of suicide in terminal illness, and it describes a series of alternative therapies for incurable illness.

Chapter 10 deals with the practical steps you can take to prevent future complications for you and your family. It gives up-to-date information on living wills, proxies, and durable powers of attorney.

Chapter 11 offers some thoughts about aging, dying, and new legislative directions. It discusses the problems of Alzheimer's disease, nursing-home placement, AIDS, and the need for organ transplants in the twenty-first century.

It is my firm belief that with knowledge, understanding, and faith, people need not fear the unknown, whether it be death, dying or the end stages of aging or illness. This thought was best expressed by Madame Marie Curie, who said, "Nothing in life is to be feared. It is to be understood."

Acknowledgments

Writing this book has been a profound intellectual and emotional experience. In the last year, I lost four close friends who had talked to me about their philosophy and feelings about dying. I am deeply grateful for the insights and motivation that they provided me in writing this book. I owe thanks to Eugene (John) Heimler, Jeanette Clark, Bob Rowe, and David Lenhof.

Among those who have provided me with thought-provoking arguments and issues, I wish to thank Gardner Bemis, Alex Roth, James Bennett, Leonard Howard, Barry Zacherle, Steve Miller, Dave Mathews, and Albert Mariani.

I give special thanks to those who have read portions of the manuscript: Robert Nathanson, Melodee Deutsch, Ida Johnson, and Wallace Johnson. Whatever errors remain are mine only.

For their support and encouragement, I wish to thank Derek Humphry, Pat Osgood, Bonnie Reilly, Dee Jay Mailer, William Cody, Bea Bennett, Colleen Roth, Cynthia Burdge, Ann Clark, James Deutch, William Dung, and Michael Chaffin.

For the useful and relevant material they provided me, I wish to thank Francie Boland, Randy Jensen, Ken Kipnis, Joe, Joyce, and Christy Cruzan, Fenella Rouse, Jeff Crabtree, Mario Milch, Derek Humphry, John Golenski, Lawrence Nelson, Laurie Dorfman, Ruth Stepulis, John Mueh, and Mitchell Levy.

I am deeply grateful to Georgia Howton and Donna Edwards for giving me invaluable assistance with library searches.

I owe special thanks to Ellen Colburn, who has been not only a wonderful friend but also a superb editor.

I am also indebted to Norma Fox, Executive Editor, and Frank Darmstadt, Assistant Editor, who have provided me with support, guidance, and valuable advice.

Last but not least, I am deeply grateful to Adrienne Burnell, my wife, for giving me emotional sustenance, encouragement, ideas, suggestions, and, mostly, enough love to carry me through the vicissitudes of writing and times of soul searching.

Grateful acknowledgment is made for reprint excerpts from the following:

George M. Burnell, "My Mother Wants To Die: A Lawyer Won't Let Her," *Medical Economics*, 19 Dec. 1988, 57–60. Copyright © 1988 Medical Economics Publishing. Reprinted by permission of *Medical Economics* magazine.

Ronald E. Cranford, "Helga Wanglie's Ventilator," *Hastings Center Report 21* (July–August 1991): 23–24. Reprinted by permission.

"Death in the First Person," *American Journal of Nursing 70* (2, Feb. 1970): 336. Copyright © 1970 American Journal of Nursing Company. Used with permission. All rights reserved.

Ann Landers, "She's Dying, but She Still Needs to Be Loved," *Honolulu Advertiser,* 26 August 1991, B2. Permission granted by Ann Landers and Creators Syndicate.

Don McLeod, "Death in the Family: New Hospital Ethics Committee Helps Patients, Families Control Latest Technology," *American Association of Retired Persons Bulletin* (May 1991): 1, 10–11. Reprinted by permission of AARP.

"The Right to Die: Questions and Answers," The Society for the Right to Die. Reprinted by permission of Choice In Dying (formerly Concern for Dying/Society for the Right to Die) 200 Varick Street, New York, NY 10014.

Peter R. Rosier, "A Jury Acquitted Me of Murder: Most Colleagues Turned Their Backs," *Medical Economics*, 1 May 1989, 42–45. Reprinted by permission of the author.

Toni Shears, "Holding on . . . Letting Go . . . ," *Advance* (Fall 1990): 2–9. Reprinted by permission of the University of Michigan Medical Center.

Harry von Bommel, *Choices: For People Who Have a Terminal Illness, Their Families, and Their Caregivers*, 2nd rev. ed. (Toronto: NC Press, 1987), 51–55. Reprinted by permission of the publisher.

"What You Should Know about Medical Durable Power of Attorney—Proxy Appointments—Health Care Agents," The Society for the Right to Die. Reprinted by permission of Choice In Dying (formerly Concern for Dying/Society for the Right to Die) 200 Varick Street, New York, NY 10014.

Contents

Why Dying Today Is a Problem for You and Your Family

DEATH ISN'T WHAT IT USED TO BE

Forty years ago, my grandfather died at home. It was sad, but everyone who knew him thought it was a natural event because he was old and very ill and had led a full and productive life. He died peacefully in his own bed after saying good-bye to the loving family at his bedside. He was in his late seventies.

Two years ago, his daughter (my mother) died in her late eighties in a hospital, with a brand-new electrical device in her chest. She was hooked up to intravenous lines and connected to a variety of display monitors, each one relaying secrets about the inner workings of her body.

At the moment of her death, my mother was receiving the best care that money could buy. But she was all alone in a private room and away from her family. I don't believe that she had as good a death as her father did. Yet she lived in a modern age that offered an advanced and sophisticated health-care system.

Ever since her death, I have been asking myself this basic question: "Does modern health-care technology answer the needs of the dying person?"

In this age, it is not likely that any of us will die at home in

1

our own beds unless we make a special request. Even then, we must assume that our request will be heard and respected.

Although our life span has greatly increased, there is no question that "life is still the cause of death" and will continue to be so, probably forever. But at the very least, we can hope for a more gentle and dignified death. Yet, as I have experienced with my own family, dying is not what it used to be. In the past, death occurred when illness or injury stopped the heartbeat, and breathing ceased. Most people expected to die at home, to let "nature take its course."

But today, the great majority of Americans die in hospitals or nursing homes, with no choice in how to spend the last moments of their lives. The reason? Modern medical technology now allows even the incurable or terminally ill to remain alive almost indefinitely. Cardiac resuscitation and mechanical life-support systems can perform vital bodily functions even in a person who is no longer conscious.[1]

At times, however, life-prolonging interventions offer little or no hope for improvement in the patient's status or quality of life. In many such cases, physicians face the thorny question: Do we treat just because we can? This is especially true when persons become incompetent (unable to make decisions for themselves because of coma or brain death) and have not indicated their preferences about life-sustaining treatments.

For example, take the *Cruzan* case, which made the headlines in 1990.[2] On January 11, 1983, twenty-six-year-old Nancy Cruzan was thrown out of a car and landed face down in a ditch. Paramedics came and resuscitated her, but she had not been breathing for twelve to fourteen minutes. When she arrived at the hospital, she was unconscious and had a lacerated liver and a contusion of the brain. In addition, the lack of oxygen she had suffered further complicated her condition. On February 7, her husband consented to have a feeding tube placed in her stomach. Rehabilitation efforts continued, but without success. Nancy remained unconscious, unable to respond to anyone around her.

Eventually, she was transferred to the Missouri Rehabilitation Center, a health-care facility operated by the state.

After four years, Nancy's parents were legally appointed coguardians. After considerable thought, they requested that the tube-feeding be stopped. The facility refused, and the Cruzans sought a court order to approve their request. As a result, what had been a medical problem for Nancy Cruzan became a legal problem for both her and her parents.

The trial court approved the Cruzans' request. The court decided that there was evidence that Nancy would not have wanted to continue receiving artificially supplied food and water. It ruled that she had a right to choose her own destiny, and that if she wanted to refuse further treatment, she had the right to do so. Furthermore, the court found that her guardians had the right to act for her.

But then, the state department of health made an appeal to the Missouri Supreme Court. Interestingly, this court's focus was the fact that Nancy was neither dead nor terminally ill, which raised the question about whether a guardian could be allowed to request on her behalf to stop tube-feeding. The court further reasoned that it was really being asked to allow the medical profession to help Nancy die by starvation and dehydration. It also determined that the question was not about life versus death but about the quality of life versus death. The court made no distinction between nutrition and hydration and other medical treatment. Moreover, the court did not consider the treatment burdensome to Nancy.

The court defined the basic question to be whether keeping Nancy alive was more detrimental to her and her parents than not keeping her alive. It also concluded that the evidence about her prior wishes to live or die was unreliable, and that her parents lacked sufficient authority to make a judgment.

By a vote of 4 to 3, the Missouri Supreme Court decided that keeping Nancy alive was better than allowing her to die. It did agree, however, that a person has a right to refuse treatment if able to make that choice.

By the time the Missouri Supreme Court made its decision, the U.S. Supreme Court had agreed to hear the case. It wanted to decide whether Nancy had a right under the U.S. Constitution to require the hospital to withdraw treatment under the existing circumstances.

The *Cruzan* case became the first "right-to-die" case to reach the U.S. Supreme Court. The Court had narrowed the question: Did the State of Missouri have a right to require "clear and convincing evidence"? And should that evidence be required as a standard before allowing the withdrawal of life-sustaining measures? The Supreme Court found that the U.S. Constitution did not forbid the State of Missouri to require such "clear and convincing evidence." In other words, the U.S. Supreme Court, in deciding whether the Missouri Supreme Court had made an error, concluded that it had not. (In the Cruzan case, the U.S. Supreme Court also reaffirmed several rulings that dealt with hopelessly ill patients, their families, and health care professionals. For further discussion, see Chapter 7.)

As it turned out for Nancy Cruzan, on December 14, 1990, Probate Judge Teel of Jasper County made the final decision. After hearing the testimony of two of Nancy's former co-workers, who testified that she would never have wanted to live in such a condition, Teel granted permission to stop the tube-feeding. He found their testimony provided "clear and convincing evidence." Nancy Cruzan's feeding tube was removed two hours later. As expected, Nancy died on December 26, 1990, much to the relief of her family.[3]

The Cruzan situation is one that any of us could face, and the case illustrates the complex web in which both the medical and the legal professions become entangled. The ultimate question is who decides about our last days on earth. What if we become "incompetent," unable to make decisions because we are comatose and brain dead? In subsequent chapters, I shall discuss the various options available now and in the future.

DOES SOCIETY HAVE TROUBLE
COPING WITH DEATH AND DYING?

Throughout history, death has fascinated us. Consider the number of operas, paintings, poems, novels, plays, and movies that deal with the subject of death. Such works, however, with very few exceptions, depict death and dying unrealistically. But in twentieth-century United States, authors and artists frequently glorify it, dramatize it, make it look worse or better than it is, or "sanitize" it. In other words, they simply deny its true nature.

The true picture of death has been clouded by myth and has often been suppressed. Even the Pentagon, at the conclusion of the Gulf War, issued a directive that caskets of soldiers killed in the Middle East should not be shown to the public.

The collective attitude toward death has led to a universal fear of the dying experience in our society. There are many reasons for such fear, and I shall discuss them later in greater detail, but suffice it to say that the fear has been intensified by our greater awareness of the possibilities of modern medical technology.

There is little question that the human body can be kept alive almost indefinitely with machines, intravenous fluids, and nasogastric feedings. And such an existence can be maintained whether or not we have any brain function left.[4]

Once we are admitted to a hospital, we may no longer have control over what will happen to our bodies. Someone else may decide about our chances of survival, the best course of treatment, and what medication side effects our bodies can tolerate in the short run or even in the long run. In other words, once the system of modern medical care takes over, we frequently lose control over decisionmaking, particularly in severe and terminal illnesses.

Statistics show that today over 80 percent of Americans die in hospitals or in institutions. This percentage is in marked contrast to fifty years ago, when only 20 percent of Americans died in hospitals or other health-care facilities, and when most of them died at home.[5]

Today, nearly two million persons die each year, and most of them have little to say about how they will die. Although all deaths are unavoidable, 10 to 20 percent of the dying might choose to avoid a prolonged and difficult death.[6] As a result, thousands of Americans recognize that terminally ill patients should have the right to ask their physicians to hasten death and to end prolonged pain and suffering. Even Barbara Bush, wife of the U.S. President, acknowledged signing a living will, commenting, "I had a dog I loved put down because I didn't want the dog to suffer. I certainly hope that someone would do the same thing for me."

The rapid advances in medical technology have forced us to recognize that dying is no longer that simple and peaceful transition that our grandparents and great-grandparents experienced. The reality is that we may very well spend the last few weeks or days of our lives in an intensive-care unit, attached to monitors, machines, tubes, and life-support paraphernalia. More than ever, it is imperative that we understand the forces that prevent us from electing the treatment of our choice. At the same time, it is important to know our rights to refuse treatment or unwanted life-support measures.

Death and the dying experience may not seem so awesome if we know that society will let us retain a sense of control and allow us to die a peaceful and painless death.

WHEN ENOUGH IS ENOUGH

Sometimes, a good death is a matter of honoring the patient's and the family's request for discontinuing life-sustaining treatments when all other medical options have been exhausted. Then, and only then, can the patient regain a sense of control and a feeling of dignity. At that point, letting go of the suffering and dying in the comfort of home on one's own terms offer the kind of peace that can lead to a good death.

Let me share the experiences of four people who chose to die on their own terms. The first, Mary, was a patient at the University of Michigan Medical Center. The next three—David, Bob, and Janet—were close friends of mine. For each, dying was a very different experience. Each one had reasons for choosing a particular course of action, and each one died peacefully.

Mary's Story

Mary, a seventy-eight-year-old retired schoolteacher, had been on kidney dialysis for the last ten years because of a failing heart and diseased kidneys. In addition, she had a cancerous tumor that was growing and causing further complications. Her husband of forty years, who had been visiting her everyday at the kidney dialysis unit, could see that Mary was getting increasingly frail and mentally disoriented and too confused to express her wishes.

One alternative her husband had considered was to discontinue treatment and allow her to come home and die without further pain and suffering. But for several weeks, despite numerous meetings and consultations with the social worker, the doctor, and peer counselors (patients on the unit who faced similar problems), Mary's husband could not reach a decision.

The staff continued to be patient and supportive. The social worker would say, "There are no easy answers. Each person and each family must do what feels right for them." One peer counselor said, "I hope it never gets to the point where someone dictates to me that I must carry on. That would be unthinkable. There are worse things than death, you know." Dr. S., Mary's doctor, patiently reassured her husband that he would not be alone in making his difficult decision, saying, "In our unit, about 20 percent of our patients die from the withdrawing of therapy."

Despite numerous meetings with the staff over a period of weeks, the husband confessed, "I'm straddling the fence, playing it by ear. Mary was not doing so well and I was ready to take her off dialysis, but she got a little better. We've had some good times since then. Right now, I'm holding off, but I don't think I'm doing her a favor, and I don't think I'm doing myself a favor."

The staff was acutely aware that he was already silently grieving the expected loss of his wife, and that he still needed more time. "Patients and families need time to absorb the reality of an illness, the complications, and what the medical team can do about them. Then, within their own desires and support system, the family can accept what the outcome will be—whether it's a cure, chronic care, a nursing home, or death," explained Dr. S. at one of the staff conferences. He cited Mary's husband as an example of someone who was working through a process. As one of the social workers put it, "I tell patients that death is a part of life, and that lots of people are afraid of death. I tell them that it will help them to know whom they would trust to make decisions about their medical care. Then they can discuss with those people at which point it would be appropriate to say, 'Enough is enough.' "

Mary's husband continued to listen and to mull over the decision. Finally, one day, in his conversation with the director of the unit and the social worker, he announced, "I think I would rather take her off the dialysis. She's suffered enough. I think that she would want that, too."

This was not an easy decision, but when Mary and her husband went home, he felt at peace with himself, and he felt that he had helped his wife retain her dignity while she was awaiting death with serenity in her own home.[7]

Mary's case is an example of what can be achieved through sensitive and careful counseling. Planning is of crucial importance to families and patients faced with the dilemma of a deteriorating condition. An experience like that of Mary and her husband is usually satisfying for patients and staff alike.

But more often than not, hospital staff are not ready to accept the "enough-is-enough" approach. Erica Perry, a social worker in the Michigan Medical Center Dialysis Unit, deplores the unfortunate attitude that is more typical in hospital practice: "We plan for births, for weddings, for many events in life, but one of the things we don't plan for is our own death. One of the tragedies in the hospital setting is not giving people that opportunity."[8]

David's Story

I met David when my wife introduced him as one of the best students in her class at the nursing school. He was a tall young man with a warm and kind face. He spoke with a velvety voice and displayed an intense interest in whomever he talked with. He was happily married, and he and his wife had become active members of the Buddhist Church in Hawaii.

After his graduation from nursing school, he worked in a local hospital despite a progressive form of diabetes, which had begun in his early teens. One day my wife told me, "I ran into a friend of David's today. He is in the hospital awaiting a kidney transplant." I thought to myself that it truly was a shame for this young man to face such a plight at the beginning of his career. I decided to give him a call to see if I could help.

"Hi, David. I'm calling to see how you're doing. I heard that there is a question of your getting a kidney transplant. Is that really true?"

"Oh, yes, it's really true. But I'm doing fine," he said in his characteristic caregiver voice.

"Well, I'd love to hear more about it. Can we get together?"

"You name the time," he added without hesitation.

We met that week in what turned out to be the beginning of a series of meetings. It became obvious to me that David needed to talk, and for my own reasons, I needed to learn more about his battle for life.

David told me that for several months he and his doctor had considered the possibility of a kidney transplant. Finding a donor, which can be a problem, was easy in his case because both his wife and his sister had offered to donate one of their kidneys. As it turned out, the kidney of an anonymous donor tested as a better match for David's kidney. So the operation was scheduled with the new donor's kidney. Unfortunately, following the surgery, the new kidney failed to function properly because the graft did not take. David was then wheeled back into the operating room for removal of the defective kidney. While on the operating table, David went into cardiac arrest but was successfully resuscitated.

In the months that followed, David, with the help of modern medicine, continued his battle against a progressive illness. He showed remarkable patience and stoicism in the face of constant frustration, pain, and setbacks.

But one day, the doctor came in and said, "David, I'm afraid that your leg has become full of gangrene, and we're going to have to operate again."

After a long pause, David broke the silence: "Do you mean an amputation, Doc?"

Looking him straight in the eye, the doctor said, "I'm afraid that's what it means, David." David looked out the window for a while, as if to say, "When is this journey going to end?" Then, after a deep breath, he said, "I guess I'll be ready when you are, Doc."

The amputation was performed without complications, but because of the previous incident of cardiac arrest in the operating room, more procedures and tests had to be scheduled. For several weeks, David underwent angiograms (the injection of contrast dye into the arteries of the heart), angioplasty (the placing of a rubber balloon to dilate the arteries inside the heart), CAT scans, and dozens of lab tests.

David's spirits were sinking slowly. He felt as if he was on an "emotional roller coaster." Yet his doctors never let him down. Like good generals in the field, they continued to wage the battle against disease. After two weeks, David experienced several strokes. He was losing the use of the left side of his body. Doctors agreed that further surgery was out of the question. It was time to reassess the battle and the casualties. After some deliberation, they agreed to hold the line and continue dialysis from week to week.

Gradually, David began to entertain thoughts of an alternative to how he was living his life. He had always been deeply spiritual and had always relied on his faith in God. At one of our meetings, he seemed eager to share with me his wish for an alternative solution to his dilemma.

"George, I don't know how to put this. For several weeks, I've been thinking that none of this battle makes any sense anymore. Perhaps it's time for me to think about alternatives."

I caught my breath and, after a moment, responded: "Well, I can see that life is getting tougher and tougher for you. What alternatives are you thinking about?"

He shifted position and gently continued, "I'm thinking about stopping the dialysis and calling it quits."

For a moment, I searched for an appropriate answer. I did not want to influence him one way or the other. Whatever choice he made would be fine with me, and I would support him in his decision.

As I reviewed my thoughts, I responded, "I think that you are entitled to your feelings about this, David. You have certainly given it your all, and I want you to know that I will support you in your decision, whatever it is."

David seemed relieved to have expressed his feelings and to have obtained some support instead of a barrage of objections and disapproval.

Another week passed, and then David told me that he had discussed his decision with his wife. She, too, had accepted his decision. They had agreed that they should slowly break the news to the rest of the family and their friends. Also, he wanted to have plenty of time to prepare them for his decision and to say his good-byes. David spent the next three weeks persuading his mother and sister that his decision to stop all treatment was the best for him. They finally agreed.

David's mood gradually changed, as if a veil of doom had been lifted from his mind. He began to appear calm, relaxed, and sometimes even lighthearted, as he had been before his hospitalization. At the end of one of our visits, he concluded, "I guess the worst is over. It's as if I had been holding back, but now I feel I can let go and feel free again." He graced me with his gentle smile as we shook hands and hugged warmly.

Later that day, he asked his doctor to release him and to let him stay on home dialysis for just a few more days. David's wife took him home on a Sunday. After four days, he decided to stop the dialysis, and a few days later, he died peacefully.

"It was a great release and a wonderful death," said his wife, who had stood by him all along. "On the last day, we held hands while he slipped away gently with a sigh."

Later, when I talked with her again, she said, "I'm so grateful that he didn't go into a vegetative state. He was conscious and clear to the very last."

Bob's Story

I first met Bob twenty years ago in an advanced tennis class. He was a history professor at a local college, where he had been voted teacher of the year by the entire student body. His classes were very popular and always overfilled. As we became acquainted, we began to share our thoughts and feelings about many current philosophical and social issues.

Later, on several occasions, Bob invited me to talk to his class about my firsthand experiences in World War II. As the years passed, we won several tennis tournaments as doubles partners and became close friends. He was a true *bon vivant*, a man who knew how to enjoy life through many pursuits and activities. He performed in plays and musicals, played the guitar, wrote music and songs, and produced several tapes and records. In addition to his love of tennis, he was a dedicated scuba diver and underwater photographer. He enjoyed his marriage and the company of his children. Even after he retired, Bob did not slow down. He continued his busy schedule of activities and even began publishing some of his writings.

One day, he developed a nonspecific pain in his shoulder. At first, he thought that he had strained a muscle while playing tennis, but the pain did not go away even after a couple of weeks. In fact, it spread to the side of his neck. Because his family physician was a good distance away, he consulted a local physician, who gave Bob a few painkillers, thinking that it was probably osteoarthritis or a pulled muscle.

Two weeks later, the pain had spread to the chest area. At that point, Bob and his wife drove to see his own doctor. Dr. Z. had known Bob for many years and admired his fitness for a man in his sixties.

"Well, Bob, I know how you feel about tests, but this time, we better go ahead and investigate this darn pain," said Dr. Z.

"Go ahead, Doc. You know how much I trust you."

A week later, Dr. Z. gave Bob the results of the test.

"I'm afraid the news is not good, Bob. The X-rays show that you have a tumor in the lung that has spread to the other organs. I can't say now for sure what the prognosis is because with therapy, you know . . . "

Seeing the look of pessimism on the doctor's face, Bob, well known for his realism, interrupted him: "Doc, just give it to me straight."

"Bob, it doesn't look good, even with chemotherapy and radiation."

Bob interrupted him again: "Just tell me frankly, Doc, will I be able to carry on all the things you know I like to do?"

Dr. Z. replied, "Well, frankly speaking, the most you can hope for is a year or so, mostly in bed and . . . "

Bob got up and said, "Doc, I've had a good life, and I don't intend to spoil it now. Just let me go home, and give me plenty of pain medicine."

Bob went home with his own morphine pump to control the pain that seemed to be increasing day by day. During the following weeks, he told his wife and children how much he loved them and how much he enjoyed being around them. He spoke frankly to a few of his friends, saying good-bye to some of them. He continued to lose weight and could not eat. His body, once so vibrant, was beginning to wither and look like a tall shadow.

One day, he stopped eating altogether and gradually became so weak that he remained in bed around the clock. He seemed at peace with himself and calm and resigned, as if he had made a final decision. On a Sunday morning, he died quietly and peacefully as his son, Patrick, lovingly played the guitar and sang one last song to him.

Later, when I spoke to his wife, Jean, she said, "At first, I didn't know what to think. Bob had told me about his wishes not to go into extended treatments. I resisted for a while; then I saw how miserable he would be without my support. I knew that he didn't want to go on with this much longer, and I expected him to take control over the situation. That's the way he led his life, and he was much too proud to let others take over the care of his body."

I praised Jean for being so supportive of Bob through their horrible dilemma. With conviction, I told her, "I do believe that Bob had a good death, given the circumstances."

Like many survivors of spouses who have had a good death, Jean seemed eager to share her feelings with friends. She said, "I'm so glad that he did it his way, with much less suffering and pain than so many people I know who have died in agony. Of course, I felt sad losing Bob, but I felt happy because he didn't suffer. Dr. Z. later told me that any other ending would have been miserable for Bob."

Janet's Story

Janet was a widow teaching public health at a university long before she underwent a mastectomy at the age of fifty-two. She lived alone, but she had a large circle of friends, whom she loved to entertain in her small condominium. As part of that circle, my wife and I became her close friends.

Janet clearly enjoyed life and seemed grateful for every day granted to her. Her life was like an open book, and she willingly shared her health problems with those who wanted to listen. Over a period of months, she had been losing weight and complaining of severe headaches that seemed to coincide with episodes of dizziness and poor balance.

One day, she approached me and said, "I believe I'm having a recurrence of my tumor; at least, that's what the doctor thinks."

At first, I was tempted to reassure her by denying the bad news, but as I would not do that with my own patients, I put on my clinical hat and said, "Tell me what that means, Janet."

She thought for a few seconds and then replied, "I guess that means going back into the hospital, going through some tests, you know, and getting more radiation or chemotherapy."

Over the next few months of treatment, she continued to lose weight. Finally, the doctor convinced her to reenter the hospital. By then, she had lost her hair, seemed too weak to walk, and was on heavy doses of narcotics.

My wife and I began to visit her regularly in the hospital. We felt like a surrogate family to her, as we knew that she had no family left. She always seemed very pleased to see us, but as the weeks passed, and as her condition worsened, there seemed to be less and less interaction during our visits. At times, she seemed semiconscious, breathing only with the help of the oxygen tank at her bedside. At other times, she would smile and say, "I'm getting more treatment, you know; they are trying new things. Now I can keep my hopes up. Of course, I am trying new prayers, too."

After several months, she looked ghastly, almost like a skeleton, folded over in a fetal position, barely breathing, and uttering strange and unintelligible sounds. Following one of our visits, I turned to my wife and said, "I don't think Janet is going to make it to the end of the month."

But much to my surprise, several months went by, and Janet was still in the hospital, lying in the same bed and hooked up to oxygen, IVs, and a nasogastric tube. The staff had moved her to a different floor, and she had graduated to a private room. She spent most of her time sleeping, and whenever she became conscious, she would start praying. She couldn't read, eat, or watch television. Yet she remained cooperative about the nursing care and seemed most grateful for the fluid and nutrition she was receiving by tubes. It was clear from our conversations that she had put her destiny in the hands of God, and to her, that meant going along with the wishes of the doctor and being a good patient. Finally, after nine months in the hospital, she fell asleep at sunset and died.

Janet, too, did it her way. Her long battle with illness was her way of believing in herself. Also, I could not help but think that it was consistent with her personality, her faith, her values, and her love of life. In that sense, she, too, had made an appropriate choice. And in the end, that seemed to be the only thing that mattered.

IS DYING A QUESTION OF DEFINITION?

Part of the confusion over the concept of dying lies in the fact that many people are not aware of the new ways of defining death. Formerly, a person who stopped breathing and had no heartbeat was considered dead. Now, brain function is also considered in the definition of death.

In recent years, we have come to recognize that there is more to a person than just a body. The brain plays a major role in providing each of us with a personality, a set of unique behaviors and traits. These, in essence, are what distinguish us from others and give us what we call our identity.

More specifically, brain function can exist at a lower level, thus enabling vital organs to continue functioning. In such a state, the person is no longer conscious and, in effect, cannot communicate with other human beings.

On the other hand, should higher brain function be preserved, the person can then relate to others in a meaningful way. This understanding is what led Margot Fonteyn, the famous British ballerina, to continue caring for her husband, who had been paralyzed from the neck down in a political assassination attempt. During a television interview, Dame Margot spoke lovingly of her husband and his survival for many years as a quadriplegic in a state of total dependency. She said that she had felt her husband's presence and warmth for all the years he was paralyzed. Her husband's higher brain function made it possible for her to maintain a relationship and to continue caring for him.

However, when higher brain function is destroyed, it raises many questions. Is there still a human being? A person with an identity? A being who can feel, give affection, communicate?

Later, I shall discuss how doctors define death with respect to brain function. But for now, let me say that the problems for most people is that they do not anticipate surviving with minimal or total loss of higher brain function. Unfortunately for families, many such persons are now lying unconscious (in coma or persistent vegetative state) in institutions for years to come. They are, in a sense, the "living dead" of our era, living without consciousness until their heart stops or pneumonia sets in.

WHAT IS THE DYING PROCESS LIKE?

Most people today have not seen a person die even though they may have experienced many losses. Although as a physician I have witnessed the death of many patients in the hospital setting, over the last two decades I have not witnessed the death of any member of my family. I cannot help wondering about the days when families would gather around the deathbed of a grandparent, when dying was a family affair. Then, death seemed to be perfectly natural, a part of the family life cycle that no one ever questioned in the way we do now. Nowadays, dying at home can occur only if a special request is made to the doctor.

Because death has become hidden from most of us, it has become more frightening. Paradoxically, our main frame of reference today is television, movies, and magazines, all of which present dying very unrealistically and unfeelingly. In reality, dying, for most people, seems to be a calm and peaceful experience. Although there are numerous literary accounts of what dying looks like to the casual observer, a systematic report did not surface until Elisabeth Kübler-Ross published her book, *On Death and Dying*, in 1969. On the basis of interviews with two hundred dying patients, she described the following five stages of dying that most people go through.[9] Although other researchers have challenged her categories, the idea of stages is convenient and has widespread appeal.

1. *Denial and isolation.* This is the stage that people experience when they first hear a diagnosis of terminal illness. It has been described as shock and disbelief: "No, not me. It can't be true." Although total denial is rare, partial or temporary denial is almost universal.

2. *Anger.* Following a short period of disbelief, feelings of envy, resentment, and even rage usually occur. Patients struggle with haunting thoughts, the most common, resonating question being "Why me?" Not uncommon at this stage are inappropriate outbursts against family members and the medical staff.

3. *Bargaining.* Kübler-Ross believes that the anger stage does not last very long and gives way to a form of bargaining to forestall the inevitable. Patients in this stage typically reformulate their plight as follows: "If you'll do this . . . then I'll do that . . . " Such bargaining may be directed to the doctor, the family, or God. The idea that predominates is that good behavior will buy more time.

4. *Depression.* The full impact of actual and impending losses becomes more real. As the illness and the treatment proceed, the gradual losses of physical strength, social status, money, independence, time, and relationships become more evident. Even the ultimate loss of life itself in the foreseeable future becomes real. A dark mood of depression is the normal reaction during this stage.

5. *Acceptance.* After a variable period of time, people in the process of dying reach a stage of calm and peace, without depression or anger. This stage, says Kübler-Ross, "should not be mistaken for a happy stage. It is almost devoid of feelings. It is as if

the pain had gone, the struggle is over, and there comes a time for the final rest before the long journey."[10]

Kübler-Ross warns us that not all dying patients go through all of these stages and not always do they go in the order described. Nonetheless, many health-care workers, patients, and families who read her books sometimes insist that they see all of these stages in dying patients, even forcing their understanding of terminal illness on others who deal with the dying. I sometimes hear physicians and nurses complain that a patient who is close to dying "has not reached the stage of acceptance about his dying and is still stuck in his denial." Other researchers and clinicians have provided new observations to correct this rigid formulation, however.

Psychologist Edwin Schneidman wrote, "Indeed, while I have seen in dying persons isolation, envy, bargaining, depression, and acceptance, I do not believe that these are necessarily 'stages' of the dying process, and I am not at all convinced that they are lived through in that order, or, for that matter, in any universal order. What I do see is complicated clustering of intellectual and affective states, some fleeting, lasting for a moment or a day or week, set not unexpectedly against the backdrop of that person's total personality, his philosophy of life."[11]

Mansell Pattison, another scholar in thanatology, wrote, "I find no evidence ... to support specific stages of dying. Rather, dying patients demonstrate a wide array of emotions that ebb and flow throughout our entire life as we face conflicts and crises." After that cautious warning, he goes on to say, "Rather, I suggest that our task is to determine the stresses and crises at a specific time, to respond to the emotions generated by that issue, and in essence, to respond to where the patient is at in his or her living–dying."[12]

Over the last two decades, I have talked to over one hundred terminally ill individuals and their families. I am now convinced that each person has his or her own way of dying, just as each had his or her own way of living. The people I talked to reacted to their final life event as they reacted to other major events in their lives. Some did it with grace, and others did it with regrets, shame, and resentment. I believe that some of those who did it with grace did so because they had a minimum of suffering and pain and because they were able to recognize and resolve residual conflicts. They ended their lives with a good death or "an appropriate death," as Avery Weisman would say.[13] Those who suffered through pain, sorrow, and emotional turmoil ended up with a bad death. In any case, it is clear that dying is as highly individual as the many other experiences of life.

Perhaps, after all is said and done, dying is just another passage in life.

HOW MUCH PAIN IS THERE IN DYING?

> *Among the remedies which it has pleased*
> *Almighty God to give man to relieve*
> *his sufferings, none is so universal*
> *and so efficacious as opium.*
> —Thomas Sydenham, 1680

Although the fear of dying in pain is one of the most commonly expressed, dying is not always painful. A report published by the National Institute of Aging suggests that dying need not be an agonizing experience. The report, entitled "The Last Final Days," analyzes the responses of a cross section of elderly Connecticut residents through interviews with relatives, friends, or neighbors three months after the study subjects died. More than half the subjects in the study died in their sleep, without pain, and with family and friends nearby. The researchers also found that more than half the subjects had still been in good health a year before, and that approximately 60 percent had been without pain the day they died.[14]

Nonetheless, pain does occur in terminal patients, although in a minority of cases. Pain is more likely to be the result of aggressive medical treatment, ordered by doctors attempting to retard the dying process with such procedures as spinal taps, oxygen tents, medications, intravenous fluids, radiation, and radical surgeries. No matter how severe, however, the pain can be controlled with adequate narcotics in the majority of cases.

Adequate control of pain depends on the physician's training in pain management. Unfortunately, some studies have shown that doctors are still poorly trained in pain control. Jamie Von Roenn of Northwestern University surveyed 1,177 physicians who had treated more than seventy thousand cancer patients. Although 80 to 90 percent of the cancer patients received relief from pain medicines, 10 to 20 percent received little or no relief. As to the reasons given for poor pain control, the study found that about one-third of the doctors surveyed did not prescribe the highest levels of pain medicine unless they thought that their patients had less than six months to live; and about 60 percent of the doctors felt that poor assessment of the patient's condition and degree of pain was another major barrier to good pain control.[15] It is true that, in hospitals particularly, doctors tend to treat pain according to standard protocols, such as a fixed dose of morphine every four hours "as needed." This essentially means that nurses are supposed to wait for the patient to complain of pain before administering the next dose of pain medicine. Studies have shown that all this protocol does is increase the patient's level of anxiety and tension because he or she dreads the expected pain.[16]

In reality, the proper dose of morphine is the one that works, even if the patient needs more than 100 milligrams every four hours or more often. Cicely Saunders, dean of the hospice movement in Great Britain, believes that the best method of helping patients live until they die is through effective pain control. She says, "Pain control, it turns out, is not so much a matter of what is in the medicine, as it is of how and when it is administered."[17]

Much of the chronic pain in cancer patients is perpetuated by the protocol of PRN, which stands for the Latin phrase *pro re nata,* meaning "whenever necessary." The PRN protocol for administering pain medication in hospitals dictates that the patient be given pain medication at the onset of pain. But the nurse will ask the patient how bad the pain is before deciding to give the pain killer. Or the nurse may inform the patient that she or he has had the usual or standard dose and should wait awhile longer before the next dose is given. Some nurses even suggest that the pain is really not that bad and that the patient should try to bear a little pain so as to use as little analgesia as possible. In reality, the only right dose of pain medication is the one that will abolish the pain, and therefore patients should never accept less than adequate pain control. Once the diagnosis and condition are known, there is no reason to subject the patient to any pain by withholding or reducing the amount of medication. The argument that addiction presents a risk is totally ridiculous, as the patient may not live long enough to become addicted. Furthermore, the research points out that the craving for relief of pain is due not to addiction or tolerance but simply to the inadequate control of pain.[18]

According to pain specialists and doctors who work with patients in hospices, the best approach is to give pain medication before the onset of pain and preferably on a continuous basis. Otherwise, the fear of pain increases pain itself by geometric proportions. Medical staff who work in hospices know too well how important it is to relieve patients of anxiety and apprehension about pain.[19]

Sometimes, I hear from patients or their families about their battles with pain and with the hospital staff over pain medication. I tell them not to accept staff resistance and to insist on more medication if they have no relief. There is no good reason today to accept less than relief of pain. In fact, terminal patients who experience pain should expect routine medication and should not have to ask for it. If you or someone important to you complains of severe pain without getting relief from proper medication because there is a fear of addiction, you should urge your physician to honor the request; and if he or she resists, you should consider changing your physician. Such resistance is not likely to occur if you have a long-standing and good relationship with a physician who knows your personality and your tolerance of stress and pain. By contrast, you are more likely to encounter inadequate pain control in an acute general hospital, where several physicians treat and medicate a patient whom they don't know well.

The best way to achieve good pain control in a terminal condition is probably through a home care program in which patients have a morphine pump that they regulate themselves according to need. This was the case with my friend, Bob, who found it easier to retain a sense of control over his body and his pain by regulating the dosage of morphine himself. Furthermore, going home in itself may provide such emotional relief that the pain seems reduced. The familiarity of home, the love and attention of one's family, the reintegration into daily household routines and decisions, and the possibilities of entertainment and pleasant diversions—all seem to have an analgesic effect that is underestimated.[20]

Once again, I wish to emphasize that addiction should not be a concern for the person who self-administers the narcotic; addiction is a trivial complication in the treatment of a terminal illness. The convenience of being able to self-regulate pain medications allows patients to carry on reasonably well and to die in relative comfort.[21]

A special word should be said about cancer pain. Although not all cancer patients experience pain, it is a predominant characteristic of the disease. It has long been recognized that the terminal management of the cancer patient in an acute general hospital is grossly inadequate. Richard Lamerton, a British physician who did a study of terminal care in the 1970s, discovered that one-fifth of hospitalized terminal cancer patients were in severe pain.[22] In contrast, 99 percent of cancer patients admitted to the St. Christopher's Hospice in London obtained significant relief from severe pain. Despite these findings, many physicians still caution medical and nursing staff against the liberal use of narcotic analgesia. RG Twycross, however, one of the foremost authorities in the world on pain control, states that the concern about tolerance, addiction, and excessive sedation is really unwarranted. He feels that any need to increase doses of morphine is more likely due to an increase in pain than to tolerance of the morphine.[23]

In the 1970s, another form of pain control gained popularity, especially in the treatment of cancer patients. It was known as the *Brompton cocktail* or *pain cocktail*. Developed in Great Britain, it consisted of an oral narcotic mixture that contained diamorphine, cocaine, gin, sugar syrup, and thorazine syrup. The main disadvantage of this mixture was that it contained fixed amounts of ingredients and prevented doctors from adjusting the ingredients to the needs of individual patients. Since then, physicians have preferred to use individual medications, which they can better regulate and monitor.

Another approach to the intractable pain of advanced cancer patients has been proposed by Balfour Mount, director of the Palliative Care Unit at the Royal Victoria Hospital in Montreal:

1. He says that it is important to determine the exact basis for the cause of pain, pointing out that pain is sometimes really due to anxiety about having pain rather than to pain itself.
2. He insists that one must treat the pain preventively, that is, before it occurs, in order to break the patient's cycle of anticipation and worry about pain.
3. He strives to achieve a pain-free state without excessive sedation and drowsiness in order to allow the patient to function as normally as possible with family and friends.[24]

It is becoming clear that there is more to pain than simple physical sensation. Pain is, as Mount points out, a dual phenomenon, one part being the physical sensation, the other part being the emotional reaction to the sensation of pain. Just knowing this will help us to understand that each person has his or her own threshold of pain which will vary according to mood, morale, and the intensity of the pain itself.[25] It is most important for the physician to understand this so as to make an accurate assessment of the pain threshold and the origin of the pain. With this in mind, Cicely Saunders said that cancer pain may be due not just to the malignancy itself, but also to emotional side effects of the treatment. She recognizes that the emotional component plays a major part that is often overlooked by practitioners. She has found that a caring figure who listens and attempts to understand the sensation of pain in the patient can bring about significant added relief of that pain.[26]

There is no question that the level of sophistication in the management of chronic pain has increased significantly since the early 1960s. Twycross recommends that other medications be added to morphine and other analgesics, particularly for advanced cancer pain, because of the severe side effects of constipation and nausea often associated with narcotics.[27] Other medications used as additives to narcotics include antidepressants, tranquilizers, cortisone compounds, and nonsteroidal anti-inflammatory drugs.

For patients with advanced cancer pain, nonpharmacological control of pain has also been used with varying degrees of success. For example, hypnosis has been shown to be effective for the 40 percent of patients who are found to be responsive to this technique.[28] Other psychological interventions have been described and used successfully. These include relaxation techniques, guided visual imagery, and psychological exercises designed to give patients a sense of power and control and a feeling that they can actually help themselves.[29]

Finally, pain from a tumor growth can be further controlled by more radiation, chemotherapy, and surgery depending on the site and size of the tumor.[30]

At this point, the most important thing to remember is that pain can be controlled in the vast majority of cases, and that an open and honest relationship with your doctor can be crucial in putting your mind at ease if the need for reassurance should ever arise.

Some readers may ask, "What about the agony of death, the pain that accompanies the last few hours of death?" Terrible suffering in the last few hours of life is a relatively rare phenomenon. In most terminal conditions, the body tends to accumulate toxic substances that build up and produce a state of narcosis or coma, so that the patients die while they are in a state that resembles sleep.

Nonetheless, it is undeniable that there are cases in which total relief from pain is virtually impossible. As mentioned earlier, the estimate is between 10 and 15 percent of the cases. In those cases, alternatives that hasten death rather than prolong suffering have been used by terminally ill individuals. The factors and conditions that may prompt the decision to elect such alternatives are discussed in detail in subsequent chapters.

An exhaustive review of the subject of pain control is beyond the scope of this book. Readers interested in an up-to-date review of the literature on chronic pain and its management and current research should consult the comprehensive *Handbook of Chronic Pain Management*,[31] by Burrows *et al.*

OTHER SYMPTOMS IN TERMINAL ILLNESS

Pain is not the only troubling symptom in terminal illness. A cluster of annoying and disturbing symptoms can occur either as side effects of radiation treatment, chemotherapy, analgesic medication, or surgery, or as a result of the disease itself.

A major symptom in many types of cancer is loss of the desire to eat. This is a particularly troubling symptom because it carries so much psychological significance to patients and their families. This loss of appetite may have many causes, including nausea, constipation, depression, or even poorly controlled pain, and tends to speed the dying process even faster than the disease itself.[32] A further complication is that the refusal to eat frustrates and upsets the family. It is important for family members to understand the basis for this symptom and to avoid badgering the terminally ill person and, instead, to be as supportive as possible.

Equally bothersome are nausea and constipation, which frequently occur early in the course of terminal illness. Having control of bladder and bowel function is of great importance to most people because it affects not only the quality of life itself but also gives a sense of control and pride. Therefore, losing sphincter control may be profoundly humiliating and disturbing. It is most important for the family to treat the situation very sensitively.

Another rather disturbing symptom is shortness of breath, which is not uncommon in the end stages of illnesses involving lung complications, and which may also affect the quality of life of the dying person. Medications and oxygen usually bring about relief, although in some cases a tracheostomy (an opening made into the windpipe) may become necessary. This procedure, too, may be upsetting to the patient and the family.

Decubitus ulcers (bedsores) may make life miserable for patients who are otherwise painfree. Meticulous skin care is necessary for those who are permanently bedridden.

In all of these conditions, the importance of good nursing care cannot be stressed enough. Even more important is providing loving care and attention to terminally ill people.

Finally, one of the most pervasive symptoms that haunt the terminally ill, and even healthy persons, is the fear of dying itself. In Chapter 5, I discuss the subject in greater detail; at this juncture, I present an overview of the problem.

WHAT IS DEATH ANXIETY?

> Getting well is not the only goal. Even
> more important is to live without fear,
> to be at peace with life, and ultimately
> death.
> —Bernie S. Siegel, M.D., in *Love, Medicine and Miracles*

Recently, a patient of mine was diagnosed as having a malignant tumor. "I really don't want to die," she said after her visit to the doctor. A few days later, she admitted that she had occasionally thought about death, but now that it was seriously staring her in the face she was overcome by fears and anxiety.

The fear of death is universal. We manage not to think about it very often. As we go through life, we tend to think that life is endless and that the ending is rather abstract—something that happens to other people, not to us.

At certain times in life, however, we become more conscious of the possibility of death, particularly when we become seriously ill, when a friend dies, or when we lose a loved one.

Balfour Mount has made a detailed study of the variety of fears people have expressed about dying. The main ones that he lists are (1) fear of pain and suffering; (2) fear of being alone; (3) fear of the unknown; (4) fear of being a burden; (5) fear of financial ruin for the family; (6) anxiety about achieving closure in relationships with others.[33]

In my counseling with patients who are dying and with families whose relatives are terminally ill, I have learned about the kinds of feelings that lead to fears. Scholars have formulated seven levels that underlie these fears and have referred to this whole syndrome as *death anxiety*.[34]

Let us briefly examine these seven levels of death anxiety:

1. We fear the experience of dying itself: Under what conditions are we going to die? Will there be much suffering? How much pain will there be? How much control will we have over the pain?

As one of my patients said to his oncologist, "I don't know if it'll be tomorrow or in a week; just promise you won't let me die in pain." The fear of suffering pain is intense in some people, and in some cases, it is even worse than the fear of death itself. Another of my patients said, "I don't know how to face death, but pain numbing is a good start."

2. The second level of death anxiety comes up frequently in conversations about nursing homes. As we are all well aware, the life span has more than doubled since the turn of the century, and the fear of a lingering death in a nursing home is, for many people, an overwhelming prospect. As a result, spending some portion of our lives in a nursing home is a distinct possibility.

A recent study of the extent of nursing-home care in this

country was done by a team at the International Research Center at the Agency for Health Care Policy Research in Rockville, Maryland. They noted that the use of nursing-home facilities more than tripled between 1964 and 1985, and that the current nursing-home population exceeds 1.5 million people. They found that the probability of going to a nursing home increases with age: 17 percent for ages sixty-five to seventy-four, 36 percent for ages seventy-five to eighty-four, and 60 percent beyond age eighty-five. Of those entering a nursing home, 55 percent will be expected to spend at least one year, and over 20 percent will spend five years or more. As one would expect, of those entering a nursing home, more women than men will spend five years or more.[35]

Becoming bedridden for months or years with little control over one's life and dying a slow death in such conditions raises considerable anxiety among many of us, not to mention the fear of becoming a burden to our families. When I visited my mother in her nursing home, I recall visitors in the hallway saying, "I'll make sure that doesn't happen to me; I couldn't stand living this way." I became aware of how anxious and demoralized others and I felt after witnessing the pitiful conditions in which nursing-home residents live month after month. We had the distinct feeling that some of those poor souls were trapped and no longer had any choices to make except to wait for a slow death.

3. The third level of anxiety is based on the fear of feeling ashamed and losing dignity. Most of us prefer to think that we will retain our pride and dignity until the last day of life.

I recall how bad another patient of mine felt. He had been a dentist who had served proudly during World War II, had taught at the university, and had raised a beautiful family. Now, he was receiving radiation and chemotherapy for a malignancy. Within a matter of weeks, this proud man had become unable to control his bowels and had lost his hair and his deep, warm voice. He looked emaciated, like a survivor of the Holocaust, and lay helpless in a hospital bed, unable to communicate his feelings and share his worst fears, having lost the pride and dignity that were so precious to him. Often, these feelings cannot be expressed or shared because the family and the hospital staff usually expect the patient to fight the disease along with them rather than to give in. For them, dying is equivalent to losing the battle rather than a road to relief and peace.

4. The fourth level of anxiety is experienced as a fear of ceasing to be or of nothingness. As I mentioned earlier, we tend to think of death as something that happens to other people, not to us. It is hard to imagine a world without our being there. This has been described as the "terror of the unknown."[36] Becker, an authority on the subject of death anxiety, says that there is nothing more frightening than the fear of not knowing.

5. The fifth level of anxiety has been related to the fear of being alone when we die and of being separated from our loved ones. Dying, like birthing, requires assistance, comfort, and companionship. Families, even when living far away, try very hard to be present when the loved one is dying. Dying persons have a great need to feel close, loved, and secure during the last few moments of their lives, and when they feel the warm touch and presence of a loved one, much of the fear is abated.

6. We also fear that tubes, machines, and devices will take over to maintain our bodily functions and control our body for the remaining weeks or months of our life. In this respect, we fear having no say in whether to choose or refuse treatment. This fear is not so intense in people who, in the past, have been able to choose the kind and extent of treatment offered to them.

7. The seventh level of anxiety is based on the fear of failure. It becomes evident when dying persons believe their lives have been wasted because their true desires were never pursued or fulfilled.

Mits Aoki, a well-known lecturer on death concepts and a professor of religion at the University of Hawaii, often says in his lectures to death counselors, "We fear death to the degree that we fear life. If you can really live your life fully, you can really accept death as a release." His theory is that if you fear life, you will keep holding on to that fear and will be reluctant to let it go at death.

Other theorists and philosophers believe that this fear is largely focused on what happens after death. Will we be judged and punished for our thoughts and bad behavior? Did we accomplish what we were supposed to do on this planet? Do we still have some unfinished business? Sometimes these fears are paralyzing. They are usually traceable to the feelings of guilt, rejection, or inadequacy that haunt many of us as we go through life. At the time of illness and just before death becomes a potential reality, people sometimes feel incomplete, unfinished, and unresolved.

Many of these fears can be dissipated, however, if we take the last opportunity to talk openly with others around us and to be true to ourselves. In my practice, I have often seen people achieve some inner peace about the prospect of dying, whether it be imminent or not, after they have had the opportunity to talk to someone they trust.

Aoki also found this to be true. In his counseling, he has observed that in order to achieve some peace of mind, the dying need to go through four major steps. He says that those who can achieve this sequence will benefit from an "appropriate death," to use the expression coined by Avery Weisman. The conditions leading to an "appropriate death" consider not only the physical aspects but also the psychological and spiritual aspects.

1. The person must settle all unfinished business with others. This may require making peace over old feuds and releasing all bad feelings toward family members and old friends.
2. The individual must "let go of the body and the ego." Professor Aoki believes that these two components will "separate" by a natural process.

   Admittedly, it is difficult for most people to understand this concept. Aoki explains it subjectively, relating the personal near-death experience he had some years ago.[37]
3. Survivors must give the dying person permission to die. Quite often, dying people who feel "unfinished" in their

relations with other people have trouble letting go and seem to struggle with feelings of unrest and ambivalence. With support, reassurance, and permission "to let go," the dying person and the family can say their good-byes and feel at peace with each other.

4. The dying person should conceive of the moment of death as an expansion beyond oneself. This concept is easily grasped by people who have faith and are devout. Those who are existentialistic, humanistic, or philosophical in their orientation must arrive at their own concept of their place in the universe.

Despite all these fears, people have managed their feelings about dying throughout human history. The experience of dying conjures up a different scenario, however, in the modern age of technology. Whether we like it or not, we may fall victim to a complex set of machines and tubes and complicated surgical and medical procedures. We may be subjected to examinations by an army of specialists, who will give us second and third opinions. Furthermore, we must understand that the modern-day physician, unlike the old-time family doctor, must practice according to the "standard of the community" and all currently available knowledge. In doing so, the physician may pay more attention to the latest laboratory results than to the feelings expressed by the dying patient. Fear of litigation may also nudge the cautious physician toward excessive tests and procedures in order to avoid a legal confrontation.

CAN WE CHOOSE OUR WAY OF DYING?

> *Just as I choose a ship to sail in or a house to live in, so I choose a death for my passage from life.*
> —Seneca (4 BC–65 AD)

As we have seen in the case of my friends, David, Bob, and Janet, dying should be a matter of personal choice. That opinion is further supported by a recent poll made by *USA Today*. The survey reported that 68 percent of those polled felt that terminally ill people should be allowed to end their lives. Another poll, by the Maturity News Service, showed that just over half the Americans surveyed felt that life-and-death decisions should be made by family members; 25 percent felt that life support should be removed only if the patient had expressed this preference; and only 7.2 percent said that life support should be continued until a patient died or recovered. Yet the courts and the medical profession continue to debate the issues as if everyone is confused and unable to make decisions.

The Cruzan case, like the *Quinlan* case in the seventies,* has reignited the right-to-die debate in lay, medical, and legal circles. It has encouraged people to bring the issues into the open for discussion.

The health professions have not directly addressed the importance of the quality of life, the personality, and the values of the patients they are treating. The ethical issues are enormous and raise many questions.

Health professionals must study those questions with the same degree of attention as the latest laboratory or X-ray finding. At which point should they ask, "What is the treatment for?" When should they stop treating? Should patients be asked what they want before they are given any treatment, even if they don't understand its subtleties? Is it really up to them? What if they can't answer because they are not conscious? Who decides then?

---

* Karen Ann Quinlan was a young woman in New Jersey who suffered irreversible brain damage and was sustained in a chronic vegetative state. Because of the confusion over criteria for the definition of death and because everyone was convinced that Karen was not dead, according to brain criteria at the time, the respirator was not discontinued until the New Jersey Supreme Court granted the relief sought by Karen Quinlan's father on March 31, 1976.

Karen was removed from the respirator in May 1976 and was subsequently transferred to a nursing home, where for nine years she remained in a vegetative state, weighing under 70 lbs. and sustained by nasogastric feedings and antibiotics. She died in June 1985.

Should they rely on the courts for all those decisions? What if there are limited resources, only so many to go around? Who should be getting the treatment? What is the physician's final responsibility? What about professional liability? Will someone sue if treatment is withheld or withdrawn? Can the hospital impose its views and policies on the patient and the doctor?

These are only a few of the questions that haunt the medical and nursing professions today. In Chapter 3, I discuss more thoroughly the current views about and answers to such thorny questions.

Before we address those issues, you must become familiar with the kinds of questions you should ask yourself.

Even doctors who care for the terminally ill do not spend much time reflecting on their own philosophy and their feelings about questions on death and dying. Most of them rely on the guidelines provided by the Hippocratic Oath (see Appendix D) for decisions on how far to go in sustaining life for their patients.

"Who cares?" said a colleague of mine who heard about my writing a book on dying. "When my time comes, I'll think about it then," he added, with a clear wish to conclude the conversation.

Yet this is precisely the problem with the subject of prolonging life or prolonging death. No one put it better than Avery Weisman, a Harvard professor of psychiatry, who wrote, "The so-called 'problem of death' is mainly problematic because we have not fully appreciated that our own psychological reticence and revulsion have prevented us from asking appropriate questions. We have been disposed to accept easy consolation and time-honored denial of death."[38]

In the next chapters, I will familiarize you with the issues that confront us when we face the medical technology puzzle.

NOTES

1. Robert M. Veatch, *Death, Dying and the Biological Revolution* (New Haven: Yale University Press, 1989), p2-3.

2. Cruzan v. Directors, Missouri Department of Health, *et al.* 497 U.S. —, 111 L. Ed. 2nd 224, 100 S. Ct 2841 (1990).

3. Ibid.

4. President's Commission for the Study of Ethical Problems in Medicine and Biomedical and Behavioral Research, *A Report on the Medical, Legal, and Ethical Issues in the Determination of Death,* (Washington D.C.: U.S. Government Printing Office, 1981), 21.

5. Ibid.

6. Veatch, 2–3.

7. Toni Shears, "Holding On . . . Letting Go . . . ,"*Advance* (Fall 1990): 2–9.

8. Ibid.

9. E. Kubler-Ross, *On Death and Dying* (New York: MacMillan, 1969), 113.

10. Ibid.

11. Edwin Schneidman, *Deaths of Man* (Baltimore: Penguin Books, 1973), 6.

12. E. Mansel Pattison, "The Living–Dying Process," *Psychosocial Care of the Dying Patient,* ed. C. A. Garfield (New York: McGraw-Hill, 1978), 141.

13. Avery D. Weisman, *On Dying and Denying* (New York: Behavioral Publications, 1972), 36–41.

14. "Death Not Always Painful," *American Medical News,* 7 Jan. 1991, 7.

15. "Pain Control Poor, Say Most Doctors," *Hemlock Quarterly* 44 (July 1991): 2.

16. Thomas Gonda and J. E. Ruark, *Dying Dignified* (Menlo Park, CA: Addison-Wesley, 1984), 120–122.

17. Cicely M. Saunders, ed., *The Management of Terminal Disease* (London: Edward Arnold Publication, distributed by Year Book Medical Publishers, Chicago, 1978), Part I: 1–10.

18. Michael A. Simpson, *The Facts of Death: Guide for Being Prepared* (Englewood Cliffs, NJ: Prentice-Hall, 1979), 46.

19. Robert W. Buckingham, *The Complete Hospice Guide* (New York: Harper & Row, 1983) 7.

20. David Carroll, *Living with Dying: A Loving Guide for Family and Close Friends* (New York: McGraw-Hill, 1985), 100.

21. Gonda and Ruark, 120–122.

22. Richard Lamerton and Sylvia Lack, eds., *The Hour of Our Death* (London: Macmillan, 1974).

23. Robert G. Twycross, "Relief of Pain," *The Management of Terminal Disease,* ed. Cicely Saunders (London: Edward Arnold, 1978), 65–98.

24. Balfour M. Mount, "Use of the Brompton Mixture in Treating the Chronic Pain of Malignant Disease," *Canadian Medical Association Journal* 115 (17 July, 1976): 122–124.
25. Twycross, 65–98.
26. Saunders, 1–10.
27. Twycross, 65–98.
28. B. Finer, "Hypnotherapy in the Pain of Advanced Cancer," *Advances in Pain Research and Treatment* 2 (1979): 223–229.
29. J. Turk and O. Rennert, "Pain and the Terminally Ill Cancer Patient," in *Behavior Therapy in Terminal Care*, ed. H. J. Sobel (Cambridge, MA: Ballinger, 1981).
30. Gonda and Ruark, 120–122.
31. Graham D. Burrows, Diana Elton, and Gordon V. Stanley, eds., *Handbook of Chronic Pain Management* (Melbourne: Elsevier Science, 1987).
32. Gonda and Ruark, 120–122.
33. Balfour Mount, "Individualism and Our Fears of Death," *Death Education* 7 (1983): 25–31.
34. Robert A. Neimeyer, "Death Anxiety," *Dying: Facing the Facts*, eds. H. Wass, F. M. Berardo, and R. A. Neimeyer (New York: Hemisphere, 1988), 97–111.
35. P. Kemper and C. M. Murtaugh, "Lifetime Use of Nursing Home Care," *New England Journal of Medicine* 324. 9 (1991): 595–600.
36. E. Becker, *The Denial of Death* (New York: The Free Press, 1973).
37. Mitsuo Aoki, "Near-Death Experiences," *Manoa*, Summer 1987, Vol. 324.
38. Weisman, xv.

CHAPTER 2

Key Questions You Need to Ask Yourself

The end comes some time; does it matter when?

—Albert Einstein

QUESTIONS FROM THE THINK TANK

Thinking about death or dying is almost an impossibility. Most of us cannot really imagine not being part of this world, or of being nonexistent, so to speak. It is hard enough to imagine anyone we love not being part of our world.

Yet, if we are to plan and organize our lives in the end stages, we must ask ourselves the right questions. What questions should we ask?

I, too, struggled with these questions, but I was fortunate enough to have an experience that facilitated my soul searching in this area. I will share with you that experience by recreating the memorable evening that made it possible.

I had joined a unique group that was dedicated to discussing the social and relevant issues of our day. The group was a self-appointed "think tank" made up of a few people who met monthly at each other's houses. The topics we selected ranged from Greenpeace to nuclear disarmament, from abortion to zero population growth, from women's rights to changing roles for men, from acid rain to nuclear accidents, from our gross national product to our foreign policy in the Middle East, and from racial policies to third-world countries. In other words, we never ran out of issues. We named ourselves the Think and Talk Group, or the TTG for short.

For one evening, the topic was the problems of death and dying in today's world of advancing technology. We also wanted to inquire into the kinds of questions we should ask ourselves long before we got too sick or too old.

The group's attendance varied, but that particular evening was fairly well attended. There were twelve people, including a dentist and his wife (the hosts that evening), an accountant, a sales representative, an attorney, a business executive, a minister, a history professor, an insurance agent, an artist, and a few others besides my wife, who teaches nursing, and me. Masculine and feminine viewpoints were represented about equally.

In a warm and friendly voice, the hostess said, "Well, friends, let's start the meeting."

"Did everyone get the list of questions I distributed last week?" asked her husband, lounging in a large easy chair.

"No, I didn't get it," said Jill, the accountant, "but to tell you the truth, I wasn't too excited about getting it either!"

"For those who didn't get it, let me read the list, so we can get started," continued the host. "Of course, you all understand that thinking and talking about death isn't the easiest thing to do. But sooner or later, we must face the music, all of us, whether we like it or not. We must think of death in the context of our lives. We must give it some meaning. We must overcome some of the stereotypes that lead to our fear of dying. Here are just a few of the questions I think we should be asking ourselves." He pulled out a list and started reading: "Just think about your own death for a minute. How much time and energy have you spent on thinking about your feelings, your beliefs, your hopes and fears about the end of your life? What if you were told that you have a limited time left to live, how would you spend it? Would it change anything about the way that you live your life? Are there things that you would like to accomplish before you reach the end? Are there things that you would want to set in order before you die? To tell the truth, are you afraid of dying? What is it you fear about dying? Where would you like to die, if it were up to you? Have you helped someone you love die a peaceful death? What would you talk about with someone who is dying? How would you spend your time together in those last few weeks or days? Have you ever thought of all the legal details that need to be attended to before your death? Do you have any unfinished business with your parents, children, siblings, friends, or co-workers that you should take care of before your own death or theirs?"

The dentist took a deep breath, paused, looked around the room as if to check over his audience, and continued: "I know, this is a long and heavy list, but I'll finish with just a few more questions and then throw open the discussion. So here are the rest. How much life support do you want to have if you have a fatal illness? If you are brain dead, how would you want your family to handle it? Have you discussed your wishes with them? With your doctor? With a friend?"

As he finished his introduction, there was total silence. To me, frankly, the questions felt overwhelming. No one seemed to know what to say or where to start.

Then suddenly a voice broke the silence, much to everyone's relief. "Let's get right into it, then. You know what Woody Allen said about dying: 'It's impossible to experience one's death objectively and still carry a tune!' So, how do you want to discuss dying, as none of us here is dying?" said David.

We knew him as a jocular sort of fellow who, as a sales representative, always entertained his customers with a ready joke.

"Come on, David. You seem to be missing the point. Now is the time to discuss it. Once you're dying, it's too late. In my business, I always bring these things up. I know people don't like to talk about it, but they can see what the consequences will be if they're unprepared," said Larry, the insurance agent.

"OK, then, let's dispense with all these introductions. Obviously, we're all having a heck of a time getting on with the topic. It must really be a supersensitive issue," added Ivan, a husky Russian immigrant, now a history professor.

At that point, the hostess cut in: "How many of you have faced death in your past?"

Again, a long pause followed.

"I'm sure many of us can recall near-death experiences," Larry commented. "I, for one, had several close encounters during the Korean war. Some of you are even old enough to recall World War II, aren't you? But are we going to swap war stories, or are we going to talk about the business of dying in today's world of high technology, just as we said we would?"

"No, I think we agreed on talking about the basic questions!" asserted Paula, a divorce attorney.

"Well, don't keep us in suspense. What is the central question that we need to resolve tonight?" asked Mike, a soft-spoken, bearded, and stocky artist.

The history professor picked this opportunity to jump in, seeming eager to talk: "As some of you may already know, I have thought about these questions, off and on, since my wife got ovarian cancer a couple of years ago. And after all she went through—you know, the chemo, the radiation, and all that stuff—we had several long serious talks."

"I bet the first question to ask yourself is whether you'll want to go the whole nine yards if you become terminally ill." David, the young sales representative, went right to the point. "Personally, I, for one, don't want to be a hero. I don't need to prove anything to myself or to anyone else. I'll be satisfied if I can just check out quietly. You know what they say about death on Madison Avenue: 'Death is just nature's way of telling you to slow down!' And that's what I believe, too."

Ivan answered, "It's not quite that simple, David. You have to think about the pain, the struggle, the humiliation, the others around you. You see, when Margaret got ovarian cancer, she already had metastases. She knew her cancer was spreading. The doctors were cautious about what they were saying, and they made no promises but they still gave us hope. So, we went along with it."

He paused for a few seconds, then continued: "I didn't know

what to think. I was an emotional wreck. But my wife was strong. She said she'd fight it and beat it!" You could hear the lump in his throat. "I didn't have the heart to let her down. I didn't know if she wanted me to fight with her or wanted me to help her die. And I didn't want to work against the doctors."

"Do you really want to talk about it, Ivan?" asked the hostess with concern.

"Yeah! This is your topic. You wouldn't want to skip over it, would you? Please let me go on," Ivan pleaded. "So, shortly after she was diagnosed, she began to feel weak and incredibly tired. Our lives began to change drastically. She couldn't go out anymore. We stopped socializing. Later, she began to feel bloated, unable to eat, and she started losing weight. Then she got sick from the chemo. Her hair fell out and she felt nauseated much of the time. We started talking about what might happen. Again, she seemed to be the strong one. Sometimes I couldn't hold back my tears. I was ashamed to cry in front of her for fear of upsetting her even more, but she would end up comforting me. She'd tell me about her visualization exercises and how she was going to overcome this enemy inside her."

Ivan seemed to tire as he related the story. He took a long pause. Total silence reigned in the room. He took a deep breath and went on: "Then she went from bad to worse. The pain became intolerable. She got only a few moments of relief from the medicines. Later, she couldn't hold her bladder. I changed her, bathed her, and cleaned her up. I held her and told her how much I loved her. We hadn't made love in months, and she told me how sorry she felt. I began to think about alternatives for her. I consulted George [referring to me], you know, our friendly psychiatrist. And he asked me if she had talked about dying."

He stopped talking again and looked around the room, as if to see if people were still listening. "Anyway, the end was no picnic, let me tell you. She looked ghastly. She knew she was slowly dying. She agreed not to go back to the hospital no matter what. She wanted to be with me more than anything else."

Ivan continued after a sip of coffee: "I don't want to drag

this thing on, but one evening the phone rang. It was George again. He had called almost every other day. Again he was wondering how we were doing. I told him that she was still hanging on, but I thought the end was near. After I hung up, I went back to her room. There she was, smiling at me. She took my hand and squeezed it, and within seconds she died."

The group was spellbound. A few people came over to Ivan and put their hands on his shoulders and said, "I'm sorry."

"I have had a great deal of time to think about what I would do if I had been in her shoes," Ivan said. "First, let me tell you, you've got to decide for yourself if you want to put up with all this pain and suffering and all this loss of control over your bodily functions, not to mention all the transformation of your personality as the illness goes on."

David cut in, feeling it was time to lighten up the mood again: "You know what they say, Ivan. Everyone wants to go to heaven but nobody wants to die!"

"At least she was in full control of her faculties," said the attorney. "I can't think of anything worse than not being mentally alert, I mean, like those people who are brain dead."

"Go on. Tell us what you think," said the hostess.

"Just imagine what it would be like to be hooked up to all those machines with tubes coming out of every orifice of your body, while you're trying to die quietly and peacefully. I know because I saw what happened to a friend of mine," Paula said in a challenging tone of voice, as if she were defending a client in the courtroom.

"What happened to him?" asked Jill, the accountant.

"He lingered on and on. He had been admitted with a head injury after an automobile accident. They found that he had brain damage, and soon afterward he slipped into a coma."

"And then what happened?" asked Robert, the dentist.

"His heart had stopped, but they used these electric paddles—what do you call them—you know, as if to jump-start his heart, and sure enough, they got his heart started again. Then they put him on a respirator. And then they hooked him up to various monitors, one for his heart, one for his brain, and one for his kidneys. They even had tubes bringing food and fluids into his veins and tubes taking fluids out of his body. It was like a freak show at the circus, a whole bloody mess, I'm telling you."

"How was it resolved?" yelled David from the back of the room.

"The poor fellow went on and on for several weeks. His poor family, they didn't know what to think or what to do. What could they do, anyway? They felt helpless, confused, out of control. No one seemed willing to talk to them about the alternatives. I myself tried to talk to his family, but they said they were afraid to talk to the doctors."

Paula seemed eager to go on. "To tell you the truth, I had not thought very much about this whole thing, so I'm afraid I wasn't much help either."

"So, what happened, for God's sake?" yelled David at the back.

"He lasted about ten weeks. Later they transferred him from the intensive-care unit to a private room. There he seemed to shrivel up in his hospital bed. People lost interest in him, or so it seemed. Then one evening, just after I had visited him, he died with all the contraptions still in place." There was a sad note in Paula's voice.

When she continued, her tone changed. "I knew then that this would never happen to me. I'd make damn sure, I'm telling you. The hospital bill alone was $175,000! And for what?"

A long silence followed. Everyone seemed to be thinking about what they would do if they found themselves in a similar predicament.

"But you can't interfere with God's will," said Joan, the hostess, after breaking the silence.

"That's precisely the point. I don't think that you are interfering with God's will if you let nature take its course. Quite the contrary, you're interfering if you let total strangers take over the control of your body and your soul with machines and monitors. I know now that they could do that only 'over my dead body.' What I choose to do with my body is my business, and when my brain is gone, I know it's time to go," Paula replied with conviction.

Robert decided to join in: "Of course, I have little to do with death in my practice, although occasionally my patients do invite me to the funerals of their loved ones. I guess one of the questions that we must ask ourselves, whether we are brain dead or suffering from a terminal condition, is 'Would we want to linger on?'"

"Yeah, that's the bottom line," Helen, a vibrant business executive, concluded with approval.

Mitsuo, the minister, who had been quiet up to this point, broke in after a pause: "I think that the way you live is the way you die. If you had a good life, then you'll have a good death. You have to accomplish what you set out to do in this life. As some of you know, I do counsel people just before they die, and I have seen a few hundred by now. You need to relieve them from the fear of dying. Some people, however, are in full control and have no fear. Let me tell you a little story about my mother."

Everyone became totally attentive. Mits, as we called him affectionately, did not speak often, but when he did, he always had something important or amusing to say. "My mother had a good life. She had raised a large family, and she had accomplished what she wanted to do. She was in her nineties. She knew that she was approaching the end. I, too, knew that the end was near. I had to go out of town to give a workshop, but I felt that, as for all my people who are about to die, I needed to tell her that it was all right to let go and not to be afraid, and that I would give her permission to die. So the day before I left on my trip, I went to see her, sat next to her bed, and held her hand. I said, 'Mother, I know the end is near, and I want to give you permission to die, even if I'm gone on my trip.' She looked me straight in the eye with total indignation and answered, "Son I don't need your permission to die. Just remember, I'm still your mother, and if I want to die after you leave, then it's my business. I'll do as I please when I'm good and ready!"

Everybody laughed, and suddenly the atmosphere seemed much lighter. Then everyone settled down for a few minutes, and we agreed to conclude our meeting soon so we could serve our refreshments to end the evening. At that juncture, my wife picked up the loose thread in the meeting.

She seemed to have prepared to speak. "Let me say a few words. Death in my view is a very personal matter. I know that since my son died, I have not been afraid to die. Each of us can relate the dying experience to a personal meaning in our lives. Sometimes, something happens in our lives—a death, an accident we witness, a serious illness we overcome, a war, or a friend's dying—that changes our whole perspective on living and on dying.

"The important thing is to keep an open mind toward your options and to keep your channels of communication open with your family. You must let others know now what you think and what you would wish for yourself when the time comes. In my teaching of nursing students, I always stress how important it is to explore how a family feels. Let me give you an example."

She took a sip of water and went on: "Recently, I visited a man in the hospice program in which I teach and consult. The man was an old Filipino, lying in bed in a moribund state, all skin and bones, dying of cancer and pneumonia. He had been lying that way for weeks. Several members of the family, including his wife, were quietly crying around his bed. Seeing them like that, I assumed that they were saddened by the impending death. I said to them, 'It must be hard to see him die this way.' To my surprise, they said, 'We aren't crying because he is dying. We're crying because he keeps on living like this in such pain and misery. We wish God would hurry up and take him soon!'

"I then found out that he was being maintained on antibiotics, unbeknownst to the family. I spoke to the doctor and relayed the man's wishes and his family's hopes. The doctor said he understood and stopped the antibiotics. The man died a few days later."

The evening was drawing to an end. I felt that I had been too quiet. I could sense that others were expecting me to say something, judging from several glances in my direction. Someone finally said, "George, you've been awfully quiet. We'd like to hear your ideas on the subject."

So I joined in. "Everybody is different when it comes to dying. I see it all the time when I see patients in the hospital or in my office. It's easy to theorize what you might do when you're well, but when you're dying, you get a different perspective on life. You begin to appreciate each day as if it is the last one. You begin to live to the fullest. It's strange that most of us don't understand this until we've had an experience that brings us closer to death, either personally or through someone we care about.

"One of the things that's hardest for any of us to imagine is our not being alive, being nonexistent, so to speak. However, it doesn't prevent us from being theoretical and having a general idea of what we'd want in case we become terminally ill or stuck in coma. But just think for a minute. Who will know what we want unless *we* tell our families and friends? Who will know unless we write it down clearly in a document like a living will, something perfectly clear, notarized, and legal? And who will know unless our doctor gets a copy of it? And who will know how we feel if we don't talk about our unfinished business with our loved ones, our friends, our children. If we are lucky enough to die with some warning, we may have time to do all these things. But just in case we don't, we should let our wishes and preferences be known regarding our dying—in case we should get stuck in some intensive-care unit!"

I felt that I was beginning to lecture, just as I do sometimes to a group of interns and residents at the hospital. So I decided to stop.

Larry, the insurance agent, picked up the ball and reinforced what I had just said: "As I said before, we must ask ourselves if we have prepared and if we have planned. Especially today. Don't leave things to luck or to others, especially the ending of your life and after. What we heard today should help us think about all this. And most of all, we need to tell somebody, sign a living will and a power of attorney, and for God's sake, talk to our doctors."

But the history professor had to have the last word. "This discussion reminds me of what Sophocles said over two thousand years ago: 'Death is not the greatest of ills; it is worse to want to die and not be able to.' "

WILL YOU BE TOLD THE TRUTH ABOUT AN INCURABLE ILLNESS?

Through experience and through training, doctors have learned not to answer questions directly about death and dying. They wait for patients to take the lead on the subject and give them a clue. The following case will illustrate the point.

When a seventy-three-year-old woman entered the hospital recently, she thought she had pneumonia. When she went home six days later, she had chosen to die.

In between, she had learned that she had a fatal illness and had to make the kind of decision that confronts a growing number of aging Americans: whether to prolong her life aggressively with modern technology or to surrender to the natural dying process. The patient, whom we shall call Marian Lee, chose to give up to death.

Dr. O'Donnell had finished a cup of tea before entering the patient's room on her Friday rounds. "How're you feeling this morning?" she asked.

"I'm not off to a good start today," said a pale Mrs. Lee. "Everything seems to hurt."

The doctor chose her words carefully as she responded to her patient. She mentioned Mrs. Lee's medical history of respiratory problems and said, "We have found some lumps on your lungs. They are tumors and appear to be spreading rapidly." She paused briefly, then she went on, "Did you have an idea that something serious was happening to you?"

Mrs. Lee nodded slowly.

Dr. O'Donnell continued, "We don't know yet what kind of tumors you have. There are so many different kinds. Some respond to treatment, but there are some that we can't do very much about." After a pause, she went on, "Mrs. Lee, you've been an avid tennis player most of your life. We may be in the final set."

"That's something I can understand," Mrs. Lee replied, a wry smile creeping over her face.

"Do you have any questions?"

"Not now, doctor."

On the patient's chart, Dr. O'Donnell noted her exchange with Mrs. Lee and wrote, "Discuss prognosis with patient and family tomorrow."

Dr. O'Donnell returned to Mrs. Lee's room the following morning, and the patient was dozing. Noting on the chart that the nurse had given the patient morphine after her complaint of severe pain during the night, the doctor decided to come back later.

That afternoon, Mrs. Lee was alert again. Dr. O'Donnell greeted her and said, "I spoke with the oncologist early this morning. We can treat some of your pain with radiation. But you might find this a miserable dragging out of a bad situation that is probably not going to improve. I'd say we might be approaching 'match point.'" The doctor knew from her longtime relationship with Mrs. Lee that she could tell her the truth.

"I understand," said the still athletic-looking woman. "My family and I have talked about my prospects, and I've told them that I want to go home. You've done everything you could, and we really appreciate that."

When Dr. O'Donnell asked her patient if she understood the implications of her decision to go home, Mrs. Lee smiled, reaching toward the doctor, who took her hand and squeezed it gently, feeling a lump rise in her own throat.

Mrs. Lee's daughter followed the doctor out of the room. "How much time does she have?"

"Perhaps no more than a few days."

"That's what we figured," said the daughter, her face reflecting her own pain.

Dr. O'Donnell signed the necessary papers to release Mrs. Lee for round-the-clock care in her home.

Five days later, the daughter called the physician to say that her mother had died peacefully during the night with her family around her. Mrs. Lee had asked her daughter to call Dr. O'Donnell to thank her for allowing her to "finish her match" with dignity.

As you can see from the case just described, direct answers are not always necessary.

It's not always easy for a dying person to get straight answers about what is going on. For one thing, some people would rather not know. On the other hand, the majority of people would rather hear the truth. Then, some physicians have difficulty giving a straightforward answer for fear it will hurt the patient, not to mention arouse their own feelings of frustration and failure.

Physician behavior has changed since the early 1960s. Not telling the truth about cancer diagnosis, for example, was not uncommon thirty years ago. It was called the practice of benign deception, and it was thought to be in the best interest of the patient.

In 1979, Dennis Novack and his associates published the results of a survey in the *Journal of the American Medical Association*. This survey had found that 97 percent of doctors preferred to tell their patients that they had a diagnosis of cancer. In contrast, in a survey taken two decades earlier, 90 percent of doctors had said they would *not* tell their patients.

Nowadays, if a patient has cancer and the doctor does not want to say so, the answer might be "I don't know yet." And if the doctor refuses to say one way or the other, the patient may interpret this refusal as a probable yes. We know through experience that most patients who are not given a clear answer about their condition will assume that they are in worse shape than they really are.

Contrary to what many people believe, learning the truth about one's condition may be upsetting for a short while, but it will not hasten death. On the other hand, not knowing the truth can produce a great deal more anxiety, doubt, and insomnia. Eventually, a patient left in the dark will try to get at the truth anyway by asking others, such as nurses, family, friends, or his or her minister. And sooner or later, the patient with a serious illness will confront the doctor with a direct question: "Tell me, doctor, am I going to make it?"

Most doctors agree that it's neither useful nor productive—in fact, it's even cruel—to tell patients that they are going to die within a certain period of time, such as in two weeks, two months, or two years. Too many wrong guesses have been made in the past. But occasionally, the patient and the family will press doctors to know approximately what time span remains, so that arrangements can be made to do what must be done. In those cases, doctors may give a range, such as six to twelve months, a year to eighteen months.

Recently, I saw a patient in my office whose roommate had died of AIDS. He himself had been HIV positive, and now he knew he had AIDS himself. When he asked me how long I thought he had left to live, I replied, "It's difficult to say, but you'd better be prepared to live one day at a time from now on." He smiled and said that he had just started to do so and, in fact, had "put his house in order."

Three weeks later, the man contracted pneumocystis pneumonia, and he died within two weeks.

HOW MUCH DOES IT COST TO MANAGE A TERMINAL ILLNESS?

Another aspect of dying is the financial burden often put on the family of the terminally ill. People spend more than 50 percent of their health-care dollars on the last few months of life. Although it is not easy to estimate the costs of medical care for terminal patients, we do know that, at this writing, the cost of treatment in an intensive-care unit reaches up to $1,000 a day. On the other hand, the cost of hospice care is considerably less, usually no more than a third. And, of course, care in the home costs even less.

Intricate technology and highly specialized staff are, in fact, very costly. One group of researchers did a study of high-cost patients in nine acute-care hospitals in the San Francisco area. They defined high-cost patients as those accruing a bill of $4,000 or more in 1981. Those high-cost patients accounted for almost 40 percent of the entire hospital revenue, and 48 percent of those who had accumulated a bill of over $10,000 had died within a few months.[2] Blue Cross and Blue Shield also did a survey of the cost of care. They found that the average American who died of cancer in 1983 incurred more than $22,000 of illness-related expenses during the last year of life, which today would be equivalent to $37,000 if cost is projected at an increase of 7 percent a year. During that last year, patients dying of cancer spent over one month in the acute care unit, which accounted for more than 78 percent of the total bill.[3]

Imagine all that expense just to keep someone alive in the midst of suffering and a hopeless prognosis.

WHO DECIDES ABOUT PROLONGING LIFE?

> *I think there is no such thing as medical ethics. There are only universal human ethics applied to specified human situations.*
>
> —Erich Fromm

Terminally ill patients frequently pose many problems for the medical and nursing professions. And imponderable questions invariably arise when the illness lasts for weeks or months. For example, who decides whether too much treatment is doing more harm than good? Who decides whether or when life-prolonging measures should be stopped? Who decides what constitutes ordinary or extraordinary measures? Who decides whether life still has any meaning or not?

These questions and many others have haunted people's minds for decades. But today, the questions are more pressing and burdensome as the technology changes from year to year. People increasingly need to think about the alternatives to living indefinitely or dying. It's true that bioethics committees are now functioning in many hospitals throughout the country, though still mostly in large centers. But in other areas of the country, only our conscience prevails. That conscience rests mostly on philosophical, religious, and humanistic traditions rather than on well-established guidelines. We need much more information and education if we want to be able to make more reasonable decisions.

In the end, the final decision rests with you. And that is why finding out as much as you can now will prepare you better for the future.

DO YOU HAVE A RIGHT TO DISCONTINUE LIFE-SUSTAINING MACHINES?

Yes, you should have such a right! However, problems arise sometimes with the medical profession and sometimes with the legal profession as well, if we have not made a written statement of our wishes. (See Chapter 7 for a discussion of landmark legal cases.)

In some instances, it is the institution that refuses to honor the patient's wishes to discontinue life-sustaining treatment or medication. The patient then has the right to request a transfer to another hospital or nursing home.

However, most physicians today will accept their patients' choices. Doctors are learning that to respect their patients' choices, even though they may not agree, is frequently the best course of action. It may not only be the best guarantee that the doctor will not be blamed later on, but it is also a way to keep the doctor–patient relationship on a positive and respectful course.

You should try to ascertain ahead of time if the doctor does in fact have a nonjudgmental and accepting attitude.

IF A PATIENT IS UNABLE TO DECIDE ABOUT EXTRAORDINARY MEANS, WHO SHOULD DECIDE?

Certainly the patient's wishes, if known, should be respected with regard to extraordinary means. Ideally, the treatment team composed of the attending doctor, specialists, nurses, a social worker, the hospital administrator, and, in some cases, a consulting psychiatrist, will convene to discuss the specifics of the situation, including the factors involving the family. In large centers, the bioethics committee of the hospital usually serves that function. The committee's role is to facilitate consensus after informing and educating everyone on the major issues in the case.

In most instances, a satisfactory solution can be reached.

WHY WON'T SOME PHYSICIANS ALLOW THEIR PATIENTS TO DIE?

You must remember that physicians have been trained to preserve life and relieve suffering. At least, that is what the Hippocratic oath advocates. Some have argued that the oath is not keeping up with the times, whereas others have maintained that the oath helps the ethical attitude we need in today's society. But many physicians regard death as a failure, and they feel uncomfortable or even upset when "a patient dies on them." It is very much a matter of attitude.

When I was an intern, one of my first patients was an elderly lady who was unconscious after a stroke. She was being maintained with antibiotics and suction through a tracheotomy. I recall how anxious I was to maintain her breathing and heart function with all the available means, thinking that my chief resident would perceive her death as "my failure." The morning after I had been up most of the night trying to keep her alive, much to my surprise the chief resident said, " What in the world are you trying to do? Can't you just let this poor old lady die in peace and stop disturbing her?"

Physicians often have a hard time telling the truth about a fatal diagnosis because they don't want to worry the patient or the family. More often than not, they try to deliver the truth with a message of hope, as no one can be sure of the future. They must remember that, in the face of an incurable illness, getting well may no longer be the major goal. The primary task should be to achieve peace of mind and freedom from fear. As Bernie Siegel recommends in *Love, Medicine and Miracles*, "Getting well is not the only goal. Even more important is learning to live without fear, to be at peace with life and ultimately death."[4]

Ideally, if you can share your feelings and express your choices of treatment with your doctor, you have the best chance of retaining a sense of control and achieving a feeling of peace within yourself. This is not to say that you must make all the decisions. You will want to know what your doctor thinks and recommends before you make up your own mind.

TO WHAT EXTENT CAN A PATIENT SHARE WITH THE DOCTOR IN THE DECISION ABOUT TREATMENT OR NONTREATMENT?

Physicians' attitudes toward their patients' participation in the decision-making process are changing. If you can share in the responsibility for your health and treatment, both you and your doctor will benefit. Your relationship with your doctor will become more trusting, and you will lighten the tremendous burden of responsibility that frequently affects that relationship. Sharing in decisions will also prevent the resentment that often results from the paternalistic attitude of some physicians.

Sometimes physicians don't like the choices patients make,

but the best in the profession explain the facts and give the odds for a good or a bad outcome. Physicians do know the statistical probabilities for serious illnesses, and presenting that information is not being judgmental. They realize that their role is to help their patients make the right decisions for themselves.

The final choice of treatment always remains yours. What the physician can give you are the facts, the probabilities, experience with that kind of treatment, and personal feelings and recommendations based on knowledge of you. But that's all. You and you alone must decide. After all, it's your body and your person that are involved.

WHAT HAPPENS WHEN THE FAMILY DISAGREES WITH THE PATIENT?

> *A man's dying is more the survivors' affair than his own.*
>
> —Thomas Mann

Mann's opinion describes a common situation. It usually occurs when a patient has reached the final stage of acceptance of death, but the family has not. That is, the family members, who are also going through the various stages of the dying experience, have not caught up with the patient's stage of acceptance and are still working through their feelings at an earlier stage. In these cases, the family must receive help to progress through their "unfinished business" until they, too, can finally "let go."

I am reminded of a college professor of art history who was dying of prostate cancer. He had metastases to the bones and had severe pain during the few months of counseling sessions that he had with me. He had reached the stage of acceptance and was ready to die. He told me that, with the help of his morphine pump, he could choose approximately the time of his death, but he could tell how much his wife was struggling with and stressed by his illness. He tried to help her and reassure her that he was alright emotionally, that he was not afraid, and that he was ready to be in peace.

When I saw her during an office visit for psychotherapy, she was still in the stage of depression and anger. Gradually, however, she began to deal with the unfinished business of his abandoning her one more time—as she complained he had done several times in the past. After she was able to forgive him for all past misdeeds, she was able to "let go." He died a couple of days later, much to her relief, because she knew that he was no longer suffering.

IF YOU WANT TO DIE AT HOME, IS THAT THE SAME AS EUTHANASIA?

Patients with incurable illnesses today can choose to die at home. This approach to care is called *hospice without walls,* and the care is given with the help of doctors, visiting nurses, and social workers.

The team of caregivers' main concern is to make the patient comfortable without resorting to artificial means, assuming that this is the wish of the patient and the family. But most of all, this arrangement enables the dying to spend their final days or weeks in the home, surrounded by love and support. This is not to be confused with euthanasia, passive or active, which consists of facilitating the dying process. (Chapter 8 includes a detailed discussion of euthanasia.)

IF YOU WANT HELP IN THE DYING PROCESS, WHAT CAN YOU DO?

The decision to forgo life-sustaining measures is something you can do today if that is your desire and if you have prepared the proper living will and durable power of attorney. (See Chapter 10 for details.)

Sometimes a patient has a well-established diagnosis of incurable illness and has reached a state of acceptance. If the family is also at peace, the patient can request the halt of all life-sustaining measures. In the majority of cases, the doctor and the institution will respect the patient's wishes. (See Chapter 7 for landmark legal cases.)

When there is conflict with the doctor or the institution, it is best to ask for another opinion, to change your doctor, or simply to transfer to another institution.

The matter of active euthanasia is another story. It refers to another person's giving the dying patient a lethal dose of drugs on the patient's request, or to helping the dying process by any other direct means. Although active euthanasia is still against the law, legislation is being considered in several states (see Chapters 7 and 8 for details).

> *Death is not the ultimate tragedy in life.*
> *The ultimate tragedy is to die without*
> *discovering the possibilities of full*
> *growth. The approach of death need*
> *not be denial of that growth.*
> —Norman Cousins

KEY QUESTIONS TO ASK
YOURSELF WHEN YOU ARE WELL

The following questions are not easy to ponder, yet, thinking through some of your answers will help you work through your doubts and prepare you to discuss these issues with your doctor, family, or friends.

1. Do you feel that life is worth living at all costs, even if it means surviving with machines, monitors, respirators, and tube-feedings?
2. Do you believe that life is worth living if you become brain dead?
3. Do you feel that stopping life-sustaining treatment is contrary to your religious beliefs or to your philosophy?

4. Do you feel that in the case of a terminal illness it would be preferable to let nature take its course rather than apply heroic efforts to maintain life?

5. Do you believe that one can have a good death as opposed to a bad death?

6. Do you attach much importance to whether your doctors understand your feelings, your needs, and your wishes concerning your death?

7. Do you care how your doctor stands on the issue of life-sustaining treatment? Would you prefer to leave life-and-death decisions with your doctor?

8. Would you feel free to discuss life-and-death decisions with your doctor?

9. If not, do you feel strongly enough about those issues so that you would consider changing your doctor?

10. Does your family know and understand your feelings and preferences about dying?

11. Would you be willing and prepared to let your wishes and preferences be known in writing?

12. Have you prepared for your family's welfare and well-being after you're gone?

13. Have you thought about organ transplantation? If so, would you be willing to donate some of your organs to save someone else's life?

14. Would you wish to find a way to terminate your life painlessly if you had an incurable illness, were suffering enormous pain, or were brain dead?

15. Would you want some aid in dying from a physician if this were legal?

This chapter has given you food for thought about dying. The questions raised in the above discussion will give rise to even more questions. They might stimulate you to do more reading in the fields of thanatology and bioethics, or they might facilitate further discussions with your peer groups.

You may choose to do your thinking privately from time to

time, or you may choose to discuss these issues with your mate, your close friends, your parents, or your grown children.

Keep in mind that these are the kinds of questions that will open up your heart and theirs to your innermost feelings. The dialogue that may ensue will free you and your family, and you and your doctor, for future decision-making encounters, especially when you get closer to the end of your life.

In the next two chapters, I explore the kinds of encounters in which these questions will facilitate your interactions. As you will see, the medical profession sometimes has as much trouble as you do in finding the right questions to ask. And knowing how to talk about death and dying, whether it is with your doctor or with your family, will go a long way toward easing the fears and anxieties that you and they might have.

NOTES

1. D. H. Novack, R. Plumber, R. L. Smith, H. Ochitil, G. R. Morrow, and J. M. Bennett, "Changes in Physicians' Attitudes Toward Telling the Cancer Patient," *Journal of the American Medical Association* 241 (1979): 897-900.
2. S. A. Schroeder, J. A. Showstack, and J. Schwartz, "Survival of Adult High Cost Patients," *Journal of the American Medical Association* 245 (1981): 1446–1449.
3. W. Hines, "Cost of Cancer Care," *Chicago Sun-Times*, 9 February, 1983, 72.
4. Bernie Siegel, *Love, Medicine and Miracles* (New York: Harper & Row, 1986), 51–52.

CHAPTER 3

What Your Doctor May Not Tell You about Dying

> *I am dying with the help of too many physicians.*
> —Alexander the Great (356–323 B.C.)

Dying used to be a simple and private affair between patient and physician. Common sense usually dictated what was best to do when the patient was ill and dying. Because complex technology is now available to nearly everyone in this country, what was once a matter simply of life and death has become a very complicated subject that encompasses a growing variety of issues related to dying.

In this chapter, I share with you the way that physicians think and feel about dying, death, and euthanasia. I believe that knowing what physicians' attitudes are will help you understand the medical profession's point of view. I hope it will prepare you to speak to your doctor about your own feelings and concerns regarding the question of dying with dignity and without pain.

THE MEDICAL TECHNOLOGY TRAP

Once admitted to a hospital today, you *may* become trapped indefinitely by a complex medical technology even if there is no hope of recovery. If you become stuck in this never-never land of an existence without consciousness, the legal system cannot or will not improve your situation. Furthermore, physicians and other staff members often become entangled in a maze of regulations that may further ensnare you and your family.

"Today, there are so many more choices and options, so many treatments, some with serious side effects, that the physician's role now primarily is to explain the various options of treatment—the pros and cons. The physician has become an adviser, not the decision-maker," says Russel Patterson, professor of neurosurgery at Cornell University Medical College.[1]

The situation has become increasingly difficult in a variety of ways. For example, advance directives, such as living wills, DNR (do not resuscitate) orders, and health-care proxies, are supposed to simplify the life-and-death decision-making process. But in practice, health professionals perceive those directives in such a legalistic way that their attitudes tend to complicate the picture.

Although the idea of providing patients with more choices and freedom of action seems to be a universally approved goal, the path finding ways of meeting these noble objectives may be littered with major obstacles.

"More and more, professionals are interested in the form rather than the substance—literally," says George Annas, Director of the Health, Law and Ethics Program at Boston University's School of Public Health. He goes on to say, "People care more about the bureaucracy and what's best for the bureaucracy than what's best for the patient."[2]

On December 1, 1991, the first federal law was passed in this area; the Patient Self-Determination Act requires hospitals, nursing homes, hospices, and home-health-care agencies that receive Medicare or Medicaid funds to provide patients with information about their right to determine in advance whether they want to have life-sustaining medical treatment if they become hopelessly sick. Patients must be informed of the relevant state laws on advance instructions such as the living will and the health-care proxy. In the living will, patients outline the circumstances under which life-sustaining treatment should be withdrawn. In the health-care proxy, patients designate a trusted person to make decisions about their care, should they become incapacitated. So when you are admitted to a qualified health-care facility, you will be advised of your right to a proxy, and you will be asked to sign special forms. These should relieve the physician of the burden of what to decide and what to do in the event of a prolonged death.

Despite these legal attempts to help patients deal with the problems involved in such a situation, few people understand the issues. It is not a matter of whether you are going to live or die, nor a question of when you are going to die. It is a question of *how* you are going to die. Most of us don't really understand this, and most of us don't really want to think or talk about it. Yet, sooner or later, we have to stop fooling ourselves.

Recall the case of Nancy Cruzan discussed in Chapter 1. That case raised the question of the right to discontinue futile treatment, all the way to the U.S. Supreme Court for the first time and allowed people to think about them in personal terms. Having a health-care proxy is no longer an option that applies mostly to other people. It has become a matter of necessity that applies to you and me.

"It's gotten to the point that if you don't have it written down, the doctors and nurses don't know what to do," says Annas.[3] But even with all the paperwork completed and all the directives explained, most of us cannot predict what the technology will be able to do to our bodies in years to come. Therefore, we are unable to anticipate what decisions will have to be made. In the end, we may have to go back to common sense.

DOCTORS AND THE HIPPOCRATIC OATH

> *Care more for the individual patient than*
> *for the special features of the disease.*
> —Sir William Osler

Many people believe that doctors are bound by the Hippocratic oath. Physicians based the oath on a tradition that had been handed down through the centuries, and that tradition began with Hippocrates, the famous Greek physician from the island of Kos, who promulgated ethical guidelines for the profession as a way of overcoming the prevalent superstitions. As time went on, the guidelines became increasingly out of date and had little relevance to the current practice of medicine. A physician historian confirmed this view when he wrote, "Time does change most things, if not all things. The passage of twenty-four centuries certainly changes the circumstances under which one must interpret facts. Thus, it seems to me, we must see these principles in their broadest sense and not be bogged down by literal interpretations."[4]

On the other hand, physicians like Richard Kravitz uphold the Hippocratic oath as particularly relevant just because of changes in society. He says that the oath gives physicians an opportunity to reaffirm their stand for good conduct and "furthermore, law is the arbiter of good conduct only in good societies. When law and individual conscience conflict, ethical codes may be a guide to physicians grappling with difficult choices."[5]

Interestingly, the Hippocratic oath says nothing about actually preserving life. It comes down to how one interprets the phrase, "so far as power and discernment shall be mine, I will carry out regimen for the benefit of the sick and will keep them from harm and wrong."

In 1948, the World Medical Association (WMA) issued an improved version of the oath, seemingly in direct response to the horrors perpetrated by Nazi doctors. The WMA issued the new version in Geneva, and it became known as the Geneva version of the "Hippocratic oath, or the Geneva oath. For the benefit of the interested reader, here is the text in full: "Now being admitted to the profession of medicine, I solemnly pledge to consecrate my life to the services of humanity. I will give respect and gratitude to my deserving teachers. I will practice medicine with conscience and dignity. The health and life of my patient will be my first consideration. I will hold in confidence all that my patient confides in me.

I will maintain the honor and the noble traditions of the medical profession. My colleagues will be as my brothers. I will not permit consideration of race, religion, nationality, party politics or social standing to intervene between my duty and my patient. I will maintain the utmost respect for human life from the time of its conception. Even under threat I will not use my knowledge contrary to the laws of humanity.

"These promises I make freely and upon my honor."[6]

As you can see, there is no reference to treatment and care for the hopelessly ill and the dying. And although the Geneva version has removed most vestiges of antiquated social references that many would find offensive today, it, too, has room for improvement in its sexist language. So, in the end, doctors must rely on their own interpretations of the oath, heeding the age-old dictum of "Primum non nocere" ("First, do no harm"). Although the oath says nothing about prolonging life for the hopelessly ill, Kubler-Ross reminds us that "patients who are beyond medical help and whose organs are kept functioning only with machines are not benefiting from this kind of management, and we should have the courage to learn when to call it quits!"[7]

IS DEATH THE ENEMY?

Contrary to what most people believe, doctors fear death as much as the rest of us. But to most physicians, death isn't just one thing. It has come to mean many things. Remember that medical tradition calls for preserving life and alleviating suffering; yet death may contradict one goal while possibly facilitating the other. Although physicians have learned to hate death as an enemy to be defeated, many physicians, especially those who see death daily or weekly, recognize death as ending pain or bringing peace at the end of a long and productive life.

"When physicians see somebody dying from a curable disease, they will fight tooth and nail to save that person. But let them be by the bedside of a failed old body, and they're not afraid of death," says Eric J. Cassell, a clinical professor of public health at Cornell Medical College in New York.[8]

Physicians do not spend much time studying or talking about death. In conferences or daily clinical activities, they focus their attention on solving the disease problem, coping with the symptoms, or finding a way to alleviate suffering.

Perhaps it is true that physicians are not programmed to think about death, and some will admit that, like most of us, they don't want to think about it. But a more likely explanation is that they get caught up in the use of technology without thinking much about when enough is enough. They become totally engaged in battling the disease process. This is particularly true when a number of specialists are on the case, none of whom really knows the person in the body they are trying to save. Specialization today encourages physicians to treat symptoms or disorders without thinking much about the patient.

The reminder from Sir William Osler to care more for the patient than for the disease has been more or less forgotten, even though most physicians heard it more than once when in medical school. The reason is that technology has encouraged further specialization as its increasing impact has been felt. This specialization led George Starkey, a cardiothoracic surgeon at Boston's New England Deaconess Hospital, to say, "Fragmentation of services leads to dealing with diseases rather than with sick people." In doing so, he says, "We use the technology to deal with the immediate problem but miss the main problem, which is that the patient is trying to die."[9]

Some doctors do think about death as an option for their patients, but they are more likely to do so if they have gotten to know their patients over time. Unlike the specialists who focus on "the problem that needs fixing" rather than the person with the problem, those physicians who are involved with their patients as persons with feelings, families, personal goals, and past histories are likely to consider death a viable subject. "When the disease process calls for futile treatment, it is not very far from talking about futility to recognizing that death is a proper topic," says Howard Spiro, professor of medicine and director of the program for humanities in medicine at Yale University.[10]

But times are changing. Just as technology is advancing at a rapid pace, experts in the field are recognizing that we must educate the medical profession about the prolongation of suffering and the futilty of treating a terminal illness. Medical schools, medical organizations, and foundations are launching new programs to meet these needs.

A new program is being offered by the W. K. Kellogg Foundation. It is called the "Decisions near the End of Life Program." This program will help educate hospital staff about current ethical issues and will raise awareness of end-of-life decisions in the hospital setting. The goal is to encourage physicians and nurses to rethink their role with their patients, but before they can do this, they must consider the role that death plays in the drama. They must recognize death as an option for their patients—for you and me—when the time comes. Preserving life is only one of the functions that physicians must perform; relieving suffering is another important duty, even if it means helping a patient die gently. "Life is an abstract good," says Spiro, "but one that has to be balanced against the very real call to relieve suffering."[11]

HOW DOCTORS DEFINE DEATH

Since the arrival of modern technology, determining when death occurs has not been easy. Before the 1960s, people thought that death occurred when the heart stopped and respiration ceased. But now that machines can generate breathing and heartbeat almost indefinitely when a person is no longer conscious, a new definition of death has had to be established. This definition was particularly urgent because a new category of bodies was now being maintained through artificial means: bodies that had no hope of returning to spontaneous breathing or consciousness. Playing an increasing role in establishing a more accurate definition of death is the evolving practice of organ transplantation.

In 1981, President Ronald Reagan appointed a commission whose purpose was to establish a "definition of death," among other ethical problems being considered.[12] The president's commission concluded that physicians must take brain functions into account. Because we know that the brain controls all the bodily functions and that these functions can no longer occur spontaneously without help from the brain, the definition of death would require that doctors establish the presence or absence of brain activity. They can do this by using sophisticated equipment, such as the brain wave test (electroencephalogram).

The importance of brain functions in determining the occurrence of death led to the concept of *brain death*, which had been studied by several French neurophysiologists since 1959. Those researchers had conducted experiments on patients in extremely deep coma and on respirators. Because they could not detect any electrical brain activity, they concluded that the patients had suffered permanent brain damage and were, to use their words, "beyond coma."[13]

Later, the concept of brain death took on a greater importance because of the new practice of organ transplantation. Doctors now needed to harvest from donors various organs, such as kidneys, hearts, and livers. The practice had been regulated by the Uniform Anatomical Gift Act of 1968, which authorized the gift of all or part of a human body for specified purposes after death. However, Section 7 of the act, failed to give an updated definition of death. It said, "The time of death shall be determined by a physician who tends the donor at his death, or, if none, the physician who certifies the death."[14] Because of the confusion, critics of the act feared that doctors would obtain donor organs by declaring a donor dead before all resuscitation efforts had been made. The problem was further complicated by the fact that an organ transplant will be successful only if the organ is removed at the earliest possible moment. If the heart function is extended mechanically for a lengthy period, as in a brain-damaged donor, the organ to be used may deteriorate beyond being usable.

In addition to relieving the uncertainty and suffering of grieving families whose relatives were in a state of suspended animation, another pressing reason for determining brain death was the tremendous burden of keeping bodies without brain function in the intensive-care facilities so badly needed by other patients.

After considerable study to establish criteria, a group at Harvard published the report that became known as the *Harvard criteria*, which identified the characteristics of a person in "irreversible coma," that is, with a permanently nonfunctioning brain:

1. Total unresponsiveness and unreceptivity. This means that the person is totally unaware of her or his surroundings and does not respond to painful stimuli.
2. No movements or spontaneous breathing for three minutes while off the respirator, which means that all spontaneous movements, spontaneous respiration, and responses to pain, touch, sound, and light have ceased.
3. No reflexes. Pupils will not dilate; eyes will not turn when the head is turned; and tendon reflexes no longer exist.
4. Flat EEG (electroencephalogram) for at least ten minutes and no evidence of any electrical activity in the brain.
5. No change in the results of the tests repeated at least twenty-four hours later.

But before the criteria can be used, doctors must rule out intoxication by drugs (like barbiturates) and hypothermia (a body temperature below 90 F), which can cause a reversible loss of brain function.[15]

The Harvard criteria have turned out to be quite reliable, and doctors have reached a consensus about continuing to apply them despite some criticisms.[16]

The president's commission finally reached a uniform definition of death, which it worded in the form of a statute, the Uniform Determination of Death Act. The act states: "An individual who has sustained either (1) irreversible cessation of circulatory and respiratory functions or (2) irreversible cessation of all functions of the entire brain, including the brain stem, is dead. A determination of death must be made in accordance with accepted medical standards."

Shortly thereafter, the American Medical Association, the American Bar Association, and the National Conference of Commissioners on Uniform State Laws approved the statute. Subsequently, the majority of states adopted it.

HOW DOES MODERN TECHNOLOGY WORK TO KEEP YOUR BODY ALIVE?

> *This is my death . . . and it will profit me*
> *to understand it.*
>
> —Anne Sexton

During a life-threatening illness, doctors can initiate a number of treatment procedures to prolong cardiac function, even without hope for recovery. Ideally, they should discuss these measures with the patient ahead of time. At the time of a terminal illness, it may be awkward or even impossible to initiate such a discussion. Yet, health-care professionals do try to involve patients or their families in these discussions early, especially when there are a few more weeks of life left.

The main problem with life-sustaining and life-prolonging measures is that, in some cases, they may provide considerable relief, whereas they produce more pain and suffering in other cases. Each case must be judged on its own merits, but above all, the patient's wishes must be known to the health team if they are to proceed with some rationale and an understanding of the individual under their care. And that individual could be you.

Possible measures include a series of techniques to provide the body with nourishment through intravenous fluids or feedings through a nasogastric tube, which is inserted through the nose into the stomach, or through a tube that is surgically inserted into the stomach (gastrostomy).

If you were to develop pneumonia in the terminal stage of an illness, you might be given a course of antibiotics, which would deal with the infection but would do nothing more than prolong the course of the underlying life-threatening illness. On the other hand, if the problem is breathing, as in the case of an unconscious (comatose) patient, the medical team might provide you with a ventilator, a machine that assists the body with breathing. This assisted breathing may go on for years without your being aware of it.

Or you might be given intravenous steroids to reduce swelling of the brain (cerebral edema).

More often than not, a health team will proceed with cardiac resuscitation by using defibrillators (electrical plates applied to the chest to restart the heart muscle) or injections of adrenalin into the heart muscle.

Sometimes an opening must be made into the trachea (tracheotomy) for the insertion of a tube (intubation) that provides an airway.

Technically speaking, there is almost no limit to the capacity to keep a body alive for years, even without brain function.

Generally, these measures occur mostly in an emergency, when the health team initiates treatment, not knowing the wishes and the circumstances of the patient. They may find out later that the patient was not well served by their interventions. In some cases, overtreatment has become the subject of litigation, when life-sustaining measures get completely out of hand.[17,18] A good example is that of Carrie, a young respiratory therapist at a large hospital, who was just injured in an automobile accident.

THE CASE OF CARRIE

Carrie arrived at the hospital with multiple compound fractures of all limbs, facial fractures, and lacerations. She was also in a coma. Shortly after her arrival at the hospital, she was placed on a respirator. In order to keep the respirator working, a tracheotomy had to be performed. Meanwhile, the trauma team went to work. They stopped the bleeding, sutured all of her wounds and lacerations, and put casts on all of her limbs. They agreed to postpone orthopedic surgery until Carrie was more stable.

Carrie's condition did not stabilize. She remained in a persistent vegetative state over the next three weeks. Then she came out of her coma. Although she seemed alert, she could barely form a few words. At that point, her parents agreed to go ahead with the surgery. Until that time, Carrie had been able to move only a few muscles in her face.

Carrie knew a great deal about her situation. She had been in the U.S. Navy's medical corps, and she was very familiar with the plight she was in. She began to signal to her parents that she wanted them "to pull the plug." Her parents conveyed Carrie's wishes to the medical team, but the neurologist advised them to wait because, in time, things would get better.

Then the trauma team removed the casts. To everyone's surprise, Carrie could not move anything. In other words, she was a quadriplegic. A magnetic-resonance-imaging (MRI) scan was performed and showed no obvious damage to the spinal cord. "These things do take time," said the doctors, instilling some hope in the parents. The real questions that remained were these: Why wasn't Carrie breathing on her own? And why wasn't she moving?

Meanwhile, Carrie continued to grimace her wishes to be disconnected from the ventilator, but the doctors pursuaded the parents to transfer her to a rehabilitation center, where she could get further care.

Carrie continued to plead with the attending physician, the lung specialist, the nursing supervisor, and finally her minister. By that time, Carrie's parents had come around to her way of thinking and wanted to put a stop to her suffering. The hospital staff, however, felt that Carrie was having an "attitude problem" and that, with proper therapy and counseling, she might change her mind. Never mind that she had to be fed through a J-tube (a tube inserted surgically into her small intestine), that she couldn't swallow, that she couldn't eat, and that she couldn't smell, cry, laugh, or do anything that would require breath. Never mind that her face was contorted in constant pain, and that she was unable to wipe the tears streaming from her eyes. The doctors did agree that this was "the worst possible scenario of someone being trapped in her own body."

Carrie's parents began to explore legal means to put a stop to this horrible situation, but the medical director warned the parents that if they continued to insist on disconnecting the ventilator, he would charge them with murder.

Eventually, Carrie got an infection in her lungs, and this time, she refused to take antibiotics. After four more weeks of the medical ordeal, she developed meningitis. She had several seizures and finally died seven months after her admission to the hospital.[19]

This case indeed shows the need for guidelines on the subject of life-sustaining treatments. In this case, we recognize the tremendous power of medicine to prolong a life. But the capacity to prolong life, as in this case, can exceed the capacity to restore health. This case also demonstrates the power of the institution over doctors, patients, and their families, who will yield to threats and coercion under the weight of administrative and public pressure.

TO TREAT OR NOT TO TREAT: THAT IS THE QUESTION

The use of treatments such as cardiopulmonary resuscitation, mechanical ventilation, kidney dialysis, intubation, maintenance antibiotics, and intravenous steroids continues to pose ethical and legal dilemmas. We face a dying process too often unduly prolonged by intensive and invasive medical treatments. Frequently, even patients like Carrie, who have decision-making capacity and express a wish to be left alone, cannot always ensure that their choices will be honored. Health-care professionals themselves are often in conflict over these issues, fearing litigation, on the one hand, and feeling compelled to "save a life at all costs," on the other hand.

The question of whether to withhold or withdraw life-sustaining treatment has received increasing attention since the early 1980s (see Chapter 7 for a discussion of specific court cases). Meanwhile, ethical experts wrestle with logical and moral arguments from the academic vantage point. I shall briefly touch on a few major points, leaving detailed analyses to the scholars.

More often than not, doctors feel compelled to continue treatment once they have started it. Somehow, they think they cannot ethically or legally stop treatment, even if it is futile in improving the patient's condition. Naturally, this compulsion has led to undesirable consequences: first, overtreatment, which in some cases has led to litigation, and second, failing to initiate treatment at all, doctors fearing that if they do begin treatment, they won't be allowed to stop.[20]

Yet the facts contradict this notion. Even the federal government has provided the opinion that withdrawing treatment is more justifiable than withholding it. At least, that's what the President's Commission for the Study of Ethical Problems in Medicine and Biomedical and Behavioral Research stated: "Whether a particular treatment will have positive effects is often highly uncertain before the therapy has been tried. If a trial of therapy is not helpful to the patient, why should anyone continue the treatment? This should be enough of a clue to stop treatment; why should anyone assume that further benefits are likely to result?"[21]

So there you have it. Your doctor should not fear stopping treatment if you and she or he can agree that it is futile. But this is not what happens in the everyday practice of medicine. The reason? Most doctors fear malpractice liability, and many worry that stopping treatment, even when stopping it is ethically justifiable, will constitute wrongful killing.[22]

Helene Lutz, a bioethics fellow at the Washington Hospital Center, has argued that this notion is based on two fallacies. The first is the assumption that the patient's death is caused by the withdrawal of treatment itself. This assumption, she says, is simply not true. The patient actually dies of the particular illness or medical problem, and not of the withdrawal of treatment. The withdrawal of treatment only allows death to occur. As in the case of Carrie, withdrawing treatment allowed the natural dying process to take place; it did not actually kill her. The machinery in this case served more purpose than to prolong the dying process, not to mention causing suffering.[23]

The second fallacy is that withdrawing life-prolonging treatment will lead to prosecution. The president's commission states: "Legally speaking, there seems to be little or no difference between withholding and withdrawing treatment. Nothing in the law—certainly not in the context of the doctor–patient relationship—makes stopping treatment a more serious legal issue than not starting treatment. On the contrary, if a doctor fails to start treatment that might be in a patient's best interest, he is more likely to be held in a civil or criminal wrong than stopping the same treatment when it has proved ineffective."[24]

Despite this clear statement about the legality of the matter, it is still more difficult psychologically for doctors to stop treatment. Ethicists who help physicians cope with these dilemmas raise the proper questions: Will a proposed treatment or procedure offer you a reasonable hope of benefit, an improved condition, and a better quality of life? Or will the treatment just prolong a dying process already in motion? Will the treatment offer relief of suffering or alleviate pain? Are the burdens resulting from this treatment excessive, or are they reasonably bearable for the amount of benefit to be gained? These are the questions that should help your physician reach a reasonable conclusion if you find yourself in such a medical condition.

Finally, one must conclude that if a treatment is medically or ethically indicated, it is simply wrong to withhold it or withdraw it. On the other hand, if there is no good reason to use a particular treatment, there should be no moral objection to stopping or withholding it.[25] Later, we discuss how you can talk openly and effectively with your doctor about these matters.

You and your doctor can mutually reach a conclusion about whether there is any justifiable reason for starting or maintaining a treatment undertaken for your medical problem, but even then, you must continue to reassure your doctor that no litigation will result and that you will provide all the forms necessary to express your wishes.

In Chapter 10, I discuss the advance directive forms that you should sign before you become ill.

NEW GUIDELINES FOR DOCTORS

Knowing all the thorny questions and problems raised by the use of medical technology does not necessarily help physicians make decisions in difficult cases where life hangs in the balance.

To address the pressing need for assistance, a group of ethics committees in the San Francisco Bay Area proposed a new set of guidelines. They called themselves the Bay Area Network of Ethics Committees (BANEC) and they represented a joint venture between the well-known Hastings Law Center and the San Francisco Medical Society.[26]

The BANEC worked on a proposed set of model guidelines for the termination of life support in institutional settings. Here are some of the highlights of those guidelines.

First, the BANEC established a principle of *patient autonomy.* What they said was that you and I have a legal and moral right to decide what we wish to do with our own lives. They called this the *right to self-determination,* which means, in the health-care business, that your doctors and nurses must collaborate with you and your family in making decisions about your health care. Of course, they cannot ignore the philosophy of the institution, but they must also take into account your values, your goals, your religious convictions, and your overall philosophy of life. This principle applies only to adults.

One problem with that particular guideline is that, if the institution has a philosophy different from yours, the doctor may end up in an awkward position. If you wanted to refuse treatment, but the institution has a policy against it, would you then have to transfer to another institution? There was such a case, *In the Matter of Requena.*[27] A patient at a hospital refused further nutrition and hydration, and the hospital refused to abide by her wishes, requesting instead that she go to another facility. The patient didn't want to do that, and the court ruled in her favor. That case established the precedent that *not all technologically possible means of prolonging life need be used in every case.*

However, the doctor's feelings and philosophy should not be totally ignored. In another case, the court asserted that a physician cannot be forced against his or her own moral beliefs to withdraw life-sustaining treatment even if the patient so desires. This is especially true if the patient can be transferred to another physician.

The moral of this story is that you had better know how your doctor stands on these important issues. It would also be wise to know in advance what is the policy of your hospital.

Second, the BANEC proposed a principle of *proportionality,* which has two parts. Doctors who will agree to forgo life-sustaining measures must take into account not only the patient's medical condition, but also his or her personal values, religious convictions, and psychological resources, and the health team must recognize that the treatment can be of no benefit and that the burdens resulting from the treatment may be worse than the condition being treated, in other words, that the treatment may make you feel worse than the disease does.

The health team must also recognize that there are times when the number of medical procedures and interventions may be disproportionately intense for an incurable illness. Why, then, apply extraordinary measures to counteract what might otherwise be the natural course of an illness?

In everyday practice, physicians use the principle of proportionality in most of the treatments they offer to you, and they do so with each patient. They weigh what is "beneficial" against what is "burdensome" and, ideally, share their thinking with their patients. But what may be beneficial to you may not be to the next patient, and doctors' wishes for aggressive treatment also vary depending on their individual philosophy, goals, and values. Thus, open communication between you and your doctor is important. Naturally, more complications arise if you have a surrogate making decisions for you.

The third guideline is what the BANEC called *informed consent*. Sometimes, doctors want to protect their patients from bad news and may choose to withhold information simply because they feel it is too unpleasant or too painful for you to hear. But this choice is wrong and is the subject of this guideline, which says that your choices of treatment should be honored whenever possible. Those choices should include your decisions about life-sustaining treatments and whether you want them withheld or stopped.

The guideline also says that you should have the right to information about your diagnosis, your prognosis, and your treatment options, including the risks and benefits involved. In other words, no information can be withheld. In practice, physicians know that patients can absorb only so much information at a given time, and it is true that a few patients would "rather not know." Dr. Kubler-Ross never tells a patient that he or she is going to die. She just talks about the "situation" and the "condition," letting patients come to their own conclusions. Nevertheless, patients need and want to know about their treatment. Only when there is a feeling of shared decision making with the physician can mutual respect and participation take place.

After you and your physician have had a good exchange on the above topics, an entry can be written into your record. Informed consent in the medical setting has become an unexpected procedure. Therefore, it should include all forms of life-sustaining measures as well.

THE AMA'S POSITION ON WITHHOLDING OR WITHDRAWING LIFE-PROLONGING TREATMENT

You should know that the American Medical Association (AMA) has issued an official statement about withholding and withdrawing life-prolonging medical treatment. Most likely, this statement will guide your physician as well. It says that "the social commitment of the physician is to sustain life and relieve suffering. Whenever the doctor's duties conflict with the choice of the patient, or the family or legal representative, the patient's choice should prevail. But when the patient's choice or an authorized proxy is lacking—as in the case of an incompetent patient without family—the physician must act in the best interest of the patient."[28]

For humane reasons, a physician may, with informed consent, do what is medically necessary to alleviate severe pain. This may include stopping or omitting treatment to permit a terminally ill patient to die when death is imminent. The physician should not, however, intentionally cause death. The physician is obligated to assess carefully the situation of the unconscious patient. Should life-prolonging treatment be continued? Does the physician know what wishes the patient may have expressed in the past? Are the family's attitudes known?

Even if death is not imminent, if the patient's coma is irreversible, the fatal diagnosis is beyond doubt, and the family concurs, it is not unethical to discontinue all life-prolonging medical treatment.

Life-prolonging treatment includes medication and artificially or technologically supplied respiration, nutrition, or hydration. In treating a terminally ill or irreversibly comatose patient, the physician must decide whether the benefits of treatment outweigh its burdens. And in all cases, doctors must try to maintain the dignity of the patient.[29]

As a policy, such a practice could have major implications, as it would apply to an estimated ten thousand permanently comatose patients in the United States. But keep in mind that most of these patients would not be alive today if it were not for the high technology available in medicine. This state of affairs has reminded physicians that they are not just supertechnicians monitoring electrolyte balance and brain-stem functions. They also serve as healers of human beings.

DOCTORS AND THE AMA'S
POSITION ON ACTIVE EUTHANASIA

Even though the AMA issued the above statement on the withholding and withdrawing of medical treatment, they have maintained a firm position on the physician's role in helping patients die. They have staunchly opposed taking an active part in assisting the patient in dying by providing lethal drugs, as is permissible in the Netherlands (see Chapter 8).

Yet surveys have shown that physicians are slowly changing their attitudes toward euthanasia. In 1961, Arthur A. Levisohn, a professor of medical jurisprudence, surveyed 250 internists and surgeons. He asked them a series of questions, among them the following: "Do you think that in the case of incurable adult sufferers, physicians are strongly tempted to practice euthanasia?" and "In your opinion, do physicians actually practice euthanasia in instances of adult incurable sufferers?" Among the 156 physicians who responded, 61 percent agreed that doctors did practice some form of euthanasia, either by accelerating death or omitting life-sustaining measures. Yet, over two-thirds would not support legislation to legalize euthanasia.[30]

In the seventies, doctors' attitudes continued to change. In a survey of doctors in Seattle hospitals, 59 percent of the physicians surveyed said they would practice passive euthanasia with a consent form signed by the patient or the family. About 25 percent said they would practice active euthanasia (would give the patient a lethal drug) with such a consent if there were a more tolerant climate and no fear of prosecution. The author concluded that the factors influencing doctors were essentially cultural.[31]

In 1974, the magazine *Medical Opinion* conducted a survey of 3,000 randomly selected doctors. Of the respondents, 79 percent agreed that people have a right to let others know about their wishes before a serious illness strikes, and 82 percent said that they would help family members by using passive euthanasia. Most interestingly, 86 percent of the doctors said that they would want euthanasia for themselves if the need arose. The magazine concluded that "the medical mandate for euthanasia is stronger than was previously known."[32]

Despite these changes in attitudes, doctors still feel reluctant to practice any form of euthanasia, offering several reasons. Some mention the fear of being sued; others speak of the commandment, "Thou shall not kill"; and others quote the Hippocratic oath, which does forbid the administration of a "deadly drug."

In the 1980s, a series of articles came out in medical magazines, including one in the *Journal of the American Medical Association* entitled "It's Over, Debbie." The article was written by a gynecology resident who gave an overdose of morphine to a twenty-year old woman dying of cancer and begging to be released from excruciating pain.[33] A series of rebuttal articles followed, and the debate continued to rage in medical circles. Despite considerable opposition and political pressure, Kenneth Vaux, a professor of ethics and medicine at the University of Illinois Chicago Medical School, defended the article. Later, he said, "It is one of the most important ethical questions of our time."

Cases like Debbie's are probably not rare in medicine. Yet doctors don't like to talk about them, even among colleagues. The fear of professional disapproval and the threat of litigation present a tremendous block to such communication. Despite the pressure to keep quiet, a few physicians are taking the risk of opening the debate further by publishing their experiences in more and more cases. It is as though physicians are waiting for public opinion to change enough to assure them that it's all right to talk about this sensitive issue. They also want some reassurance that they need not fear being sued.

In 1987, the State of California made a survey of residents' attitudes toward end-of-life decisions. Of the respondents, 90 percent believed that incurably ill patients should be allowed to have all medical care stopped, and more than 80 percent believed that next of kin should have the authority to "pull the plug" on life-support systems of patients who have no hope of recovery.

In 1988, the American Medical Association made its own survey of 1,000 physicians in active practice. Among those physicians, 78 percent favored withholding or withdrawing life-support measures from hopelessly ill patients, but only if the patient or the family made the request.

These surveys show that the trend among physicians has been to lag behind public opinion about carrying out patients' decisions to ending their suffering. At least, that seems to be what physicians are saying in public, even though it may not be so in practice.

The Opinion Research Center of the University of Chicago reported a consistent trend in the increase in public approval of euthanasia. In 1947, the survey showed that 35 percent of the population approved of euthanasia; in 1973, the approval had climbed to 50 percent, and in 1983 to 63 percent.[34] On the other hand, a Colorado survey of physicians in 1988 reported that only 35 percent would carry out euthanasia, in certain cases.[35]

Another survey of 2,000 physicians conducted in 1991 by *Physician's Management* magazine revealed that almost 30 percent of the respondents felt that there were circumstances in which a physician would be justified in causing a patient's death. Among those respondents, 58.5 percent said that they themselves had removed life-sustaining therapies in certain circumstances. The strongest obstacle perceived by these physicians to their wish to help patients in the dying process was the fear of legal consequences. When the threat of legal involvement was removed, the number of physicians agreeing to help their patients would increase dramatically. Those who would help a comatose patient by removing life-support measures at the request of a spouse would increase to 88 percent. The fear of prosecution seems to remain one of the most serious barriers for physicians who wish to provide aid in dying for patients and their families.[36]

Despite pressure to keep quiet, a few physicians do take the risk of fueling debate by publishing their experiences with some of their patients. Such a major report made the news when an internist at the University of Rochester, Timothy E. Quill, former director of a hospice program, reported a different kind of case in the prestigious *New England Journal of Medicine* in March 1991. This is the story he told.[37]

THE CASE OF DIANE

Diane was a young woman who came to see Dr. Quill because of a rash and constant fatigue. He had known Diane for eight years and had witnessed her ability to overcome a traumatic past. She had grown up in an alcoholic family and had overcome family crises, vaginal cancer, and depression. As Quill came to know her, he had learned to respect her and to admire her ability to overcome adversity and to face problems with courage and determination. She was brutally honest and incredibly clear, and she had developed a strong sense of independence and confidence.

The presentation of her complaint was common enough so that, as a matter of routine, Quill decided to check her blood count. The result showed a low blood count and some rather unusual white blood cells. In a rechecking, much to the doctor's dismay, the test came back indeed revealing abnormal white blood cells. He convinced Diane to come to the hospital for a bone marrow biopsy. By then, Quill had raised the possibility of leukemia. Hearing the word seemed unbearable to her. "Oh, shit, don't tell me that," she said in a frightened voice.

The biopsy confirmed the worst: acute myelocytic leukemia, a rare and virulent form. In the face of the tragic news, they looked for any sign of hope. The current statistics showed that chemotherapy brought success about 25 percent of the time; out of that group, 50 percent might survive if they underwent bone marrow transplantation. But during the weeks of chemotherapy, there was always the chance of repeated infections, loss of hair, and other side effects. Hematologists agreed that survival was a matter of a few months at best. Despite pressure from the oncologist, Diane returned to Quill and told him that she did not want chemotherapy. She said that she had talked it over with her husband and her son and that they supported her decision. She had come to the conclusion that she would suffer unspeakably during the process of treatment from the lack of control over her body, from the side effects of chemotherapy, and from the pain and anguish.

Quill spent a considerable time exploring all the options open to Diane. After several days, it became clear that she had made up her mind that she wanted to die. As a former director of a hospice, Quill explained the various ways of providing pain relief in the final stages of dying, but Diane had apparently already made up her mind. She requested a prescription for barbiturates. It was clear that she was not depressed, and she was maintaining her relationships with her family and close friends. Quill wrote the prescription and made sure that she would know how much to use.

During the following months, Diane spent time with her son, her husband, and her closest friends. As time went on, severe symptoms began to appear. She became weak and tired and complained of intense pain. Despite help from visiting hospice workers, she continued to decline. What she feared most was beginning to become her reality: increasing discomfort, dependence, and hard choices between pain and sedation.

One day, she called up her closest friends and asked them to come over and say good-bye. She also called Dr. Quill to let him know that she wanted to say good-bye to him as they had agreed.

During that last visit, it was clear to the doctor that she knew what she was doing, that she was sad and frightened to be leaving, but that she was even more terrified to stay and suffer. In their tearful good-bye, she said that she was sure to see him again at her favorite spot on the edge of Lake Geneva.

Two days later, Diane's husband called to say that Diane had died. She had said her final good-byes to her husband and her son that morning, and she had asked them to leave her alone for an hour. When they found her later, she seemed at peace, covered by her favorite shawl. Quill went to her home to visit the quiet husband and son. They all talked about what a remarkable person she had been. They seemed to have no doubts about the course she had chosen or about their cooperation, even though the unfairness of her illness and the finality of her death still seemed overwhelming to them all.

It is to Quill's credit that he had the courage to publish this honest and poignant story about his patient, given the current constraints of our society and its laws. His article not only raises our awareness but, even more creditably, has brought into the open what is probably the practice of many physicians in this country, even though it is not openly acknowledged. Undoubtedly, the article will continue to raise discussion within the medical profession to a more realistic and responsible level.

REACTIONS TO DR. QUILL'S CASE

Arnold Relman, editor of the *New England Journal of Medicine*, had an interview with the *Medical Ethics Advisor*, a publication for health-care professionals and executives. In it, he defended Quill's actions when they were compared with the situation described in the famous article entitled "It's Over, Debbie." Relman was definite in comparing the two instances: "What the doctor says he did in the 'Debbie' story is something that few if any doctors in their right mind would do." In referring to Quill's case, on the other hand, he said, "What Dr. Quill did is something that many doctors do, or think they ought to do." He concluded, "The author is to be commended. It required courage. The law has to catch up with what is the moral and ethical consensus of the community."[38]

Since the publication of the Quill article, reactions from colleagues have been supportive and approving. Endorsing Quill's report was Stuart Wesbury, president of the American College of Healthcare Executives and a member of the American Society of Law and Medicine's Advisory Board on Institutional Ethics Committees. He said, "This is the kind of case that needed to happen.

I'm excited about this contribution." He believes that Diane's case will help future debate on how life-and-death decisions should be made.[39]

George Annas, a professor of health, law, and ethics at Boston University School of Medicine, agrees that the Quill case is simply "a good description of good medical practice" and "what one would hope that any reasonable doctor engaged in treating the terminally ill would discuss with his patient." In an interview with the press, Annas reiterated that the doctor's actions were legal and made sense. He added, "I want this guy as my doctor. The vast majority of people in the United States would want somebody like this as their doctor."[40]

Another bioethicist, at the University of Minnesota, Arthur Caplan, had this to say: "From my point of view, this story comes as close as I can imagine to a morally defensible role for a physician in the suicide of a patient."[41]

Still, the debate is exploding with dissenting opinions. John Wilke, a Cincinnati-based physician who serves as president of the National Right to Life Committee, says that he was very disturbed by Quill's article. In his opinion, this sort of reporting is "designed to legalize physician assisted suicide." As a spokesperson for physicians who are characterized as "prolife," Wilke makes this point: "We have a jury system and we have judges. There are various things that come to play within our system of legality that ameliorate or even remove guilt at times, but we let the jury decide and we let the judge decide. We don't change the law." Then he adds, "Killing patients is wrong, and we should never change that law. The problem today is patients who someone else thinks ought to die. The problem is getting them to die."[42]

HOW DOES A BIOETHICS COMMITTEE WORK?

Our hospital first established a biomedical ethics committee several years ago. Those invited to join represented a variety of disciplines within the medical center: internists, surgeons, family practitioners, pediatricians, gynecologists, a psychiatrist, nurses, legal counsel, an administrator, and a patients' advocate. From time to time, outside consultants and nationally known experts on ethics joined the group.

The purpose of the committee was simply to improve the quality of medical ethical decisions regarding the provision and withdrawal of treatment and care. Additional goals were to educate and inform the hospital staff, to develop policies and guidelines, and to provide consultation. A primary function was to facilitate the decision-making process in cases of terminal illness where withholding or withdrawing treatment was at stake. The committee wanted not to make decisions for others, but to provide support and to help sift through the issues and the facts. The study done by the president's commission mentioned earlier found that over 50 percent of the committees surveyed focused on helping physicians, and that about 25 percent counseled and gave support to patients and their families.[43]

For the first few months, the committee proceeded to educate itself, learning to ask the right questions and discussing hypothetical cases. Gradually, physicians began to present cases with which they needed help in reaching a decision with patients or their families.

The committee provides an open forum for any physician to come and discuss problems she or he is having with terminal patients in the hospital or in hospice care. For example, the members of such ethics committees help raise the right questions: "Should the patient be told about his/her terminal diagnosis? Does the patient have a right to die and a right to refuse treatment? Does a patient have a right to actively end his/her own life? Under what conditions can the family make treatment decisions for the patient? Should the hospital staff be involved if the family chooses to have passive euthanasia? What is the hospital's responsibility in preserving and maintaining dignity in the dying patient?"[44]

The answers to these questions are not easy, and usually there are no direct answers, just compromises. More often than not, the real help comes in being able to negotiate a compromise by facilitating communication between the physician, the patient, and the family, especially in cases where the patient is incompetent or unconscious. In short, bioethics committees see their function not as making decisions for others, but as facilitating the decision-making process among all the parties involved in the care of the patient.

It is important to not think of bioethics committees as rubber stamps for decisions made by others or as debating forums. They just want to explore enough facts about the patient's illness and the factors pertinent to the person lying in that hospital bed. Then they want to help the guardian or the next of kin make an informed decision in planning for the final care of the patient.

Most ethics committees have a wide representation of disciplines and viewpoints, which allow the members to express a wide array of opinions and feelings. The exchange is usually informative, inspiring, creative, and often therapeutic for both staff and families.

Bioethics committees are serving an increasingly vital function by raising awareness of the issues surrounding dealing with the terminally ill. They also encourage dialogue among the physicians themselves. Death and dying are no longer subjects to whisper about behind closed doors. It is finally OK to discuss them in broad daylight in a conference room.

QUESTIONS TO ASK YOUR DOCTOR WHILE YOU ARE STILL WELL

Ideally, you should develop a relationship with your doctor long before you are gravely ill. Get to know each other well enough so that your doctor understands you as a person with a particular lifestyle, and certain goals and values. Very importantly, share your general philosophy and attitude toward death and dying (see Chapter 5 for more on the philosophy of death and dying).

If you visit your physician during an illness, you need to find out how easy it is to get your questions answered. Doctors tend to favor patients who ask intelligent questions, assuming, of course, that you know what questions to ask. And you may want to be selective about asking the right number of questions so as not to appear too demanding.[45] Here are just a few examples.

Questions regarding tests:

1. What is the purpose of these tests?
2. Are there any risks involved in these tests?
3. How long will it take to get the results?
4. What would happen if I chose not to have these tests?
5. Will I have to take much time off from work to go through these tests?

Questions regarding medications:

1. How will the medications help my symptoms?
2. What are the most common side effects?
3. What will happen if I don't take these drugs?

Questions regarding your condition:

1. Can you tell me the diagnosis?
2. What causes it?
3. How will the treatment work?
4. How long will I need this treatment?
5. Will there be any side effects of this treatment?
6. When will I get well?

Questions before surgery:

1. What are the risks and benefits of this surgery?
2. What are the alternatives and their benefits and risks?
3. What is my prognosis if I choose not to have the surgery?
4. What are the risks of anesthesia?
5. Could you help me to speak to persons who have had this surgery?
6. Will I have much pain or discomfort after the surgery?
7. When will I be able to go back to work?

QUESTIONS DEALING WITH DEATH AND DYING

Questions about death and dying are the most difficult questions to ask, and the most difficult for physicians to answer. However, you may want to be sure that you get some straight answers, so that you are not dismayed if the time comes when you need assistance in dying. When discussing these issues, make your own judgment about whether you have the right doctor for yourself. It will be more difficult to make that determination at the time of an acute illness.

It is best not to be cajoled by kindly and paternalistic answers such as "Don't worry, I won't let you suffer," or "Leave it to me," or "I won't let my patients die in a lot of pain." Don't trust such answers, especially those that are so general. Be direct with your questions.

1. If my condition presented no hope for recovery, would you favor disconnecting life-support equipment?
2. Would you use this equipment regardless of the prognosis of hopeless terminal illness?
3. Would you object to giving me medicines that would control my pain?
4. If I had a terminal illness, would you be concerned about my becoming addicted to morphine?
5. How do you feel about a living will? About a durable power of attorney?
6. Would you be willing to give me enough medicine to allow me to die?

The doctor may not be able to answer the last question directly because, as we have seen, it is still against the law to participate in euthanasia, but the way your doctor answers ought to give you an idea of his or her general philosophy. And if your doctor gives you a lecture or belittles your remarks, you will be amply forewarned.[46]

In any case, it is most important that you determine where

your doctor stands on these issues so you can put your mind and your family at ease.

LOOKING FOR THE RIGHT DOCTOR

> *Die, my dear Doctor, that's the last thing I shall do!*
> —Lord Palmerton (1784–1865)

It is important to get satisfactory answers to your questions because living wills, although legal and accepted in thirty-nine states, are not enforceable unless the physician and the hospital have no objection to complying with them. The only way to be sure is to discuss this matter well in advance with your doctor. You need to find out if your doctor will meet your needs before you attempt to exercise that last right.

Call your local hospitals and ask for their physician referral services. If you belong to a health plan, ask for a recommendation from your health plan representative, another health plan member, or the patients' assistance office. If you are having trouble locating a physician, call your state or county medical society, which will give you the names of several physicians. Make a fifteen- to twenty-minute appointment to discuss personal issues. You will find that most doctors today will be receptive to your needs.

For your interview, come well prepared with your questions. Share your concerns and your reasons for inquiring about the doctor's view. Be candid and say that you will appreciate an open and frank answer to your questions. After some general questions, bring up the issue of the living will and your general feelings and attitudes toward death and dying that is, if you know enough about them. Of course, you will not really get to know the doctor's approach to illness until you are actually ill, but you and your doctor should know something about each other by then.

Before you schedule the interview with your doctor, you need to think about your own values. In the next chapter, I discuss the kinds of questions you need to ask yourself before you meet with your doctor.

NOTES

1. Quoted in D. S. Pinkney, "Advance Directives Make Patient's Wishes Known," *American Medical News*, 7 Jan. 1991, 9–10.
2. Ibid.
3. Ibid.
4. J. H. Leversee, "Hippocrates Revisited: A View from General Practice," in *Hippocrates Revisited: A Search for Meaning*, ed. R. Burder (New York: Medcom, 1973).
5. R. Kravitz, "Hippocrates," *The Pharos* (1984).
6. Derek Humphry, *Final Exit* (Eugene, OR: Hemlock Society, 1991), 24–28.
7. Elisabeth Kübler-Ross, *Questions and Answers on Death and Dying* (New York: Macmillan, 1974), 78.
8. F. J. Skelly, "Death Is Turning into a Pressing Issue for Practicing Physicians," *American Medical News*, 7 Jan. 1991, 5–6.
9. Ibid.
10. Ibid.
11. Ibid.
12. President's Commission for the Study of Ethical Problems in Medicine and Biomedical and Behavioral Research; Report on the Medical, Legal and Ethical Issues in the Determination of Death (Washington, DC: U.S. Government Printing Office, 1981), 21.
13. Ibid.
14. Uniform Anatomical Gift Act (1968) Section 7(b).
15. Ad Hoc Committee of the Harvard Medical School to Examine the Definition of Brain Death "A Definition of Irreversible Coma," *Journal of the American Medical Association* 205 (1968): 337.
16. J. Korein, *Brain Death: Interrelated Medical and Social Issues* (New York: New York Academy of Sciences, 1978), 6–10.
17. *Leach vs Shapiro* (1984), 13 Ohio App. 3rd 393, 469, N.E., 2nd 1047 (Ct. App. 1984).
18. *Leach v. Akron General Medical Center* (1982), 68 Ohio Misc. 1 426 N.E. 2nd 809 (Com. Pl. 1980; 1982).

19. "Doctors Dithered: Carrie Suffered," *Hemlock Society Newsletter* 37 (1989): 6–7.
20. President's Commission for the Study of Ethical Problems in Medicine and Biomedical and Behavioral Research, Deciding to Forgo Life-Sustaining Treatment (Washington, DC: U.S. Government Printing Office, 1983), 76–77.
21. Ibid.
22. H. A. Lutz, "Ethical Perspectives on the Right to Die: A Case Study," in *To Die or Not to Die: Cross-Disciplinary, Cultural and Legal Perspectives on the Right to Choose Death,* ed. A. S. Berger and Joyce Berger (New York: Praeger, 1990), 29.
23. Ibid.
24. President's Commission, 19, 76–77.
25. Lutz, 29.
26. Lawrence J. Nelson, "Model Guidelines for the Development of Institutional Policy on the Termination of Life-Support and Commentary, Part I," *Clinical Ethics Report* 3 (1, Winter 1989): 1–8.
27. *In the Matter of Requena* (1986), 517 A. 2nd 434 (NJ Sup. Ct. App. Div. 1986).
28. American Medical Association and Council of Education and Judicial Affairs, *Withholding or Withdrawing Life Prolonging Medical Treatment* (Dearborn, MI: American Medical Association, 1986).
29. Ibid.
30. A. A. Levisohn, "Voluntary Mercy Deaths," *Journal of Forensic Medicine* 8 (2, 1961): 68.
31. N. K. Brown, "The Preservation of Life," *Journal of the American Medical Association* 211 (5 January (1970)): 97.
32. B. T. Scott, "Physicians' Attitude Survey: Doctors and Dying: Is Euthanasia Becoming Accepted?" *Medical Opinion* 3 (1974): 31–34.
33. "It's Over, Debbie," *Journal of the American Medical Association* 259 (1988): 272.
34. G. A. Kanoti, J. P. Orlowski, "Ethical Perspective on the Physician's Role in Patient Death," *Physician's Management* 31 (1991): 69–72.
35. Ibid.
36. Mac Overmeyer, "Physicians' Views on the Right to Die," *Physician's Management* 31 (1991): 41–45.
37. Timothy E. Quill, "Death and Dignity," *New England Journal of Medicine* 324 (1991): 691–694.

38. American Health Consultants, "Accounts of Assisted Suicide in Journal Advances Debate," *Medical Ethics Advisor* (April 1991): 44–47.
39. Ibid.
40. Daniel Q. Haney, "Doc Goes Public on Aiding Death: A N.Y. Internist Writes of Giving a Cancer Patient the Means to End Her Life," *Honolulu Star Bulletin*, 6 March 1991, A-1, A-12.
41. Ibid.
42. American Health Consultants, 44–47.
43. Therese A. Rando, *Grief, Dying and Death* (Champaign: IL: Research Press, 1984), 420–430.
44. Ibid.
45. Harry van Bommel, *Choices: For People Who Have a Terminal Illness, Their Families, and Their Caregivers*, 2nd rev. ed. (Toronto: NC Press, 1987), 51–55.
46. Humphry, 24–28.

CHAPTER 4

Hard Choices,
Tough Decisions

*The last of human freedoms is the
ability to choose one's attitude in
a given set of circumstances.*
—Victor Frankl, Professor of Neurology and Psychiatry,
University of Vienna Medical School

IS DYING A QUESTION
OF INDIVIDUAL FREEDOM?

Who ever thought that death would be a matter of choice? In the past, people were guided by simple axioms like "Death will come when nature takes its course" or "Death will come when God's will is done." Taking someone's pulse used to be the way of determining death. When the heart stopped, it was a sure sign of death. Even Groucho Marx, playing Dr. Quackenbush, who was taking a patient's pulse, joked, "Either this man is dead, or my watch has stopped."

But nowadays, dying is no longer a simple matter, and as a colleague recently told me, there are worse things than dying today; You could get stuck with treatments you don't want and procedures that won't let you die in peace.

In the past, when one was in a terminal illness, the doctor provided supportive care—now called *palliative care*—and prepared the family for the transition from life to death; then, people really did view death as a transition. With the evolution of modern technology, doctors are more likely to see death as a medical failure and therefore the enemy. They will approach a family with the apologetic statement, "I'm sorry, we did everything we could," as if no one were ever supposed to die. Doctors sometimes feel that every symptom and every condition must be treated with all the measures that technology can provide. This attitude has led to the feeling that "Sometimes, we treat because we can, not because we should," and sometimes, the patient's feelings are left out of the decision.

The questions that remain unanswered are: To what extent do we or our family retain a choice in making decisions about treatment? And what kind of dying experience can we expect for ourselves? If we become terminally ill, how much choice do we really have? Are we entitled to know all the alternatives and options for treatment? Will doctors feel comfortable in sharing the decisions with us?

But even doctors have a difficult time making decisions. At times, they even disagree on such things as whether the patient has actually died, should be resuscitated, or should be treated. Without advance directives, doctors tend to favor aggressive interventions and active treatments toward a "cure." It is only after all aggressive treatment has failed that they may decide to switch to nonaggressive treatment. Sometimes, doctors cannot decide and vacillate between one course of treatment and another. This is especially true if the patient is suffering from a terminal illness like advanced cancer. Initially, aggressive treatment may be given with radiation and chemotherapy, but as the patient's condition continues to worsen, persisting with aggressive treatment becomes a less clear choice.

At that point, what are the options? In the absence of a written directive about the patient's preferences in the given situation, should the patient, if able, state his or her wishes or preferences then? Will the doctors listen? Will they be able to remain objective in their discussions with patient and family? Will their own values play a role in their determining how much more treatment should be given? Will the patient be strong enough at that point to make a truly informed decision?

These are not easy questions for anyone. The main issue is the locus of control in making further decisions for treatment. How much control will the patient retain? If you are in such a situation, you should ask your doctor to give you enough information to allow you to think carefully about your options. The debate over the freedom to choose and the patient's ability to retain control is taking place in various circles of experts in ethics, medicine, law, philosophy, theology, and public policy. It may turn out to be the most important debate of the 1990s.

In his book *A Graceful Passage*, Arnold Beisser writes, "The awesome decision to live or die belongs not to the courts, to attorneys, to hospitals, to doctors, to nurses, or to any other group, but to the person whose life it is. The support of others is vital for an informed decision, so family, friends and professionals can be of help, since they can help in the individual's free choice. And the most important choice one ever has is between life and death."[1] In this chapter, I review the highlights of our society's current arguments, which you need to know in order to make informed decisions for yourself or your family.

IS DEATH THE ISSUE OR IS DYING THE PROBLEM?

Although the moment of death remains an issue that some experts like to debate, for most individuals like you and me the real issue is whether dying itself will be a problem. The question most people silently ask themselves is whether they can avoid or even prevent a lingering death. Derek Humphry, the president of the Hemlock Society, says that it is not death but the dying that is most frightening.

If you look at the causes of death today, they can be broken down roughly into three categories: (1) communicable diseases; (2) sudden deaths (accidents, suicides, homicides, and some cardiovascular diseases); and (3) chronic illnesses. Of the three categories, communicable and infectious diseases have assumed less importance, and accidents are becoming more important because of biomedical interventions that can produce bad scenarios of dying. For the most part, deaths fall into the category of chronic illnesses and may be slow and lingering because of the slow decline that characterizes most of these illnesses.

In the United States, over 2 million people die each year. According to one study, 87 percent of all deaths are due to chronic conditions,[2] and according to another study, 50 percent of deaths occur within twenty-nine months of the onset of the disease.[3] These statistics imply that about 4 million people are in the process of dying each year. Relatively few will die at home. The old familiar scene of the family gathered around the deathbed of the dying parent is an image of the past. The fact is that today most people die in hospitals, the most conservative estimate being at least 80 percent.[4]

Choosing to die when one has incurable illness has received little support so far among public policymakers. When Arthur Koestler, the famous seventy-seven-year old writer, and his wife chose to end their lives in London in March 1983, the debate over choosing death over life was stirred up again. Koestler had decided that suicide—or self-deliverance, as it is called by proponents of euthanasia—was preferable to the agony of advanced leukemia and debilitating Parkinson's disease.[5]

After stories about the lingering deaths of celebrities, the climate of public opinion is changing gradually. A Harris poll on the right to die taken in the mid-1980s revealed that 75 percent of Americans believed that an incurably ill person should have the choice of withdrawing life-support systems. This is easy to understand because most people today fear a lingering death or a life suspended in limbo. Montaigne, the sixteenth century French essayist wrote, "Death is the moment when dying ends." But today, more than ever, it is our goal to shorten the time between the start of dying and death.

IS DYING A MEDICAL OR A LEGAL DECISION?

People have rights, not technologies.
—George Annas, medical ethicist and attorney

Sometimes experts wonder, "When should we stop treating this patient?" implying that it's up to the treating team to decide. They often think of the patient as an object that has no deciding vote. What they should be asking is "When should it be morally or legally feasible for the patient to refuse medical treatment, even if that refusal means that dying will be hastened, or at least not prolonged?" In Chapter 7, we discuss several landmark cases in which such decisions had to be made, creating headlines in the media and focusing interest on the courts.

It is not unusual for a medical team to decide to treat a patient even when they do not know for sure whether the patient is dead or alive. In other words, treatment may proceed because there is evidence of a heart beating in a chest. But is there a live person in that body? In some cases, this remains a real and thorny question. Has death actually taken place?

Medical and ethics experts like to debate the issue at great length, and if they can't agree or decide, they turn the matter over to legal experts. Unfortunately, even the legal experts can't be sure, but they will offer opinions and decisions based on the letter of the law, which may not be in the best interests of the patient or the doctors.

For example, take the case of Clarence Nicks.[6] On May 7, 1968, this man had been severely beaten in a brawl by several assailants. The beating resulted in his admission to the hospital in a comatose state; his brain waves were flat and he had stopped breathing. In the modern definition of death, this man was dead. Yet his heart was still beating, and to keep his heart beating, Nicks was put on a respirator. Although he was pronounced dead by one physician, another physician disagreed, believing he was still alive. Nevertheless, surgeons transplanted his heart into John Stukwish, a sixty-two-year-old man suffering severe heart disease. Meanwhile, the attorney for the assailants, who were being charged with murder, claimed that Nicks, the victim, could not possibly have been dead before his heart was removed. That is, if anyone was responsible for Nicks's death it was the surgeon who had removed his heart. Although there was no disagreement over the technical facts of the situation, there was still considerable question about the technical and legal interpretation of what constitutes "death." It is a fact that most states, although not all, use the so-called brain definition of death. However, the debate continues between the medical and legal professions about whether death is a legal or a medical concept, as was clearly the problem in the Nicks case.

Although death may not be one of your current concerns, your family could end up with a serious legal problem, a situation that would be most unfortunate and embarrassing for them. In Chapter 10, I discuss how to prevent such ambiguities and embarrassing situations by obtaining and completing the appropriate documents.

CHOOSING OPTIONS IN THE HOSPITAL

> *I sometimes entertain what for me is the ultimate horror story—being in a hospital where the health care system has taken over my life and moves inexorably toward decisions about me in which I would have little or no say. That seems very grim indeed, helplessly being kept technically alive without choice.*
> —Arnold Beisser, *A Graceful Passage* (1990)

Where people die greatly determines the number of biomedical intervention they'll receive. Cases in hospitals abound to illustrate that machines, resuscitation, aggressive procedures, surgery, and artificial nourishment and hydration through tubes can prolong the process of dying.

Throughout life, people are used to making decisions for themselves, but when they are diagnosed as having a life-threatening illness, they are suddenly transported, with their families and friends, into a totally foreign environment called the *American health care system*. There they must listen to various professionals and specialists who speak a foreign language called *medicalese*. As patients, they must acquiesce to taking a series of uncomfortable and scary tests. Without notice, they must be prepared to make drastic changes in their schedule, lifestyle, and commitments. Finally, the doctors expect them to make decisions and choices that, in the truest sense, deal with life and death.[7]

During this time in the new environment of the "health care system," people often behave like strangers in a foreign land. They are frequently bewildered by the strange customs, rules, uniforms, and language spoken by the "specialists." Patients, as they are suddenly called, may even ask, "Which one of these doctors is really my doctor?" or "What am I supposed to ask? Why do they need to do surgery to find out what's wrong? Why are they insisting on chemotherapy?"

Most people can't even imagine, in the midst of these complexities, that they have any right to participate in decisions about or choices of treatment. So it is not surprising that they feel a lack of control over their own destiny.

Yet, I believe that, if given enough assistance in interpreting information and knowledge, most people can understand technical information sufficiently to make intelligent treatment decisions. Of course, they must sometimes take the initiative by asking the appropriate questions, and they must express their wishes to participate in the treatment decision. They need information, and doctors and nurses are the ones who control the flow of information. But doctors don't always assume that their patients wish to know very much about their condition, and sometimes they also exclude patients and their families unintentionally, particularly when medical conditions and laboratory results change rapidly, and poor or no communication takes place. Without information, people remain in the dark. They should therefore insist on information. For example, a patient with suspected cancer should ask, "What is the result of my biopsy? Do I have cancer? What are my treatment options? What are other alternatives? What are the side effects of the different treatments? How will these treatments interfere with my daily life? May I obtain a second opinion?" These were the questions asked by my friends, David and Bob, discussed in Chapter 1, before they could make up their minds about what to do.

As a rule, people with life-threatening illnesses who make decisions about their treatment consider several factors. They examine the basis for their reasons to want to let go rather than fight the disease by using all the medical technology available today. Among the factors that they consider is their experience or knowledge of the particular illness. For example, do they know someone with a similar illness? What was the outcome?

They also consider such things as their previous lifestyle and quality of life. My friend, Bob, placed a great emphasis on his inability to continue the active life that was so important to him. Yet, it is curious that health-care providers tend not to be sympathetic with the general argument that life is no longer worth living.

Another factor for the seriously ill person is the burden versus the benefit of the treatment. Traditionally, physicians are the ones who place much emphasis on this aspect of treatment decisions. It is true, however, that health professionals have a "cure orientation" that leads them toward aggressive treatment decisions. It is only when doctors see poor tests results and poor responses to treatment that they will agree to stop treatment and turn to so-called palliative care. Doctors tend not to discuss these results with patients and families unless they are specifically asked. They tend to believe that most patients don't really want to know, even when the patients ask questions. And it is true that more often than not the anxiety that the illness provokes will lead the doctor to be protective of patients and their families. Sometimes, the information may be very complex, and the doctor may feel that it is nearly impossible to present a balanced view of the problem without injecting a high dose of anxiety.[8]

When illnesses are characterized by a roller-coaster course, doctors may choose not to share the information they have, but the inevitable result is that patients get confused. Sometimes, families invest high emotional stakes in the outcome of treatment, and doctors who pick up those feelings may choose very aggressive treatment because it is expected.

In their book *Life-Death Decisions in Health Care,* Degner and Beaton recommended that the health system designate a health professional to represent the views of patients and their families as a type of patient advocate. Such a person would help patients and families in deciding about treatment options and would arrange for emotional support whenever it is needed. Although this recommendation may appear too revolutionary for the current system, with an increasingly complex technology and a very busy medical staff, the proposed model has merit.

PROLONGING LIFE OR PROLONGING DEATH?

> *Man's chief purpose is to Live, not to exist,*
> *I shall not waste my days trying to prolong them.*
> *I shall use my time.*
> —Jack London (1876–1916)

Whether one is prolonging life or prolonging the dying process is not an easy distinction to make. In this section, I wish to show that this philosophical debate depends on several considerations. For one thing, the question is different for a terminally ill person and for the person who is well. The same question produces different answers from the terminally ill patient, the attending doctors, the nurses, the philosopher, the theologian, and the ethicist. I do not have any more answers than the clinicians and scholars in the field. All I wish to do in this section is to discuss points of view and encourage you to make up your own mind.

From the Patient's Viewpoint

There is a fundamental difference between a person who is about to die in a short time and one whose dying is being prolonged for weeks or months. The person who is about to die will do so without complications and without much delay. On the other hand, the person who is dying slowly may have to decide whether continuing treatment is still worthwhile or whether the burdens of treatment are much greater than the benefits resulting from it. That is, the person may feel that life is being prolonged for no useful purpose and at the cost of terrible suffering.

All people should have the right to refuse treatment if they can give good reasons to themselves, especially if they find that the pain and suffering caused by the treatment are worse than the disease itself. Even then, they must be able to negotiate this position with the medical staff, who may feel obligated to pursue the treatment, and who may be responding to professional and legal obligations rather than to purely humanitarian considerations.

I recently heard of the case of a forty-one-year-old woman who had to go to the hospital several times a week for kidney dialysis. She had been doing this since she was nineteen, and she had decided that she no longer wanted to endure life on these terms, feeling that her way of life was not allowing her to contribute anything to society or even to herself. All her waking time was devoted to arranging the schedule for her treatments. She felt no satisfaction and fulfillment from this activity and could see no change in the years ahead. She had discussed her feelings many times with her physician and her family, and although they tried repeatedly to dissuade her, she seemed to have reached an irreversible position after several years of soul searching. Finally, she convinced her doctor that she wanted to stop the dialysis, and she asked for his help.

Because she knew that without medical help she would die in severe pain, she asked her doctor to help her stop the treatment in the hospital and make her "comfortable" during her last days. He agreed to do so, but as soon as she reentered the hospital, she was reconnected to the dialysis machine, much to her dismay. She refused to go on the machine, and the hospital promptly discharged her. The doctor then ordered home nursing care and administered her pain medication on house calls. Nine days after her last dialysis treatment, she died quietly and peacefully.

Hospitals may not be the place to receive the treatment of your choice. They are not prepared to help patients die, and they certainly will not cooperate with a patient's wish to get help in dying, even despite the feelings and opinion of your doctor, as in the case above.

From the Health Professional's Viewpoint

Opinions about whether one has the right or the option to make decisions about prolonging life or not prolonging dying vary considerably within the medical profession.

Prolonging life has its downside, particularly when it is confused with prolonging the dying process. It was with this thought in mind that the American Medical Association (AMA) issued the following statement to the medical profession in 1986: "Life prolonging medical treatment includes medication and artificially or technologically supplied respiration, nutrition and hydration. In treating a terminally ill or irreversibly comatose patient, the physician should figure out whether the benefits of treatment outweigh its burdens. At all times, the dignity of the patient should be maintained."[9]

Despite this admonition, the medical and nursing professions are still caught in a conflict set up by society. As Beisser writes, "Committed as they are to saving lives, hospitals, doctors, and nurses are caught between the twin legal pressures from malpractice insurance on the one hand and 'right to life' legislation on the other, the system keeps people alive, whatever the quality of discomfort they feel or what their wishes are.[10]

From the Church's Viewpoint

Even Pope Pius XII in his statement on the "Prolongation of Life" agreed that an anesthesiologist is not expected to use artificial respiration in cases that are considered "completely hopeless."[11] In fact, he even went beyond that statement in recognizing that some treatments may do some good, but only by inflicting serious pain and suffering. Yet, in the medical setting, busy doctors sometimes continue to treat because the technology is available or because families continue to pressure them and insist that everything possible be done.

Whose Viewpoint Really Matters?

The decision to continue treatment should be a personal one, if the person is competent to make choices and decisions. The pain and suffering from radical surgery, the nausea from chemotherapy, or the anguish from kidney dialysis are enough justification to refuse treatment, and this choice should therefore be respected.

Other valid reasons should be respected as well when the treatment prolongs the burden of the disease itself, as in the last stages of cancer complicated by pneumonia. In this situation, if the doctor decides to treat the pneumonia with penicillin, the penicillin will eradicate the pneumonia, but it will only delay inevitable death of the underlying disease. Many years ago, pneumonia was considered a benevolent friend because it helped the terminally ill die quickly and painlessly.

The question remains whenever technology is being applied to a very ill person: Are we prolonging the dying or are we prolonging the living? People are not sure. Neither the medical nor the legal professions are sure either. Many doubts persist at this stage of our knowledge. Most scholars agree that a person's choice should be respected, but under what circumstances? That is where disagreements arise. Principles of morality, religious dogma, traditions in medicine, legal rulings and statutes, and beliefs in civil liberties are all invoked by their proponents in the name of fairness, the sanctity of life, or faith in God.

Walter Bortz, a former president of the American Geriatrics Society and a clinical professor at Stanford Medical School, writes the following in his book *We Live Too Short and Die Too Long:* "Philosophically, I favor euthanasia. As I removed the tube from my patient this morning, I now await his death in a few days. Why wait, you may ask. If what the family, and I, and all others want is for him to have a dignified death, why not just give him a barbiturate and curare and hasten the event? The answer is that the medical system is not ready for that; and I'm not sure that we can ever develop procedures which will be 'airtight' enough."[12] And so the debate continues.

Sometimes people get confused over what is standard, or ordinary, treatment and what "extraordinary," that is, what is beyond what most people would expect. Still, it is a very complex question that covers not only the personal views and values of the individual but also the ever-expanding list of new treatments. Cardiopulmonary resuscitation (CPR), radical surgery, hemodialysis, and transplant surgery for example, may be extraordinary treatment if their result is only to prolong the dying process. On the other hand, they are considered "ordinary" if they usefully and meaningfully prolong life.[13]

ARE FOOD AND WATER A TREATMENT IN TERMINAL ILLNESS?

The question becomes even more complicated when one deals with the use of nourishment and hydration. Those for and against withdrawing or withholding food and water have offered their views, many pointing out that the dilemma is at best filled with uncertainty.[14] Some have pointed out the medical profession's mixed messages: sometimes agreeing and sometimes disagreeing that the right to self-determination should be respected.[15] Some express a fear that physicians may withdraw nourishment indiscriminately and may, if permitted to do so, extend the discontinuation of food and water to the retarded, the confused, the psychotic, the senile, and the handicapped; in other words to all persons they perceive as having limited social value.[16]

Some scholars point to the fact that most people perceive food and water as a basic sign of nurturance and a minimum commitment to the well-being of another person.[17] Some people say that providing food and water is not a treatment. Others say that, on the contrary, food and hydration are indeed "ordinary" treatment, particularly when they are provided artificially through a nasogastric tube, intravenous lines, gastrostomy (the insertion of a tube into the stomach through the abdominal wall), or hyperalimentation (food introduced into the body through a needle inserted into the subclavian vein, the large vein under the collarbone). Although there have been decisions about the termination of purely medical treatment, there is no consensus on withholding or withdrawing food and water.[18]

The conflict is best illustrated in the landmark *Conroy* case. In 1985, Claire Conroy was an eighty-four-year-old resident of a nursing home in New Jersey. She had advanced heart disease, diabetes, high blood pressure, and a gangrenous leg. For months, she had been lying in a fetal position, moaning and groaning, unable to speak, and constantly pulling at her bandages, at her nasogastric feeding tube, and at her urinary catheter. She lacked bowel control and had almost no ability to swallow. She was expected to die within a year even with continuation of the tube-feeding, but the doctors agreed that, if the feedings stopped, she would die within a week. They also thought that her death might be painful.

Her only relative was a nephew, Thomas Whittemore, who had been appointed her guardian. In his capacity as guardian, the nephew applied to the court for permission to stop the nasogastric feeding.

In the months that followed, a trial court approved the removal of the tube, reasoning that life had become permanently burdensome to the patient, and therefore that prolonging her life was not only pointless but cruel. But a guardian *ad litem*—a court-appointed guardian, as distinguished from her nephew—decided to appeal the decision to a higher court.

The appellate division reversed the lower court's decision, reasoning that the right to terminate treatment should be reserved to patients who are brain dead or in a persistent vegetative state. This court was of the opinion that withholding nourishment would hasten death, as opposed to simply allowing the illness to take its natural course. Later, the nephew appealed to the New Jersey Supreme Court. This court also found that Conroy's circumstances did not satisfy the criterion of having made her prior wishes clear and it did not feel that supplying nourishment was inhumane and produced unavoidable pain and further suffering. In essence, this court agreed with the appellate court that the withdrawing of nourishment would hasten death. On the other hand, the court said that Conroy would have satisfied their criteria if she had indicated her wishes in a living will.[19]

In the 1987 case of Hilda Peter, a sixty-five-year-old nursing-home patient in a persistent vegetative state who had been maintained for two years simply by a feeding tube, the New Jersey Supreme Court reached the decision that forceful feeding *was* a medical treatment that could be forgone, and that *the real cause of death was the underlying disease and not the forgoing of artificial feeding.*[20] Hilda Peter died a few days after her feeding tube was removed.[21]

And so the debate continues. In the 1986 statement quoted earlier, the American Medical Association had clearly said that "life-prolonging treatment includes medication and artificially or technologically supplied respiration and nutrition or hydration." Nevertheless, the American Nurses Association stated in 1988 that under most circumstances it is *not* morally permissible for a nurse to withhold or withdraw food or fluids from persons in their care.[22]

Some nurses offer a note of caution against such a blanket policy. As Mary Ellen Wurzbach, an assistant professor of nursing at the University of Wisconsin, writes, "Many of our patients will be unable to make decisions or will have a difficult time making choices about their care." Administering care within the context of when to withhold or withdraw nutrition and hydration presents the ultimate challenge to the nurse's sense of humanity. If the challenge is met, the client, the family, and the nurses's belief in human dignity will be supported.[23] If the challenge is not met, however, all concerned will suffer moral distress.[24]

In the daily practice of medicine, one cannot adhere to abstract principles and armchair arguments. Joseph Fletcher, President-Emeritus of the Right to Die Society and Visiting Scholar of Medical Ethics at the University of Virginia School of Medicine, writes, "Life is good . . . but it is only one of several goods, and in some cases it is better to let life go. This means that quality of life is the guideline, not any doctrinaire 'sanctity of life.' " To health professionals dealing with the practical problems of day-to-day care, he offers the following admonition based on years of experience: "My moral guidelines are often called situation ethics, so called because it decides what is good or right according to what actual situations indicate as the most beneficial course to follow in the actual situation, rather than 'applying' some abstract 'principle.' "[25]

Meanwhile, the question of artificial feeding is taking on a greater significance as an increasing number of people in the country are kept alive. The latest estimate is that between 10,000 and 60,000 people are kept alive by tube-feeding alone in hospitals and nursing homes.[26]

Although the courts in eighteen states have ruled that patients have the same right to refuse feeding tubes as to refuse other medical treatment, in the *Cruzan* case a majority of the U.S. Supreme Court issued the decision on June 25, 1990, that, "Artificial feeding cannot readily be distinguished from other forms of medical treatment." Nonetheless, the Court did agree to let the states decide for themselves. Remember that the *Cruzan* case was finally settled by a local court that determined that "clear and convincing evidence" was present to show that in the situation she was in, Nancy Cruzan would have wanted to stop all feeding.[27]

The implications and legal aspects of these and other cases are discussed in greater detail in Chapter 7.

THE RIGHT TO REFUSE TREATMENT
IF YOU ARE NOT TERMINALLY ILL

Earlier, I discussed the case of a woman who had been on kidney dialysis for many years and had asked her doctor to help her die after she had made a conscious decision to end a life of suffering. There are other conditions that do not cause terminal illness but that raise serious questions about what options a person has to stop the suffering associated with illnesses. Examples are amyotrophic lateral sclerosis (ALS), an incurable condition also known as Lou Gehrig's Disease; polio; and severe cerebral palsy. In these cases, what are the options?

These diseases may affect all the motor functions of the body, leaving the individual with enormous obstacles to a minimal quality of life, until, eventually the respiratory muscles are affected. People, courts, and the medical profession have been able to accept the rights of individuals who are terminally ill or are in a persistent vegetative state to stop all treatment if they have expressed their wishes in a living will, but with regard to competent persons who are not terminally ill and wish to exercise their rights to choose different options, another controversy is taking place.

One such case, which received much publicity in 1983, was that of Elizabeth Bouvia. She had a difficult life, having suffered since birth from a severe form of cerebral palsy that made it almost impossible for her to move or speak. But through valiant efforts, she gradually learned to speak, although not clearly. Later, she learned to get around in a wheelchair. Eventually, she made a life for herself. She succeeded in attending college, getting a master's degree, and becoming a social worker. She later married and kept house for her husband. After some time, she developed painful and incapacitating arthritis. At that point, her marriage failed and ended in divorce, and she moved in with her parents.

After a while, Bouvia's parents admitted that they could no longer care for her. She was totally bedridden and suffered continuous pain. Her doctors decided to withhold her pain medication because they feared she was becoming addicted. She was all alone, in constant pain, and without any resources or any hope that she would ever get better. At that point, she decided to check into a hospital to obtain sufficient nursing care while she starved herself.

When she entered the hospital, she was immobile except for being able to move a few fingers of one hand and a few muscles of her face and head. She was totally dependent on others for her care. Arthritis gave her severe and continuous pain, for which a tube in her chest automatically pumped morphine. Besides the arthritis, she had constant pain because of her inability to change her position.

She did not know that the hospital would object to her request to starve herself. So she decided to seek an injunction from the court to prevent the hospital staff from inserting a tube or performing a gastrostomy. Although the court recognized that she had a right to refuse treatment, it did not feel that she had the right to end her life, especially with the assistance of society.[28] And that is where the confusion arose: the court could not force the hospital staff to help her in her plans to end her life. Therefore the staff resumed forced feeding.

Bouvia checked out of Riverside Hospital and tried to live in a variety of arrangements while her condition continued to deteriorate. Eventually, she entered High Desert Hospital in the County of Los Angeles. Again, she sought an injunction from the Court of Appeals of the State of California. This court, favoring the right of the competent patient to self-determination, ordered the hospital staff to remove the nasogastric tube and prohibited replacing it without Bouvia's consent. Judge Lynn Compton, who presided over the California Court of Appeals, made this final statement about Bouvia: "Whatever choice Elizabeth Bouvia may ultimately make, I can only hope that her courage, persistence and example will cause our society to deal realistically with the plight of those unfortunate individuals to whom death beckons as a welcome respite from suffering."[29]

During the 1980s, there was considerable press coverage of the *Bouvia* case. The reactions were extreme. Some people felt outraged that Bouvia could "affront society" by requesting to assist her in dying. The right-to-life organizations objected on religious and moral grounds. Others, like human rights groups, feared that to grant her wish would lead to death camps and to a holocaust mentality. Still others felt that her actions implied that all disabled persons were really cowards and had a wish to die. Even medical experts felt the need to reassure the public by asserting that pain could safely be controlled and that no one needed to fear the suffering from pain.

In his book *A Graceful Passage,* UCLA psychiatry professor Arnold Beisser, who is himself a quadriplegic as a result of polio and who has lived in an iron lung most of his life, wrote, "The real tragedy [for Ms. Bouvia] is that the fate of this one human being was completely out of her hands, and had become a matter for public policy debate." Later, in his analysis of Bouvia's case, he wrote, "Who am I to say that it should have been enough for her? It is she, and she alone, who must live in her body, and if any of us wish to assume responsibility for how she wished to do that, should we not also be required to suffer her agony?" In his conclusion, Beisser claims that Bouvia was given a sentence worse than death: a life without meaning.[30]

As it turned out, Bouvia decided not to have the feeding tube removed, and ironically, at the time of this writing, she is still alive. What was most important to her was to obtain a feeling of autonomy over her body and her destiny. The sense of empowerment that is taken away first by the disease and later by the medical or legal establishment is what many patients wish to recover. Whether they will act on their newly acquired freedom to choose death over life is quite a separate matter.

Amyotrophic lateral sclerosis (ALS) also gradually affects all the voluntary muscles of the body and eventually the respiratory muscles as well. Only the person who lives in that body can really tell what pain and suffering are occurring. No one else can really appreciate or judge what has to be endured. Should those with ALS have some choices? Should they have the freedom to decide how long the respirator should be continued? Should they have the right and privilege to expect a painless and peaceful ending to their suffering?

Take the case of Laura Marazzo, who had an advanced case of ALS. Her motor functions had deteriorated to such an extent that she was bedridden, unable to move, unable to swallow, and completely dependent on a respirator. The only way she could communicate was by jerking her lower jaw in response to questions. Like Bouvia, she had reached a point where life was becoming intolerably painful and pointless. She, too, wanted the freedom to choose and to retain control over her body and her destiny, whatever her ultimate decision.

In January 1991, Judge James A. Gowan in Suffolk County, New York, ruled that Marazzo was competent because she could communicate by her jaw movements her wishes to be disconnected from the respirator. He then said, "She has the right to determine the course of her medical treatment, or stated in the reverse, to decline medical treatment if she so desires." He was basing his opinion on the fact that, in the United States, a competent adult has an absolute right to reject unwanted medical treatment of any kind.[31]

It is this principle that has guided courts and medical experts in cases of patients who are terminally ill or in persistent vegetative states, especially if they have living wills or other advance directives. But many rational individuals find it difficult to understand why some people would choose death over life.

Cases of quadriplegic patients or those suffering from ALS, like Laura Marazzo, who wish to be disconnected from ventilators or feeding tubes are not uncommon. To date, almost every court decision has respected the patient's right to reject treatment.

Meanwhile the controversy continues. Thomas Marzen, an attorney for the Indianapolis-based National Legal Center for the Medically Dependent and Disabled, said, "They [the disabled] are made to feel that it's time for them to go. There's a kind of message that's being transmitted that their lives are not worth living."[32] On the other hand, Ronald E. Cranford, a renowned neurosurgeon and medical ethics expert at Hennepin County Medical Center in Minneapolis and one of the nation's most vocal right-to-die advocates, disagrees: "I don't agree with the right-to-lifers that it's a likely scenario, although in some situations patients may feel an obligation not to burden their family. . . . However, I don't think that's true in the cases I've been involved with or in most cases."[33]

Susan M. Wolf, an attorney and associate for law at the Hastings Center, a bioethics think tank in Briarcliff Manor, New York, expressed a different opinion. She says that the real problem, as she sees it, is not a matter of denying the refusal of treatment, but simply a lack of social services. To emphasize her point, she says, "It's not enough to vindicate people's right to refuse life-sustaining treatment; it's also critically important that we pay attention to all the cutbacks in services that we've seen in recent years." She feels that these people need support and services, not just the right to refuse treatment. But she agrees that it's proper that the courts stand ready to vindicate the right to refuse treatment; whether people choose to exercise it is quite a separate right.[34]

And so it seems that society is slowly moving toward change. Many people are beginning to recognize the importance of retaining control over their destiny. In the decades ahead, we may find that society will allow us to get the treatment of *our* choice, to accept or refuse extraordinary treatment, and to retain the feeling of control that is so important to our dignity and peace of mind.

CHOOSING DEATH

> To die—to sleep—
> No more; and by a sleep to say we end
> The heartache, and the thousand natural
>   shocks
> That flesh is heir to.
> —William Shakespeare, *Hamlet*

People sometimes wonder if there is a moral difference between *not* doing something to prolong life and doing something deliberately to end it? In either case, the issue of having personal autonomy over one's life is a basic question if not a right. Many organizations and groups in the country oppose this viewpoint, and it is beyond the scope of this book to discuss in detail the expert arguments about choosing not to prolong dying and choosing death. For such an analysis, I again refer you to the excellent discussion by Robert M. Veatch in his book *Death, Dying and the Biological Revolution.*

As mentioned earlier, the famous writer Arthur Koestler decided at age seventy-seven to end his life. It seems that his suffering from advanced stages of leukemia and Parkinson's disease was the motive for his decision. His suicide touched off violent reactions on both sides of the Atlantic. Although in England and in most of the United States, suicide is not a crime, most religious groups condemn it as "self-murder." And incidentally, in all countries, assisting anyone in suicide is against the law.

Religious groups that feel that no one has the right to take a life except God were shocked by the news of the suicides of Dr. Henry P. Van Dusen and his wife, Elizabeth, in 1975. Van Dusen, who for many years had been president of the Union Theological Seminary in New York and a world spiritual leader, had lived a full and creative life. When severe handicaps set in, the Van Dusens saw that they would become increasingly dependent on others, even to the point of the most basic biological functions, and they feared a total loss of dignity. They left a letter explaining in detail to their family and friends that they were not acting out of despair nor were they rejecting their faith in God or their belief in life as the highest value; they wished to exercise their God-given free will to prevent the inevitable loss of all dignity. Mrs. Van Dusen died the day after taking an overdose of sleeping pills; Dr. Van Dusen, unfortunately, did not die until two weeks later, after being taken to a nursing home.[35]

Another case that made great fanfare in the news was that of the New York artist and psychotherapist Jo Roman, who committed suicide on June 10, 1979. Roman had stated openly that she believed in the right to "self-determination." In fact, she was writing a book on the subject.

Roman had planned to live until her seventies with the hope of avoiding senility. When she learned in March 1978 that she had breast cancer, which had allegedly spread to the lymph nodes, she decided to schedule her self-deliverance much sooner. She turned down radiation and surgery but accepted chemotherapy. Later, she found that the chemotherapy was too debilitating and decided to discontinue it.

Meanwhile, she finished her book, entitled *Exit House*, which was published posthumously in 1981. The book recommends that a social agency be created to help the terminally ill who want a "gentle suicide" without complications or obstructions. Then she arranged for an hour-long videotaping of the preparation of her suicide, which was televised by the Public Broadcasting Service under the title "Choosing Suicide" on June 16, 1980. As expected, this public display of autonomy had a very disturbing impact on most people. In the tape, Roman defended her actions by saying, "Why should I have pain? . . . I don't have to have a day of pain."[36]

Many people considered Roman's position extremely narrow and selfish. Ironically, the autopsy showed that the cancer had not spread to the lymph nodes, and she could have lived more productive years. One could argue whether she made a right and moral decision, but the true underlying motive was, as most psychiatrists would agree, her fear of losing control and her wish to retain it at all costs. Others would argue that she exercised her right to self-determination and autonomy, both of which also refer to the right to choose or to refuse further medical treatment. Of course, she went much further than that.

Some have argued that Jo Roman used poor judgment and that she could have lived a few more good years, especially as her cancer had not spread (although she didn't know it at the time). Others have accused her of being self-centered and of having ignored the pain she was causing others, although on the surface she had the open support of her family. Another way to explain Roman's decision is to look at the so-called balance-sheet phenomenon. This kind of thinking occurs in the so-called balance-sheet suicide, in which the person with an intolerable medical condition weighs the benefits against the burdens of living, including the chances of improvement, and finally concludes that death is the optimal choice. Doris Portwood, who has also written about rational suicide in her book *Common Sense Suicide*, perceives this act as the final right of the individual in our society today, especially of the ailing elderly.[37]

Over the last several years, I have seen a few AIDS patients who have welcomed the opportunity to talk about their choices of living and dying. Most of them did not take any active steps when the end was near, but knowing that they could exercise some control was enough to give them peace of mind until the end.

In Chapter 8 I discuss more extensively the right-to-die movement in the United States and elsewhere.

TOUGH DECISIONS IN SPECIAL CASES

As public awareness of the effects of declining health and lingering death is increasing, people and professionals alike feel more freedom to talk openly about the subject. Such questions as aid in dying, euthanasia, and the right to "pull the plug" are receiving increasing attention in the lay and medical press.

Sometimes patients with an incurable disease seek deliverance by ending life. Because this is not easy to do, they seek help from the medical profession. But aid in dying is still considered illegal, and most physicians will decline to provide such aid, at least openly, in today's climate. As attitudes are gradually changing, a few physicians are beginning to publish accounts of such cases as the following accounts, which tell two unusual stories that illustrate tough decisions following hard choices for both the patient and the doctor.

Sometimes physicians become frustrated in dealing with their colleagues and take over the care of their loved ones in an attempt to reduce their suffering. In the first case, the doctor assisted his wife in committing suicide after she was diagnosed as having terminal lung cancer. He had hoped to get support from colleagues in his community and from public opinion by appearing on a local television show. Instead, he got into serious difficulty with the law and the medical profession.[38] This is his poignant story.

THE CASE OF PATTY

Patricia Rosier had been diagnosed as having cancer of the lungs with metastases to the brain and the adrenal glands. She knew her diagnosis and the fatal outcome awaiting her. Her physician had told her that she had days, possibly a few more weeks, to live. Her pain was under reasonable control, although her continuous vomiting was almost unbearable.

Patty had heard that her death might be horrible. She was obsessed with the fear of losing control, and retaining control was extremely important to her. She could also see how her deteriorating condition was affecting her husband, Peter, a respected pathologist. He seemed totally demoralized and had become severely depressed, to the point of suspending his medical practice at age forty-five. He managed to maintain the household with the income from disability insurance

During one of their intimate moments, Patty told Peter that

she would like to end her life by taking an overdose of drugs. He said that he would like to die with her. After further discussion with their two children, he agreed not to do so.

Patty had made up her mind, and she set a date for her suicide. She arranged to have a last supper with her family and closest friends. She ordered champagne and lobster from a caterer and organized the evening as a formal affair. It was a poignant and memorable event with everyone toasting the "Lady."

Because of her flair for style, she wanted to share her experience with others and agreed to appear on Fort Myers, Florida, television to talk about her cancer and the effects of chemotherapy. Later, she agreed to a second interview to announce that she would be dying soon, not mentioning her intention of suicide.

On her last night, she asked Peter to call the TV station for a final interview, which they granted. Many people who knew Patty sensed that she was preparing to die on her own terms and that she would do so without waiting much longer.

That evening she gathered her family together—her husband, her two teenage children, her stepfather, her two stepbrothers, and her aunt—and announced that she wanted to have one last intimate moment with her husband before saying good-bye.

Patty and her husband retired to the bedroom and made love one last time. At midnight, they came out to the family room where everyone was gathered. Patty kissed everyone good-bye and went back to her bedroom.

Before preparing for bed, she made sure to vomit up her dinner so she would have an empty stomach for better absorption of the pills she was planning to take. Then, in the presence of Peter, she took twenty Seconal and washed them down with a glass of water. That dose had been determined by Peter, who had asked a colleague what was the lethal dose. Unfortunately, that was only the minimal lethal dose, not necessarily the one that would work.

Patty spent the entire night in a deep sleep, and by the next morning, she seemed to be in a deep coma. Peter began to realize that he had made a mistake in the dosage. He began to feel that he had failed her. He felt desperate and could not bear the thought of seeing her disappointment at awakening. Realizing that she could not take additional Seconal and morphine in her comatose state, he panicked and called one of his colleagues, who came over to find Patty breathing shallowly. Peter asked the doctor for a large dose of morphine, but the doctor left in a hurry, visibly shaken by the request. Somehow, Peter got the doctor to agree to leave 8 milligrams of morphine, which he injected into Patty's buttocks in front of her stepbrothers. Even hours later, Patty had not stopped breathing, and Peter ran out to ask another doctor for help. He obtained four morphine suppositories from that doctor and immediately gave them to Patty.

Hours later, she was still breathing and did not seem to be dying. It was evident that all the drugs combined had not been potent enough. Everyone was in a state of turmoil. By then, it was noon of the next day, twelve hours since Patty had taken the first drugs. At that point, one of her stepbrothers said that, if he had enough guts, he would go into the bedroom and smother his sister to get it over with. Soon after, Patty's stepfather said, "Enough is enough." He went into the bedroom, followed by his sons, put his hand over Patty's mouth, and suffocated her. She died without regaining consciousness.

After they emerged from the bedroom, the stepfather and his sons agreed not to mention the incident to anyone.

Following the cremation, the grieving began. Still reacting to the traumatic events, Peter began to write a book about the experience as a way of finding some relief from his grief. He even went so far as to look into the possibility of producing a television play about Patty's life, but his script was rejected by several producers. He returned to the television station that had offered Patty her three interviews and appeared on television admitting that he had assisted Patty in her suicide. As Peter found out, that was to be one of the biggest mistakes of his life. The interview was seen by the state attorney, who immediately launched a criminal investigation.

The investigation led to testimony from the stepbrothers and stepfather, who were offered immunity for disclosing the details of the incident. They confessed to the suffocation, but no charges were filed against them. Nevertheless, the state attorney decided to pursue the matter in a trial, pressing three charges against Peter: first-degree murder, conspiracy to commit murder, and attempted murder, using Peter's manuscript as the main piece of evidence.

The trial went on. It was clear from all the evidence that Peter did not have a chance. The defense, prepared by two brilliant lawyers, Susan and Stanley Rosenblatt of Miami, took the prosecution by surprise. They pointed out the self-righteousness of the prosecutors who were using Patty's stepfather as a "whipping boy." The defense underlined the flimsy nature of the supporting evidence and reached right into the hearts and minds of the jury members.

On December 1, 1988, after three hours of deliberation, the jury of five men and seven women reached a verdict of "not guilty," acquitting Peter Rosier on all counts. The jury even declined to consider five lesser counts that had been favored by the judge.

Later, Rosier wrote an article in *Medical Economics* emphasizing the emotionally traumatic aspects of the experience, in particular, the lack of support by his medical colleagues. He wrote: "Apparently, a jury of non-physicians found it easier to address the subject than my colleagues did . . . . Following weeks of testimony, it took the jury in my murder trial only three hours to acquit me of all charges. Since the trial, I've asked myself what could have made this nightmare less painful. If only doctors had gotten together and said, 'We don't know the answer to this. We're not supporting Rosier or opposing him. But this is an issue the community should look at. How are terminally ill people treated, and what should a doctor's role be?' That kind of discussion never occurred. The medical profession hid its head in the sand . . . . I have no interest in leading a crusade for euthanasia. But when a terminally ill person makes an informed, rational decision, the government should stay out of the patient's room. Each individual owns his own life. Patricia Rosier owned hers, and she made her own decisions. If I could pick a memorial to Patty, it would be that the trial and publicity lead to legislation giving the terminally ill more control over their destiny."[39]

This rather sad story is one of many that are advancing the level of discussion and bringing the subject into the open, but most people are still afraid to talk about the problems involved in terminal illness. Everyone should choose her or his own way of dealing with the issue. Some would prefer to have more control over their decisions, and others would rather put themselves in the hands of God. The problem is not to decide what is right or to know what is righteous. The problem is the "conspiracy of silence" that exists in our society concerning terminal illness. People need to know if they can act autonomously and privately, and if they can exercise some choice in these end-of-life decisions. In Chapter 10, I discuss appropriate ways to gain peace of mind with appropriate preparations.

Sometimes, even choosing to let nature take its course may become a problem. Just refusing the help of modern technology in favor of natural ways of dying may lead to unforeseen complications. This is what happened to my mother and me when a self-righteous group of people decided to impose their wishes and values on my mother's and my beliefs. At the age of eighty-eight, my mother was not allowed to live out her life without interference from others. I will tell her story as I wrote it in an article published in *Medical Economics*, a journal with national circulation.[40]

MY MOTHER'S STORY

My mother might have finished her rich, full life with dignity until the end. Instead, a self-righteous lawyer condemned her to a living hell.

My eighty-eight-year-old widowed mother had Alzheimer's disease, and it had advanced to the point where she had to be placed in a nursing home. A year passed. Then her internist phoned me with disturbing news: "George, your mother's pacemaker is going to need a new battery." Dr. Brown (not his real name) continued, "But because of her age and deteriorating health I think we should talk it over."

We discussed her condition and history in detail. Mother had been an active businesswoman most of her life. I had vivid memories of her as a young woman—how she'd saved my life as we fled from the Nazis; how she'd encouraged me in my darkest moments to pursue my education and career. We had a close, loving relationship.

In the last few years, she'd become painfully aware of her failing memory and inability to get around. Now she was in chronic congestive heart failure, confused, incontinent, and almost blind. She couldn't watch television and didn't know where she was, what day it was, or even what had happened a minute earlier. All she could do was stare at the ceiling and submit to being fed, changed, and medicated. The quality of her life could only get worse, according to her doctor.

"I need time to think it over and talk with the rest of the family," I told him. I agonized over the situation for several days, reviewing it with my wife and other members of our family, remembering how adamant Mother had been in making me promise not to let her "vegetate" in a nursing home. It had broken my heart when I was forced to put her in the very place she's feared so much.

Knowing that she was completely dependent on her pacemaker, we decided to "let nature take its course." Artificially prolonging a life that had lost all meaning to Mother would be cruel and degrading. But before I had a chance to tell the doctor of our decision, he called me.

"George," he said, a note of alarm in his voice, "I just received a letter from the pacemaker supplier. It's threatening me with legal action if I don't replace the battery!"

I couldn't believe my ears. The only explanation I could

think of was that the company was afraid my family would sue if the pacemaker failed.

Brown quoted from the letter: "I am sure you are aware that a failure to replace her pulse generator due to the wishes of family members . . . would leave any participating parties open to possible legal and ethics actions. In the absence of a living will . . . such a failure to replace her pulse generator borders on indefensible passive euthanasia and cannot be condoned."

Brown went on, "Forget the suggestion I made to you a few days ago. You can understand my position, can't you?"

I was furious. "You mean, the fear of litigation prevails over sense and compassion?"

We agreed to do nothing until we talked it over in a few days, but before that could happen, I got another call from Brown.

"The city prosecutor's office called me," he said. "They're coming over to investigate."

What could this mean? Brown had no idea what was going on, but he had had enough. He asked me to let him admit Mother to the hospital so the battery could be replaced.

My wife and I talked it over. She's a nurse, and we'd just finished writing a book on dying, death, and grief, so we were well informed on the ethical questions. I called Brown back and told him we'd decided to stand firm.

The next day, someone from the prosecutor's office phoned me, demanding an interview. We set an appointment for the following afternoon. An hour later, the hospital administrator called. He wanted to meet with the hospital's lawyer, my mother's cardiologist, and Dr. Brown. I insisted on a telephone conference that would include my lawyer. It took place later the same day.

"We understand what a difficult position this situation presents for you and your mother," the hospital's representative said, "but you must understand that this issue is likely to create legal complications."

I couldn't blame Brown and the hospital for being frightened. After all, I'd be placing my own practice, my reputation, my livelihood, and my relationship with my colleagues on the line to save my mother from an impending collision with uncompassionate technology. I almost caved in.

To ensure that my mother's pacemaker wouldn't fail in the nursing home, subjecting us to possible prosecution, we all agreed to have her admitted to the hospital for telemetry. And we agreed to present her case to the hospital ethics committee as early as possible.

The following day, a deputy city attorney and an investigator showed up at my office. "A complaint has been registered with our office by a pacemaker company," the lawyer said, "and we're here to investigate for possible criminal action." I tried to remain calm, and I thought the interview went very well. They said they felt there was no criminal intent and left, telling me they'd let me know the outcome of their investigation.

I went to the hospital that evening to visit Mother. She was wired to the monitoring machine, and she had no idea what was going on around her. When I mentioned that she might get a replacement battery for her pacemaker, she turned to me and said in a rare moment of lucidity, "I know you love your mother."

The choices stood out in stark contrast. The cardiologist had explained that replacing the pacemaker battery carried a 5 to 10 percent risk of complications from infection. If the procedure were successful, she faced several years of further degeneration, followed by eventual death from acute pneumonia or congestive heart failure. Without a new battery, he said, Mother's death would be swift, painless, and uneventful.

It should have been an easy choice, and I knew exactly what Mother would have wanted. She didn't have a living will, but she had expressed her wishes often. The hospital's ethics committee was unanimous in supporting our decision to let her go peacefully.

Then the deputy city attorney called with less forthright support: "The prosecutor understands the issues in your mother's case and he remains sympathetic, but he can't give you any assurance that no further proceedings will ensue."

"What does that mean?" I asked.

"That means we won't pursue the matter, but we can't give you a full guarantee at this point," he replied.

A family-court hearing was held. The judge appointed me my mother's guardian, with the observation that as her son I would act in her best interest. I felt relieved.

I still surmised that the pacemaker supplier was trying to force me to have Mother's battery replaced for fear of a lawsuit, so I decided to call the company president. I explained my motivation and told him I wasn't the least bit interested in suing and would happily sign a waiver.

"I don't agree with your decision," he said, "but I don't feel it's my place to interfere."

Then my office called. My mother had signed the consent form agreeing to the procedure. How could she have any idea what she was signing?

I called the hospital attorney immediately, and he agreed the consent form was invalid. But I was beginning to learn that I could take nothing for granted, so I rushed to the hospital, just in time to prevent Mother from being wheeled into the operating room. No one had bothered to inform the surgical suite nurses that the operation had been canceled.

When I returned to the office, the prosecutor's office called. "Another complaint has been registered about your mother; we're obligated to look into it again."

Who had filed the complaint? The attorney for the pacemaker company, I was told. Furious, I called the company president and demanded to know what was going on.

"I didn't place another complaint," he said. "I don't know what you're talking about."

"Your attorney filed the complaint," I told him.

"He's acting on his own behalf," the company president said. "I'm no longer using his services. Good-bye and good luck."

Now I was steaming! I called this self-retained lawyer and demanded to know whom he was representing and the grounds for his complaint.

There was a long silence. Then the answer came: "You and your mother do not have the right to pursue the course for terminating a life by withholding the procedure in question."

"May I ask who gave you the right to take this matter into your own hands?"

"I represent a right-to-life organization in this matter, and I am prepared to have you removed as legal guardian if necessary and pursue it all the way to the Supreme Court."

I asked him to consider meeting with me, my attorney, and an authority on ethics the following day. To my surprise, he agreed.

When we met in my attorney's office, I noticed that the right-to-life lawyer had brought another man with him, introducing him as the proposed new guardian for my mother.

We went back and forth with legal and ethical arguments, citing chapter and verse of case law and precedents, debating the technical reasons for keeping my mother alive or letting her die. None of the right-to-life lawyer's arguments considered her feelings or wishes nor those of her family.

Finally I turned to my nemesis and asked, "What will it take to satisfy you in this case?"

"All you have to do is let your mother have her new pacemaker," he replied. "If this isn't done, I intend to fight all the way to the Supreme Court."

I was furious and frustrated, but I couldn't bear the emotional and financial costs of such a battle. I gave in.

Mother promptly received a brand-new pacemaker, supplied by a different company. She went back to the nursing home, physically a bit stronger. But she didn't know where she was. Propped up in a wheelchair, she was being dragged to meals and bingo, but she merely sat and stared. And she waited.

About a year later, she was readmitted to the hospital because of heart failure. I visited her daily, but she didn't seem to remember my visits. She barely recognized me and gave me a vacant smile. She seemed so far away and so distant. In her private room, she lay there, totally unaware that she was hooked up to wires connected to display monitors with flickering lights and to intravenous tubing planted in her arm. All alone, in the midst of hospital bells and paging calls, she died a few days later. I have often wondered what she would say if she only knew that her body was kept alive so long under those conditions.

The pacemaker company attorney responded to my article in this way: "I sympathize with Dr. Burnell but believe that his intensely personal account misses a crucial point. Any party to a treatment regime has a right, if not a duty, to insist that this regime be aggressive and life-saving in the interests of the patient's civil rights; the only exceptions to this can be instances in which strict standards of medical and judicial review have been met." For these and other reasons, he felt that her condition did not justify the refusal to replace the pacemaker, even though I had obtained approval from the court and the hospital ethics committee.

The two preceding cases illustrate the kinds of conflict people and professionals may encounter in today's climate. The confusion seems to involve questions of definitions, legal terminology, matters of values and belief systems, personal rights, and current standards of care in the community. The debate over "whose life is it anyway" and "whose decision is it anyway" will continue to occupy the experts and the public at large for years to come. More than ever, the public needs to be well informed for progress to occur.

NOTES

1. Arnold R. Beisser, *A Graceful Passage: Notes on the Freedom to Live or Die* (New York: Doubleday, 1990), 171.
2. Ann R. Somers, "Long Term Care for the Elderly and Disabled," *New England Journal of Medicine* 307 (1982): 222.
3. Raymond S. Duff and August B. Hollingshead, *Sickness and Society* (New York: Harper & Row, 1968), 307.
4. President's Commission for the Study of Ethical Problems in Medicine and Biomedical and Behavioral Research Deciding to Forego Life-Sustaining Treatment: Ethical, Medical and Legal Issues in

Treatment Decisions, Vol. 1 (Washington, D.C.: U.S. Government Printing Office, 1983), 17.

5. Elizabeth Ogg, *Facing Death and Loss* (Lancaster, PA: Technomic, 1985), 25.

6. Robert M. Veatch, *Death, Dying and the Biological Revolution: Our Last Quest for Responsibility* (New Haven, CT: Yale University Press, 1989), 4.

7. Lesley F. Denger and Janet I. Beaton, *Life-Death Decisions in Health Care* (Washington, D.C.: Hemisphere, 1987), 135–140.

8. Ibid.

9. American Medical Association, "Statement of the Council on Ethical and Judicial Affairs" March 15, 1986.

10. Beisser, 22–23.

11. Pope Pius XII, "The Prolongation of Life," *The Pope Speaks* 4 (Spring 1958): 393–398.

12. Walter M. Bortz, *We Live Too Short and Die Too Long: How to Achieve and Enjoy Your Natural 100-Year-Plus Life Span* (New York: Bantam Books, 1991), 253.

13. J. J. Paris, "When Burdens of Feeding Outweigh Benefits," *The Hastings Center Report* 16 (1986): 30–32.

14. G. J. Annas, "The Insane Root Takes Reason Prisoner," *The Hastings Report* 19 (1989): 29–31.

15. Editorial, "Mixed Messages," *Hospital Ethics* 1 (1988): 14–15.

16. P. D. Derr, "Why Food and Fluids Can Never Be Denied," *The Hastings Center Report* 16 (1986): 28–30.

17. D. Callahan, "On Feeding the Dying," *The Hastings Center Report* 13 (1983): 22.

18. R. Priester, *Reading Packet on Withholding or Withdrawing Artificial Nutrition and Hydration, Center for Biomedical Ethics* (Minneapolis: University of Minnesota, 1988).

19. *In re Conroy*, (1985) 321 N.J. 486 A. 2nd 1209.

20. *In re Peter*, (1987) 108 N.J. 365, 529 A. 2nd 419.

21. Society for the Right to Die, *Right to Die Court Decisions*, Vol. 2 (New York: Author, 1987), NJ-4.

22. American Nurses Association, Committee on Ethics, *Guidelines on Withholding and Withdrawing Food and Fluids*, (Kansas City: Author, 1988).

23. Mary Ellen Wurzbach, "The Dilemma of Withholding or Withdrawing Nutrition," *Image* 22 (1990): 229.

24. A. Jameton, *Nursing Practice* (Englewood Cliffs, NJ: Prentice-Hall, 1984).
25. Joseph Fletcher, "Geriatric Psychiatry: The Case of the MI, DNR, ECT, NG, and DOD," *Psychiatric Annals* 16 (July 1986): 411–413.
26. Society for the Right to Die, "Artificial Nutrition and Hydration" (New York: Author, 1990), 1–2.
27. Ibid.
28. *Bouvia v. County of Riverside,* Calif. Superior Court (December 16, 1983) No. 159780, 1–9.
29. *Bouvia v. Superior Court of Los Angeles,* (1986) 179 Cal. App. 3rd 1127, 225 Cal. Rptr. 297.
30. Beisser, 118.
31. American Health Consultants, "Patients Who Choose Death May Not Be Aware of Alernatives," *Medical Ethics Advisor* 7 (April 1991): 47–48.
32. Ibid.
33. Ibid.
34. Ibid.
35. Ogg, 26.
36. Ibid., 28.
37. Doris Portwood, *Common Sense Suicide: The Final Right* (Los Angeles: Hemlock Society, 1980), 32–33.
38. Peter R. Rosier, "A Jury Acquitted Me of Murder: Most Colleagues Turned Their Backs," *Medical Economics,* 1 May 1989, 42–45.
39. Ibid., 45.
40. George M. Burnell, "My Mother Wants to Die: A Lawyer Won't Let Her," *Medical Economics,* 19 Dec. 1988, 57–60.

CHAPTER 5

Do You Have a Philosophy of Living and Dying?

There is no cure for birth or death
save to enjoy the interlude.
—George Santayana

In this age of technology, we are becoming increasingly aware of the need to think about decisions regarding death and dying. In the 1970s, "death with dignity" became a popular concept that was openly discussed. In the 1980s, the concept grew to encompass the right-to-die movement. All of us faced with these new concepts need to ponder basic philosophical ideas about the meaning of death. In this chapter, I want to encourage the reader to think about a personal philosophy, particularly in the context of recent developments in life-supporting and life-extending technology. We review some thoughts and philosophical theories expressed by writers, clinicians, philosophers, and ethicists on the subject of death and dying.

WHAT ARE THE MEANINGS OF DEATH?

The more absolute death seems, the more
authentic life becomes.
—John Fowles, *The Aristos* (1964)

All religions and philosophies have recognized death and dying as a challenge. As Plato said, "Those who tackle philosophy aright are simply and solely practicing dying, practicing death all the time, but nobody sees it." In busy lives that entail surviving in a competitive society, who has time to develop a philosophy of death? Unless one is fighting a life-threatening illness or has lost a loved one, it is difficult to pay much attention to the circumstances of dying or to the meaning of death. Occasionally, after recovering from a serious illness or narrowly escaping death after a close call in an accident, however, we are forced to ask ourselves a few crucial questions: Are we enjoying life as we expected to? Are we accomplishing what we set out to do? Are we contributing to society as we had hoped to? Are we achieving the goals we dreamed of? Are we providing for the physical and emotional needs of our family? What if something serious happened to us? Are we prepared to deal with the decisions and consequences of a terminal illness or the uncertain outcome of an accident? It is those questions that lead us to reflect on our mortality and the tenuous thread that holds us to this life. The truth, then, is that a philosophy of dying is really a philosophy of living. As Montaigne, the French philosopher, said, "Whoever teaches people how to die, teaches them how to live."

Sometimes, those insights don't come to us until we are on the threshold of life and death. As my friend, Bob, said to his doctor before preparing to go home for a peaceful death, "Doc, I've had a good life; I've raised a good family, taught all I wanted to teach, traveled the world over, and most of all, I've received much love and have given all the love I could give. I couldn't ask for more." As I reflect on his remarks, I realize that most of us take every day of life for granted, and we tend to put things off to the future. This practice may be acceptable when we are young, but as age creeps up, it becomes an increasing problem. Only those like Bob who have lived a full life arrive at the end of their lives with no regrets, no sense of being robbed of extra life, no feeling of being unfinished.

If we have no regrets, dying will not seem to be so formidable an enemy. As a patient of mine said, "If I die tomorrow, I won't have any regrets because I've lived my life to the fullest.

I didn't hold back. Of course, I took some risks, but it was worth it."

Others, after a diagnosis of cancer, emphasize the importance of the small things in life, like U.S. Senator Richard L. Neuberger, who said, "I have a new appreciation of things I once took for granted—eating lunch with a friend, scratching my cat Muffet's ears and listening for his purrs, the company of my wife, reading a book or a magazine in the quiet of my bed lamp at night, raiding the refrigerator for a glass of orange juice or a slice of toast. For the first time, I think I actually am savoring life."

Sooner or later, we have to come to terms with the fact that it is not a matter of whether we are going to die but when and how we are going to die. The earlier we can accept the reality of a finite existence, the sooner we can go on with the business of living. Death is not and should not be viewed as a catastrophic event, because death is as much a part of life as birth, procreating, and aging. Aging itself is a terminal illness in the sense that it progresses to a natural conclusion. Life and death can be viewed as part of a natural cycle. But the end of our lives will be easier to accept if we have met most of our expectations. Then we feel that our life was well spent, and we have no regrets.

Before his death in 1970, psychologist Abraham Maslow, recalling his feelings after a recent heart attack, wrote of the satisfaction he felt in just having completed what he considered his most important work. He said he had done his best in this work and that he had come upon a good time to die . . . . He compared his life to a good ending in a play.

What meaning each of us finds in life is special and unique. German psychiatrist Victor Frankl, who survived the concentration camps, said, "The meaning of life differs from man to man, from day to day and from hour to hour. What matters, therefore, is not the meaning of life in general, but rather the specific meaning of a person's life at a given moment . . . . One should not search for an abstract meaning of life. Everyone has his own specific vocation or mission in life to carry out a concrete assignment which demands fulfillment. Thus everyone's task is unique as is his specific opportunity to implement it."[1]

What if life has lost its meaning? Should we throw it away? This might be the case in a terminal illness, when there is nothing left except a life of suffering and continuous sedation with heavy medication. Some would say that, if we have no further control over life and no further usefulness, death becomes the true meaning. Whether one accepts life after death or not, inasmuch as death is a fact of life, it has a meaning in itself.[2]

Many books have been written on the philosophy and psychology of death, and the consensus is that each and every one of us must arrive at our own philosophy of death, which is basically a philosophy of living. Lisl Marburg Goodman said that the more complete one's life is, the more . . . one's creative capacities are fulfilled, the less one fears death . . . . People are not afraid of death per se, but of the incompleteness of their lives.[3]

Through the ages, we have tried to work out a strategy to cope with the prospect of dying. The hedonists of early Greece concentrated on enjoying the pleasures of life as much as possible till the end. The pessimists, on the other hand, decided that life was so awful that death was bound to be the lesser of two evils. Others thought that the whole argument was a waste of time. Euripides, another Greek philosopher and playwright, simply concluded, "Where I am, Death is not; and where Death is, I am not; therefore, there is no reason to worry about death."[4] That was the same conclusion that a friend of mine reached on learning that I was writing a book on the problem of dying today: "I don't think I want to think about it just now; death isn't something that concerns me now. I'll deal with it when the time comes."

Even that last example reflects one of the ways in which we look at the meaning of life and death. Discussing the meaning of death when one is not faced with the imminent prospect of dying is very different from doing so when death is a potential reality within a short time. As a young patient who was dying of AIDS said to me, "I see life in such different terms now; it's as if everything suddenly is so clear and so simple." I couldn't help thinking what a shame it was to have to wait so long to understand life so clearly.

The reality is that it is difficult to think about death before being faced with it. Kastenbaum and Aisenberg, two psychologists who studied the psychology of death, concluded that people think of death in three special ways: impersonally, interpersonally, and intrapersonally.[5]

In the impersonal way, we tend to see death with a sense of distance, as something that we watch on television, for example. We see pictures of dead bodies in reports of war, accidents, and plane crashes. In them, we see the death of strangers, and we tend to disassociate it from our own lives. Death is just another form of information on the daily news.

In the interpersonal way of experiencing a death, we are apt to feel a deep sense of loss, sometimes even to the point of intense pain, depending on how close our relationship was to the dead person. In a way, we experience the death of some part of ourselves. The degree to which we experience this loss varies from moment to moment and according to the degree of intimacy we had with the dead person. This is the experience of grief.

Finally, the third way of thinking about death is intrapersonally. This way is almost unthinkable because it is difficult to imagine ourselves as being nonexistent. It is easier to think about the little deaths that we encounter in our daily living, when we feel loss of self-esteem, loss of health, loss of a job, loss of an organ or limbs, or even the loss of loved ones. In their book *Dying Dignified,* Gonda and Ruark suggested that how we cope with past losses may give us a clue to how we may cope with our own death.[6] This idea is further substantiated by Kamath, who reviewed the lives of fifty well-known historical figures, such as Albert Einstein, Mahatma Gandhi, William Shakespeare, John Keats, Lord Byron, Franz Kafka, O. Henry, and Winston Churchill, and how they met their deaths. How those people lived their lives was how they coped with dying. George Washington, for example, was remarkably calm and composed, even to the point of checking his own pulse moments before his last breath.

Kamath observes that most people die in the same style in which they lived. He concludes that although a good life does not guarantee a painless end, it surely results in a peaceful end.[7]

Regardless of our past coping, establishing a philosophy of death is a useful thing that everyone should do. This may be even more true today, as dying in the hospital has become such a complicated affair. It is imperative that we give some thought to the matter because so many people may be involved in changing the trajectory of our journey toward the end of life.

Avery Weisman, a psychiatrist who worked with dying patients, noted that "every individual dies to his own life; what his passing signifies to his survivors is apt to change. For almost everyone, however, the meaning of death is that it is a *universal negative,* repudiating and nullifying the objectives so sought in life . . . . Given a choice, healthy people would opt for a timely death that shortened suffering, because death is thought to be destructive of pain, as well as everything else."[8]

On the other hand, Frankl saw in death the potential for a more hopeful and meaningful experience. He said that the prospect of death gives us one more reason to find meaning in our lives. He emphasized the need *not just to be,* but *to be someone,* which he viewed as the drive for "meaning."[9] Frankl added that even at the very end of life, no matter how much life one has wasted, it can be redeemed by flooding one's life with meaning and purpose in a final phase of growth. Then even dying can have a purpose.

Elizabeth Kübler-Ross put it in another way. She called death the final stage of growth. Thus, she said, we can approach death by learning to die just a little every day making each day count. She wrote, "In order to be at peace, it is necessary to feel a sense of history—that you are both part of what has come before and part of what is yet to come. Being thus surrounded, you are not alone; and the sense of urgency that pervades the present is put in perspective: do not frivolously use the time that is yours to spend. Cherish it that each day may bring new growth, insight, and awareness. Use this growth not selfishly, but rather in service of what may be, in the future tide of time. Never allow a day to pass that did not add to what was understood before."[10] This highly idealistic philosophy helps some people make life more meaningful, at least in terms of love, devotion, and service, but the ultimate meaning, Frankl argues, is probably beyond the capacity of humans to comprehend.

Cultural and ethnic factors also influence individuals in their philosophy of death and living. In India, for example, there is a concerted effort to deal with death in the here and now. Eastern schools teach that all human beings go through a cycle of deaths and rebirths that will continue indefinitely until, in one of these lives, one gets in touch with the ultimate reality and merges with it. At that point, the person brings the series of cycles to an end. The underlying message is that rebirth is a greater evil than death, and that the hope is not to avoid death, but to avoid rebirth, usually by hard and dedicated spiritual work.[11]

Philippe Aries describes the development of Western attitudes toward death from the Middle Ages to the present.[12] His main thesis is that the prevailing attitude toward death in the United States has been denial, an observation documented by almost every writer on the subject of death and dying.

HOW DOES RELIGION INFLUENCE OUR THOUGHTS AND FEELINGS ABOUT DEATH AND DYING?

> *"General,"* murmured the tactful
> clergyman at Ulysses S. Grant's
> bedside, *"your time has come and the
> angels are waiting for you."*
> *"Waiting are they,"* roared the General,
> *"waiting are they? Well, Goddamn
> 'em, let 'em wait."*
>
> —Apocryphal

The thought of death and dying stirs up in us a sense of dread and annihilation. As Jonathan Swift said, "It is impossible that anything so natural, so necessary, and so universal as death should ever have been designed by providence as an evil to mankind." We have had to develop strategies to cope with our perceptions of death. Both organized religions and age-old philosophies have provided answers for all who have sought relief from what Becker has called "the terror of the unknown."[13]

Through the ages, we have believed in a world of spirits. Death for the most part is seen in thousands of religious sects as a crisis, a transition in which we gain a new status. Whether in Judeo-Christian, Islamic, or Eastern religious concepts, one central idea that emerges clearly is that, while the body disintegrates, some entity or power seems to persist, and that power, spirit, or entity is somehow transformed into a permanent state. Contemporary Eastern and Western religions differ in emphasis but not in essentials. In the East, one achieves salvation through contemplation and mysticism. In the West, one achieves it through hard work and righteousness.

The United States, despite erratic church attendance, still considers itself a religious culture.[14] Religion encompasses both a sense of belonging to a larger whole and a sense that our present era is connected to the past. The overall feeling is that our sense of history makes our individual lives more meaningful.

One of the main premises in religion is that life is a gift. Some might say that it is a gift from God. Others would say that it is a gift because we never earned it. In terms of death and dying, the idea of life as a gift has a particular meaning. If life is a special status conferred through creation, the recipient is expected to become a responsible participant who amplifies the gift of existence.[15] In other words, the religious individual is expected to ask such crucial questions as "Why is the world the way it is? Why do pain and evil exist?" Or as Rabbi Harold S. Kushner put it, "Why do bad things happen to good people?"[16]

One answer offered is that the gift of life is not fully acknowledged in our culture; therefore individuals do not find opportunities to achieve all they might. This, according to J. D. Morgan, a professor of philosophy at King's College in London, Ontario, is because the "North American philosophy" is somewhat ambivalent. On the one hand, he says, we admire achievements and accomplishments, such as building malls, repairing satellites, landing people on the moon, and transplanting organs. Our slogans reveal that "It's the bottom line that counts," and that there is a "cost of doing business." We live in a society where we want to "get things done." We "worship the dollar," we cherish a "busy and active life," and we continue to strive for an ever-improving "standard of living." Those attitudes toward life generally give us satisfaction and fulfillment.

On the other hand, do material achievements give us any answer to the question of whether we will make any meaningful difference in another person's life? Does materialism tell us anything about the existence of a life after death? It is true that most young, healthy people are not really interested in the existence of a life after death. But for someone in a crisis, such as at the critical time of a terminal illness, the concept of immortality may prove to be useful. Morgan concludes that our North American culture is in a constant state of tension between its two aspects: the emphasis on "efficient doing and living" and the spiritual side of life. He feels that sometimes we sacrifice the spiritual aspect of human existence to the pursuit of achievement.[17] Meanwhile, philosophers continue to argue the merits of the spiritual viewpoint versus the more existentialistic or even atheistic viewpoint in dealing with the final stages of life. Referring to groups of believers and nonbelievers, Lisl Marburg Goodman concludes, "On second thought, to the atheist, death is the end; to the believer, the beginning; to the agnostic, the sound of silence."[18]

SOME THOUGHTS ON IMMORTALITY

The idea of a second birth is found at all times and in all places.

—Carl Jung

Since the dawn of history, we have asked the questions, "What is death?" and "How shall we think of it: Should we welcome it or should we fear it?" Perhaps one of the most soothing strategies for dealing with the concept of death has been to believe that humans have an existence beyond the current one, in other words, that death is not the end of the individual.[19]

As we have seen, thoughts about death have been influenced by philosophies and religions, the latter in turn creating theories and dogmas that have helped believers cope with death anxiety and fear of the unknown. Religious thought, as we know it today, is often concerned with the mysteries of resurrection, rebirth, and relationship to a higher power. In the search to devise ways of dealing with the idea of death, philosophers, theologians, and writers frequently find themselves in very different camps, especially on the subject of immortality.

Simone de Beauvoir, in speaking of her mother's death, said, "Religion could do no more for my mother than the hope of posthumous success could do for me. Whether you think of it as heavenly or earthly, if you love life, immortality is no consolation for death."[20] Other writers have affirmed their belief in immortality with passion or reasoning, using different arguments. Catholic writer and twentieth-century Spanish philosopher Miguel de Unamuno writes in *The Tragic Sense of Life*, "For the sake of a name, man is ready to sacrifice not only life but happiness—life as a matter of course. 'Let me die, but let my fame live! Death is bitter, but fame is eternal.' . . . "If there is no immortality, of what use is God?"[21]

Freud came from a different philosophical perspective but reached similar conclusions about immortality: "Our own death is indeed unimaginable, and whenever we make an attempt to imagine it we can perceive that we really survive as spectators." Hence the psychoanalytic school could venture on the assertion that at bottom no one believes in his own death, or to put the thing in another way, in the unconscious every one of us is convinced of his own immortality.[22]

The belief in some kind of immortality may have practical implications for extending the end stages of life. Implicit in the concept of immortality is the idea that death is a transition to something better.

Ethicist Robert Veatch argues that there are two alternatives: to hope to extend mortal life as we know it in our present existence or to hope for immortality. One can accept that immortality is ideal; an extended mortal life is equally acceptable, although not necessarily better than what we have known all along. Veatch recognizes the dilemma between wanting to pursue immortality, on the one hand, and wanting to be satisfied with the mere extension of mortal life, on the other. He writes, "I have always found one of the most perplexing dilemmas in philosophy to be whether one ought to pursue an ideal that probably can never be achieved or should, instead, accommodate to the real world and pursue the relative ideal, which is the best course once one concedes that the ideal cannot be achieved."[23]

As to how such thoughts affect the problem of extending life, Veatch concludes that idealists will not reject the extension of mortal life even if they think that there is nothing to be gained by it, but realists may have to be convinced that extending mortal life is a good thing to do. Should these considerations be taken into account when ethicists and policymakers sit down to decide on policies that influence prolongation of the life span? After a detailed analysis, Veatch concludes that humans can lessen the fear of death in two ways. In some cases, individuals can make use of our scientific and technological advances to challenge and overcome certain "evil" deaths. In other cases, individuals can use their intellectual and humanistic skills responsibly to decide that death should not be challenged any further.[24]

QUALITY VERSUS QUANTITY OF LIFE

For to live is to function. That's all there is to living.
—Oliver Wendell Holmes on his ninetieth birthday

It is not unusual to hear about people who have put off pleasurable pursuits until it's too late to enjoy them. Many of us know people, maybe ourselves, who postpone ordinary pleasures because they are so busy earning and accumulating wealth and possessions that they have no time to truly enjoy the fruits of their labor, their relationships, or their families. One does not have to postpone enjoyment of life into an indefinite future in order to give it some meaning. As Samuel Johnson said, "It is more important that we live than that we die. In fact, dying is of no importance whatsoever, since it is so temporary a condition."

Some people attach a great deal of importance to the duration of life, but who can say that a life is more complete and meaningful because it has lasted eighty or a hundred years? Maybe we are now all that we will ever be. Maybe this is the last book we'll ever read. Maybe we have eaten our last meal. We do not understand the total meaning of our destiny. Yet we tend to equate long life with prospects of fulfilling our destiny and reaching our goals. What we refer to as our destiny might well be fulfilled in a very short span of life. Even if the poet John Keats had lived longer, would he have surpassed himself? Or, for that matter, Shelley, Byron, or Mozart? They all died young. Yet it is hard to imagine how they could have improved on their work.

In the total scheme of a human life, it is hard to assess that life in terms of its quality rather than its quantity. Our Western way of thinking is obsessed with measuring life the way we measure time. We talk about it "ticking away," as if we are parties to a contract that entitles us to seventy or eighty years of full and productive life.

Psychiatrist Michael Simpson believes that we are too concerned about measuring life. He says that no one has read the small print in the contract of life because it says that there are no guarantees of time at all. The truth is that, no matter how hard we try, we won't get "it" all done "in time." In his book *The Facts of Death*, he asks, if the average person living seventy years uses up 394,200,000 breaths, does that mean that those who die after 127,563,854 breaths have wasted their time and their breath? Of course not. The important thing is to recognize that life is fleeting and that pleasures and good feelings may stop between one moment and the next.[25]

We may become so obsessed with the importance of time that we are in a constant hurry to use every bit of it as if death were imminent. We are not guaranteed any particular period of time; some of us may live to ninety-eight, and others may die today. But if we have lived fully and lovingly, we will feel that our lives were very worthwhile whenever death comes. We all remember certain precious and memorable moments in our lives that are probably worth more than a lifetime of dull and ordinary hours.

How we assess the quality of our lives is highly individual. No one can really decide what constitutes quality for us except ourselves. Someone who pities a poor soul lying helplessly on a bed in a nursing home is projecting her or his own viewpoint in saying, "I wouldn't want that to happen to me. I couldn't stand it." The person lying there, however, may no longer be able to express any feelings. How, then, is one to judge the quality of that life? As we have seen, the courts are reluctant to become involved with quality-of-life issues, as in the *Cruzan* case. The answer lies in allowing people to make choices long before they end up in a nursing home.

It is helpful to have a philosophical basis for coping with the prospect of dying. A constant focus on death can be painful and unhealthy. Even if we have been told that we have an incurable illness, it is important to go on with living rather than to deny life. It is at such times that we become impressed by small things of life, recognizing how insignificant are the day-to-day things that we viewed as problems. We realize how ridiculous are those arguments and quarrels we have had with people who are very important to us. The old saying "Live each moment as if it were your last" may sound simplistic, but it sends a meaningful message. It reminds us that we should not wait till we hear the diagnosis of an incurable illness to decide to live more fully. This does not mean that we should become obsessed with the passage of every minute; instead, we should be prompted not to waste our energy on conflicts over relatively trivial matters. Rather than asking if there is life after death, we should ask the more important question: "Is there life before death?"[26]

My deceased friend, Eugene Heimler, a professor of social work and a survivor of the concentration camps like Frankl, developed a theory of living that he called "human social functioning." He felt that five key questions should be asked by any individual who is facing a critical point in life, including death: Have I achieved my ambition in life? Do I feel hopeful for the future? Do I feel that life has meaning? Has life given me enough scope for self-expression? And when I look back, do I feel that life was worth the struggle?

Heimler worked out a method of quantifying the answers on a 20-point scale. For instance, the answer to the first question might be estimated to be worth 15 points, the second 10 points, and so on. If you answered each question with a maximum score in the affirmative, you would get 20 points for each answer, or a total of 100 (which, according to Heimler, is rather unrealistic and improbable). Your answers may vary not only at different times in life but even from one week or one day to the next. In some way the total score may serve as a kind of philosophical barometer.[27] The Heimler scale of human social functioning has been used successfully with various populations, including the terminally ill.[28,29]

WHAT IS AN APPROPRIATE DEATH?

> *He is miserable who dieth not before he desires to die.*
>
> —Thomas Fuller

Avery Weisman, a professor of psychiatry at the Harvard Medical School who is also on the staff of Massachusetts General Hospital, coined the term "appropriate death" after working with hundreds of dying patients. An appropriate death is the kind of death each of us would want if we had a choice. For example, some of us would like to die in our sleep; others would prefer to die surrounded by family members; others are interested especially in dying without pain; and some would prefer to die for a particular purpose or cause. In some ways, an appropriate death resembles the death resulting from a "rational suicide," inasmuch as the death is chosen by the person and coincides with that person's principles, goals, and needs.

Weisman says that appropriate death occurs when individuals have found peace within themselves and with others and have achieved their life goals. If a person is to be helped to die in this manner, Weisman says, "he should be relatively pain-free, his suffering reduced, and emotional and social impoverishments kept to a minimum. With the limits of his disability, he should operate on as high a level as possible, even though only tokens of former fulfillments can be offered. He should also recognize residual conflicts and satisfy whatever wishes are consistent with his present plight and with his ego ideal. Finally, among his choices, he should yield control to others in whom he has confidence. He also has the option of seeking or relinquishing key people."[30]

Obviously, not everyone can achieve such lofty ideals, but any small step toward making death a purposeful event is a gain. And even though most of us cannot determine when and how we will die, we can allow ourselves to think that the possibility of an appropriate death does exist and therefore achieve some peace of mind until the time comes.

OVERCOMING THE FEAR OF DYING

The fear of death is more to be dreaded than death.

—Publius Syrus

The term *death anxiety* has emerged since the early 1960s as a result of the considerable literature on death fears. Generally speaking, a dying person experiences four categories of fears: (1) religious fear, which is based on the fear of damnation, retribution, and punishment in the afterlife; (2) fear of pain, based on the anticipation of emotional and physical suffering; (3) anxiety about separation and fear of abandonment, based on a fear of being separated from loved ones, fears of being alone, and fear of leaving the familiar things of life; and (4) existential fear, based on not knowing what will become of us after death, and on being nonexistent.

Psychologists and clinicians have studied death fears extensively in patients, college students, and various other populations. The reader who is interested in the details of these studies should read the excellent review by Neimeyer in *Dying: Facing the Facts*.[31] I present here only highlights from the death anxiety studies.

It appears that women tend to have more fear about personal death than men, although the reasons are not clear. Perhaps women are more willing than men to express their fears.

Another interesting finding is that, contrary to what was formerly believed, medicine as a career does not necessarily correlate with an increase in death anxiety. On the other hand, certain occupations with high death risks, such as firefighting and law enforcement, are more likely to be associated with death fears.

Researchers have also found that illness per se is not necessarily accompanied by death fears. The way individuals adapt to illness is probably the key variable here. Personality factors play a major role. In general, persons with strong traditional religious beliefs tend to have less death anxiety.

Not surprisingly, individuals with a history of depression and anxiety tend to have more fears of dying. Conversely, individuals who are more self-actualized are more comfortable with their mortality.

Persons who have a greater sense of control over their lives have less fear of death than those who feel that they have no control over their destiny. I suppose that this feeling of control extends to control over the circumstances of one's dying.

Finally, a surprising finding is that death education does not reduce death anxiety. On the contrary, it may even increase it.[32]

Many other fears have been expressed, but most prevalent since the early 1970s has been the fear of being trapped by life-supporting measures while in a hospital.

Nevertheless, a feeling prevails among the general public that having more control over treatment and diagnostic procedures while in the hospital will help reduce not only death fears but, more specifically, fears about the dying experience itself.

After his heart attack, Maslow referred to his "post mortem life," which he keenly enjoyed: "If you're reconciled with death or even if you are pretty well assured that you will have a good death, a dignified one, then every single day is transformed because the pervasive undercurrent—the fear of death—is removed."

When I questioned a few of my oncologist colleagues about what they would do if they were faced with a cancer that had spread widely, the answer seemed clear. "I would not fight it; I'd make sure that I went on to a peaceful and painless death," said one oncologist. Another put it in another way: "I don't think I would put up with it; I have made arrangements with a friend to help me out of my misery." Both told me, however, that these were not declarations they would share openly, not even with some of their colleagues.

In a study conducted in Canada, a questionnaire asked lung cancer specialists how they would want to be treated if they themselves had advanced lung cancer. With advanced disease but no symptoms, only 5 percent said they would want chemotherapy. In advanced disease with symptoms, those who would opt for chemotherapy rose to only 16 percent.[33] The researchers concluded that the treatment preferences of these oncologists differed from the treatment recommendations in the standard textbooks, and that these findings should be taken into account when patients face similar situations. They felt that doctors should treat their patients as they would like to be treated themselves.

In a study with a similar design, researchers asked urologists, medical oncologists, and radiation oncologists in Britain, Canada, and the United States how they would like to be treated if they had various types of bladder, kidney, or prostate cancer. Of special interest is the fact that, after being faced with various grim scenarios of advanced cancer, these physicians' choices varied widely when they were asked to choose between surgery, chemotherapy, or radiation. In general, these doctors tended to choose the treatment modality connected with their own specialty; radiologists opted for radiation therapy, oncologists for chemotherapy, and surgeons for surgery. Also notable is the fact that, in general, the British doctors chose more conservative approaches than the American and Canadian doctors, who chose radical surgery or combinations of surgery and chemotherapy.[34]

As a psychiatrist, I have worked with many dying patients, and in my attempt to help them, I have learned a great deal about their fears. Almost all of my patients with a terminal illness have welcomed the opportunity to share their feelings, doubts, and concerns with someone who would not avoid the subject. It is known that even psychiatrists as a group have not paid much attention to patients with terminal illnesses, because of their own personal discomfort with the topic and also because of the pain and hurt that follow on losing the patient.[35]

Yet working with dying patients can be a very satisfying and enriching experience. Knowing that I can relieve the suffering of individuals so obviously in distress gives me a great feeling of satisfaction and a sense of having done something worthwhile. It is also a way to work through one's own thoughts, anxieties, and philosophy about life and dying. Let me share such an experience with you.

Brian was a forty-five-year-old bank executive who had been referred to me after being diagnosed as having AIDS. When he first told me about his diagnosis, I readily made the assumption that he had been living in an "alternative lifestyle." When he first appeared at my office, he was a tall, well-dressed slender man with a very distinguished appearance. He reminded me somewhat of Gregory Peck, the famous actor. He had a gentle smile and deep-set brown eyes that seemed to denote an intelligent and mature mind behind them.

In our first meeting, I learned that Brian had contracted AIDS through contaminated blood during a transfusion for hemophilia, a blood-clotting deficiency. When I asked him how he felt about the diagnosis, he told me that he couldn't believe it: "I am not promiscuous. I have never been an intravenous drug user. I am not a member of a minority or indigent or homeless. I have not slept with a bisexual. I am happily married to a faithful wife. I don't fit any of the stereotypes. I was angry at first, then depressed, worrying that nobody would believe how I really got AIDS."

When I asked about his interactions with his doctors, Brian said that they had tried to reassure him about doing everything possible to keep him comfortable, mentioning pain killers, antibiotics, and even new experimental drugs, plus the availability of hospice care. But Brian went on to say that he was afraid to take the new drugs because of their side effects; yet he was afraid that by not taking them, he might miss out on a possible "miracle cure." He expressed his fear of dying an undignified death. When I asked what that meant, he painted this graphic picture: "Everybody running around and prolonging your life when there is no life. I mean, if I slipped into a coma, I wouldn't want these heroic efforts. All those measures for an unresponsive body seem like a desecration. When I see these cardiac emergency teams rushing to hospital rooms, it makes me almost physically sick. Not so much for young people, but for old people or incurable ones like me, it seems cruel. All these cardiac maneuvers—airways, injections, and pacemakers—they seem to be done more for practice than because of caring about someone's life. Frankly, I would rather be at home."

Brian went on to say that he thought he would have more choices being at home. He talked about being able to decide when to say good-bye to his loved ones, about trying to find out how to die in peace. He said that his wife, who was a social worker, was supportive of his views and would be sure his wishes were respected. He talked about not wanting to waste money on a burial but preferring cremation for environmental reasons.

When I asked what he thought about what happens after death, Brian explained that, even though he did not consider himself a devout person, he did believe in some kind of natural order in the universe, not a heaven or hell concept, that makes everything work. He said that conversations with his wife that explored some spiritual questions had been very helpful to him at this very vulnerable time. He also expressed his great concern about unintentional but hurtful responses from people who, through ignorance, were prejudiced against and rejecting of people with AIDS. Then he wondered aloud why we as a nation are so very fearful of dying, when it is not such a terrible thing if we would just let it happen.

I listened carefully and encouraged him to tell me about the things that were on his mind. I could sense the impact that his story and his comments were having on me as a physician and as a person who had also made some improper assumptions.

In a following session, we talked about his plans to deal with the future. I was impressed by the degree to which he had thought about and talked through many of the issues with his wife. In careful statements, he spoke of his interest in talking to his doctors about not continuing treatments: "I really don't see why I should. I don't have any pain. I am just waiting to see what will happen. Meanwhile, I have a job to do. Because of ignorance, people are afraid of AIDS. It's like it was the Plague. Even doctors and nurses have these fears, and the stigma is out there. If I can change just one person's bias and prejudice about this condition, I think my death will not be in vain. And my wife will carry on my work when I am gone. But for now, we'll enjoy our precious times together, taking long walks and laughing, as we have always done."

When I mentioned that I was writing a book on life-threatening illnesses and asked him what I should put in the book, his answer was, "Death isn't the worst thing that can happen to you. We're born and we must die. It's part of the whole cycle of things. When I remember how beautifully my parents died, I'm not afraid. But your book should help spouses and families cope with terminal illness in their loved ones. Your book should address having the freedom to make choices about the end of one's life. And I hope you will mention how important it is for people to not judge others who are ill. And tell them that it is especially important for people with AIDS and cancer because they really need love, understanding, and acceptance. Because they fear being trapped in a hospital, show them how to enjoy everyday living so that when it is no longer possible, they will understand that it is time to die."

That was one of the most meaningful sessions for both of us.

CAN YOU RETAIN A SENSE OF CONTROL IN TERMINAL ILLNESS?

It is not a new idea that a doctor must obtain informed consent before any kind of medical procedure. Judge Benjamin N. Cardoza of the U.S. Supreme Court made this clear in his opinion in a classic legal case in 1914.[36] He concluded that "Every human being of adult years and sound mind has a right to determine what shall be done with his own body."

The ability to retain control in medical decisions was further reinforced in 1960 by Kansas Supreme Court Justice Alfred Schroeder, who wrote: "Anglo-American law starts with the premise of thorough-going self-determination. It follows that each man is considered master of his own body, and he may, if he be of sound mind, expressly prohibit the performance of life-saving surgery, or other medical treatment. A doctor might well believe that an operation or form of treatment is desirable or necessary but the law does not permit him to substitute his own judgment for that of the patient by any form of artifice or deception."[37]

Over the last three decades, physicians have increasingly involved patients in health-care decisions. In fact, participation in the decision-making process with the physician may turn out to be the most important change since the early 1960s. Several writers—for example, Norman Cousins[38] and Bernie Siegel[39]—have emphasized this point in their discussions of medical care in the technological age of medicine.

As more information about the details of treatment and the complications of major diseases becomes available, doctors do expect patients to take a larger role in making decisions about what kinds of treatment to choose or whether certain types of treatment are even desirable. Other factors, such as quality of life, personality traits, and values in life, are key elements that are considered in the equation of treatment choice. When my elderly father-in-law had a recurrence of a hernia, his physician made it clear that, at his age, the risks of surgery might outweigh the benefits of having the hernia repaired. Nevertheless, the decision was up to my father-in-law. He decided against surgery.

Retaining or regaining a sense of control in the course of a serious illness is more than a change of mood or attitude. It has been shown that it has definite impact on the brain, the endocrine system, and the immune system.[40] Physicians are well aware of the numerous cases in which a catastrophic illness took a different course from that expected. There may be several explanations for these so-called spontaneous recoveries. But the sense of regaining control is the one characteristic that stands out. Norman Cousins reports the case of a physician who had a bout with cancer. The diagnosis was unequivocal: the cancer had spread to the lungs, the lymph nodes, and the liver. The doctor recounted his story: "My oncologist friend came right out with it and said I had perhaps three or four months to live. I said nothing to my wife about it at the time but held a dialogue with myself. I decided I was not going to accept the prediction. I was going to fight it. I was going to put all my mental and physical energies into doing the fight. For a month or two, I went downhill, lost weight but not confidence. Then, little by little, the tide began to turn. I began to regain weight and strength. When I got through the sixth month, I knew the cancer didn't have a chance. How long ago was that? It was about eight years ago."[41]

Each patient today has a different set of expectations. One may want aggressive treatment at all costs, and another may prefer conservative treatment or no invasive treatment at all.

This new attitude about individual choice has become the most important factor in determining the quality of the doctor–patient relationship in this age of medical technology. Failing to find out exactly what the patient wants can lead not only to distrust and recriminations but even a malpractice suit. Therefore, it is most important that you share your thoughts and desires with your doctor to avoid any misunderstanding. Your expectations should be clearly expressed.

Because most doctors are trained to take the initiative and make decisions on their own, if you wish to have an active part in the decision making you need to make this known as early as possible. Most doctors will welcome your involvement, providing that it is not perceived as being obstructive. There must also be trust and respect, as participation will not make up for a lack of rapport with your doctor.

A paternalistic and condescending doctor loses the respect of an increasing number of patients. Although a few patients still prefer to leave the decisions entirely to the physician, an arrogant approach usually dilutes trust, and in the patient suffering with a terminal illness, it can also reduce hope.

More and more, American doctors are recognizing the need to involve their patients in making decisions about treatment. Studies have shown that such involvement is beneficial because patients retain a great sense of control over their lives. Sheldon Greenfield, Sherrie Kaplan, and J. E. Ware of the UCLA School of Public Health conducted four separate studies on the health status of patients with ulcer disease, hypertension, diabetes, and breast cancer. In each group, half the patients were given general information regarding self-care and the other half were given a talk on how to take a more active role in their medical care. The training sessions included an explanation of the patient's medical record, the basis on which the treatment had been determined, and coaching on what questions to ask, how to negotiate, and how to maintain "focus" on medical care issues. The researchers found that the health status of the patients who had increased control was much better than that of the other patients, who did not have control. Health status was found to be improved through evaluations of audiotapes of office visits, questionnaires, and physiological measurements.[42]

Recently, a friend of mine, an active woman in her early seventies, complained of chest pain and was diagnosed as having serious blockage in her coronary arteries. The doctors impressed on her the seriousness of her condition, the need to get an angiogram (X-ray that shows the heart's circulation after a dye has been injected into the arteries), and the possibility of bypass surgery if the blockage proved to be serious.

Despite considerable pressure by her doctors, my friend decided against the angiogram, preferring to rely on nitroglycerine patches and pills. She felt that she could maintain the quality of her life just as well that way. Her physician husband, along with her friends, continued to support her in her decision. "If my time has come to go, then I'd rather go while I'm doing what I like to be doing rather than what someone else thinks I should be doing," she said at the end of one of her tennis matches. Three years later, she was still playing her two sets of tennis with all the verve and enthusiasm she had shown over the years. For her, retaining a sense of control and having a choice in making decisions was more important that opting for potential improvement through diagnostic procedures and surgery.

THE POWER OF HOPE

> Hope is the thing with feathers
> That perches in the soul
> And sings the tune without the words
> And never stops at all.
> —Emily Dickinson

In the last few years, I have met with hundreds of patients who were caught in a life-or-death struggle. In many of these patients, the will to live and a strong feeling of hope played a significant part in how they handled the terminal stages of their illness. The messages they got from their physicians had an enormous effect not only on the way they perceived their illness but also on the course of the illness. Psychologists have known for a long time that panic, fear, and resentment are powerful forces in intensifying an illness. Physicians, too, have come to understand how psychological support and hope in treating patients influences the outcome of illness, even serious terminal cancer.

William M. Buchholz, an oncologist, wrote in the *Western Journal of Medicine:* "As I was eating breakfast one morning I overheard two oncologists discussing the papers they were to present that day at the national meeting of the American Society of Clinical Oncology. One was complaining bitterly: 'You know, Bob, I just don't understand it. We used the same drugs, the same dosage, the same schedules, and the same entry criteria. Yet I got a 22% response rate and you got a 74%. That's unheard of for metastatic lung cancer. How do you do it?'

"The other doctor answered, 'We're both using etoposide, Platinol, Oncovin, and hydroxyurea. You call yours EPOH. I tell my patients I'm giving them H-O-P-E. Sure, I tell them this is experimental, and we go over the long list of side effects together. But I emphasize that we have a chance. As dismal as the statistics are for non-small cell, there are always a few percent who do really well."[43]

Norman Cousins, well known for his books on the relationship between emotions and illness, also emphasized the importance of hope in the struggle with a terminal illness. In his book *Head First*, he admits that serious illness does produce states of melancholy and even severe depression. In cancer, for example, the occurrence of depression is almost universal. Over the last few decades, numerous studies have shown that depression has a profound impact on the outcome of illness by affecting the biochemical balance of the immune system.[44] Sandra Levy and her colleagues at the University of Pittsburgh and the Pittsburgh Cancer Institute found that depression behavior (fatigue, listlessness, and apathy) was associated with a decrease in the activity of natural killer (NK) cells in fighting the spread of tumor in breast cancer patients.[45]

Another study substantiated the effect of depression on immunological effectiveness. Janice Kiecolt-Glaser and her colleagues at Ohio State University found that highly depressed patients had significantly poorer DNA (genetic) repair capability in immune cells exposed to irradiation than did less depressed individuals, and that both depressed groups fared significantly worse than psychologically healthy individuals.[46]

One of the cardinal signs of depression is the loss of hope. Therefore, treating the depression may have a significant impact in possibly restoring hope and thus restoring the effect of the immune system. Of course, such treatment is to be construed not as an alternative to chemotherapy, but as a way to strengthen the body's response against the toxic chemicals used in cancer treatment.

Most doctors today recognize how powerfully treatment outcome is affected by a patient's positive emotions, such as hope, the will to live, determination, and optimism. Medical technology alone may not be enough to overcome all the forces acting in a terminal illness, and although technology such as cardiovascular surgery, the implantation of cardiac pacemakers, and medications with serious side effects can produce another ray of hope for some people, it is not without complications and has no guaranteed outcome.[47]

Some people prefer to focus on the quality of their lives and take a conservative approach to treatment. According to Kubler-Ross, individuals with terminal illness tend to experience two distinct types of hope. At the beginning of the illness, the hope is likely to be associated mostly with the prospect of cure, treatment, and the prolongation of life. This hope is usually shared by all who are around the patient, including family and medical staff. But as the prospect of cure becomes improbable (although not necessarily impossible, as so many exceptions do occur), there is a shift to another kind of hope. The new hope deals with unfinished business, the hope of minimizing pain and ensuring a future for one's children, and the wish to see that those left behind will be safe and secure.[48]

Patients who sense that their time may be limited by a terminal illness become acutely aware of how they are spending the time left to them. They hope to live long enough to resolve past conflicts or hurts and to bring about a sense of security and peace for their loved ones.

A new dimension of hope has entered our minds in the rapidly evolving age of medical technology. Now we hope that we will not be trapped by ongoing treatment in a complex medical system where medications, side effects, monitoring machines, and legal forms can dictate the course of our lives. If we wish to retain a sense of control and hope, we must look ahead and think about the problem before it happens. We cannot predict how we will feel when faced with terminal illness, but the very fact that we have given it some thought and shared it with our family, closest friends, and primary-care physician may be sufficient to provide the hope we have of a dignified end.

ABOUT THE FREEDOM TO CHOOSE

> *Questions of Fate have become questions of choice.*
> —Justice Marie Garibaldi, New Jersey Supreme Court

Fear of dying has become more concrete in the minds of people recently. When the book *Final Exit* by Derek Humphry, president of the Hemlock Society, first appeared, several thousand copies were sold out within its first week in the bookstores. The book shot up to the bestseller list of the *New York Times* and remained there for many months. As a manual on how to end one's life in the case of a terminal illness, the book seems to be answering the need of thousands of people in the country. At least, it is providing information that people would like to have in case things get too painful to endure.[49] People seem to be demanding more control by seeking more freedom to choose

death if they wish to end their suffering. No longer do they want
to be at the mercy of the medical profession in their final days.
According to David Shaffer of the Columbia University College
of Physicians and Surgeons, the popularity of the book can be
explained by a "disproportionate fear of being kept alive in an
inhumane way."[50] Several chapters in the book discuss how doctors and nurses can help patients end their lives, but laws bar
such interventions, and the American Medical Association remains opposed to this practice. Some doctors disagree. About
one out of ten primary-care physicians has taken such actions,
according to a survey done by *Physician's Management* (discussed
in Chapter 3). The debate about how much freedom an individual should have in deciding whether to live or die if faced with
a terminal illness remains highly emotional. Partisans pro and
con have their own stances, but shouldn't personal suffering and
personal distress remain one's own business? I discuss euthanasia and assisted deaths in Chapter 8.

WHEN IS IT WORTH PROLONGING LIFE,
AND BASED ON WHOSE VALUES?

> *Better to die of good wine and good*
> *company than of slow disease and*
> *doctor's doses.*
> —William Makepeace Thackeray

Perhaps one of the most difficult issues to ponder is whether
or not life is worth prolonging with the help of life-support
measures. How do you decide, if you are still competent to do
so? We have discussed in somewhat general philosophical terms
the quality versus the quantity of life as perceived by the individual. But the dilemma becomes more critical when different parties are involved in making that decision. When does medical
treatment become futile, that is, have no purposeful medical benefit? What is the right of the individual and the family in asking
for such treatment, even in the face of medical futility and staff

disapproval? Whose values should prevail? Those who based theirs on the principles of medical practice or those who based theirs on the rights of the individual?

What about religious or lay groups in the community who hold views contrary to yours? Do they have a right to impose their views? There are minority groups that do commit laypersons to similar views. Some Orthodox Jews, for example, consistently maintain that life is to be preserved, at least until the patient is in a moribund state. Groups in the community who identify themselves as "right-to-lifers" adopt a similar position, although with regard to competent patients, their position is more a "duty-to-life." You may recall the problem I encountered with such a group described in Chapter 4, when dealing with my mother's decline.

Now that death with dignity has become an expectation in our minds, it does not seem possible when decisions are taken away from us. The reasoning sometimes is that the patient must be treated as a child in need of careful "management." The metaphor of the parent–child relationship has been long recognized by medical sociologists, but it now rarely occurs. Furthermore, because of the current laws on the right to self-determination, it is illegal to adopt this stance, especially in relation to decisions involving treatment and medical interventions.

It has been said that physicians sometimes treat just because they can. They justify their actions by the injunction "to preserve life at all costs." This injunction, however, is based on the belief that life is always a good thing, regardless of its burden. That belief is not shared by everyone, but it does exist within the professional association of physicians.

In practice, however, physicians do make exceptions to the "preserve-life-at-all-costs" philosophy. They do adhere to the general policy that, in selected cases, the patient is allowed to die. Ironically, in some cases, a conflict arises when the family insists on preserving life at all costs, even when the doctors deem this approach unwise.

The case of Helga Wanglie illustrates the crucial philosophical dilemma involved in prolonging life.[51] This is the kind of case that will stimulate your thinking on the subject, and I recommend that you try to discuss your thoughts and your feelings about this case with someone you trust and respect.

Helga Wanglie was an eighty-six-year-old woman who, on December 14, 1989, broke her hip after slipping on a rug in her Minneapolis home. After successful treatment of the hip fracture at the Hennepin County Medical Center (HCMC), she was sent to a nursing home.

On January 1, she developed respiratory difficulties and had to be readmitted to HCMC and put on a respirator. Initially, Mrs. Wanglie was conscious and alert, aware of her surroundings, able to acknowledge pain and discomfort, and able to talk with her family. Over the next few months, several attempts were made to wean her off the respirator, but Mrs. Wanglie did not seem to be capable of breathing on her own.

On May 7, she was transferred to another facility that specialized in caring for patients dependent on a ventilator. On May 23, she had a cardiac arrest but was successfully resuscitated and then transferred to another acute-care hospital in St. Paul. By then, she had suffered severe and irreversible brain damage. Because of the extremely poor outlook, the doctors and the hospital ethics committee reviewed her case and decided to speak to the family about the possibility of stopping all life-sustaining treatments. They explained to the family that Mrs. Wanglie would most likely never regain consciousness and that she could go on living in her present state for many years. They pointed out that medicine had nothing further to offer and that, at this point, medical treatment could serve no purpose whatsoever.

Much to everyone's surprise, Mrs. Wanglie's husband, her daughter, and her son declined the offer to discontinue the respirator. In fact, they insisted on continuing all life-supporting measures and made arrangements for Mrs. Wanglie's transfer back to HCMC, where they felt she had received better care.

Mrs. Wanglie was readmitted to HCMC on May 31, and during the weeks that followed, she received continued aggressive treatment with respirator support, antibiotics for recurring bouts of pneumonia, artificial feeding, and special fluid and electrolyte replacement. The diagnosis on admission was "persistent vegetative state secondary to severe brain damage." Several consultations were obtained from neurologists and pulmonary specialists, and all agreed that she continued to be in a persistent vegetative state and to suffer from chronic lung disease. They also concurred that she could never be freed from the respirator. The prognosis was considered extremely poor because of the multiple medical complications, the brain damage, and her inability to breathe on her own. They concluded that the respirator would not improve her condition and was of no substantial benefit to her.

The doctors explained to Mr. Wanglie that his wife was unaware of her surroundings and of his visits and that her chances of improvement were nonexistent in their opinion. Nevertheless, the husband replied, "That may be true, but we hope for the best." He stated that his reasons for wishing further treatment were partly religious and partly personal. He felt that only God could take life and that doctors "should not play God." However, he admitted that before her admission to the hospital, he had had no idea what her views on the matter were because they had never discussed these issues.

In the weeks that followed, the conflict between the medical staff and the family continued to grow. Intensive treatment was being given, despite the feeling of futility that reigned among the medical personnel. The ethics committee met again and this time recommended that the hospital err on the side of continuing treatment with the hope that better communication with the family would eventually lead to some kind of resolution of the conflict between the family and the hospital staff.

After further discussion, the family agreed to a do-not-resuscitate (DNR) order but stood fast when it came to removing the respirator. More family conferences were held in November and December. Finally, on December 3, Mr. Wanglie sent a letter to the hospital saying, "My wife always stated to me that if anything happened to her so that she could not take care of herself, she did not want anything done to shorten or prematurely take her life."

Shortly after, the hospital medical director answered with the following letter: "All medical consultants agree [with the attending physician's conclusion] that continued use of mechanical ventilation and other forms of life-sustaining treatments are [sic] no longer serving the patient's personal medical interest. We do not believe that the hospital is obliged to provide inappropriate medical treatment that cannot advance a patient's personal interest. We would continue life-sustaining treatment on the order of a court mandating such treatment. In view of the extraordinary nature of your request [to continue treatment], we ask that you file petition to obtain such an order by December 14."

The family waited but did not file the petition. In the hope of getting a conservator who would consider nontreatment despite the family's objections, the hospital decided to file the papers with the Fourth Judicial District Court, Hennepin County, on February 8. The major argument advanced by the hospital was that they could not be forced by the family to render treatment against their feeling that it was not in the patient's "best personal medical interest." The hospital was willing to help the family transfer Mrs. Wanglie to another facility for further aggressive treatment, including respirator support, but that solution became a problem because the family could not find a willing provider.

By the time the case was heard on May 28, the cost of Mrs. Wanglie's care had been approximately $800,000, borne by Medicare and Physicians' Health Plan, a local health maintenance organization (HMO).

On July 1, Probate Judge Patricia L. Belois in Hennepin County rejected the hospital's request to name an independent conservator to review the case and to decide whether life support to Mrs. Wanglie should be continued. She ruled that Oliver Wanglie, eighty-seven years of age, was "best qualified" to represent the interests of his wife.

Mrs. Wanglie died on July 4.

The Wanglie case is unusual in that the family's argument was the reverse of that usually advanced by most families. Families usually wish to seek the cessation of life-support measures and run up against the resistance of the hospital staff or the institution. In the Wanglie case, the family demanded that extraordinary measures be continued while the hospital staff wanted to take the patient off the respirator. Philosophical arguments were advanced by the medical staff on one side and by the family on the other. Ethicists spend time thinking about arguments that defend one side or the other and help to provide us with a rationale to justify our own position, no matter what it might be. Let us briefly review the ethical arguments in the Wanglie case.

MORALITY, POLITICS, OR SCIENCE?

When the life of a comatose patient hangs in the balance, various philosophical, ethical, and legal arguments are stated by families and experts to justify their positions. But whose arguments should prevail? Whose principles should be upheld? Whose decisions should be respected? Should the dissenters reach a decision on an adversarial basis, as is too often the case in the judicial arena?

In relation to the Wanglie case, one could argue that physicians do not really have the right to prevail over the family's decision. Furthermore, who is to say that the doctors' moral stance was any more valid than that of the husband? Are doctors more qualified to make moral judgments because of their medical expertise? One could argue quite convincingly that, in reality, few doctors have had any training in medical school in dealing with ethical problems.

What doctors do know better because of their expertise is the futility of further treatment in a given case. They are trained in making diagnoses and prognoses; therefore, they can make reasonably educated guesses about the likelihood of a change in outcome. In the case of Helga Wanglie, they could state with reasonable certainty that the chances of recovery were virtually zero. Others, however, may argue that doctors do make mistakes and that there are cases, although rare, in which patients have come out of a coma. Still others will argue that the medical profession is just not concerned with outcome, but also with what is "medically appropriate."

After several years of debate, the Society of Critical Care Medicine issued a report in December 1990 on the question of forgoing life-sustaining treatment of the critically ill. The report stated, "Treatments that offer no benefit and serve to prolong the dying process should not be employed. In the light of a hopeless prognosis, the indefinite maintenance of patients reliably diagnosed as being in a persistent vegetative state (PVS) raises serious ethical concerns both for the dignity of the patient and for the diversion of limited medical and nursing resources from alternative applications that could offer medical and nursing benefit to others. The PVS patient should be removed from the ICU [intensive-care unit] unless it is not possible otherwise to meet the patient's nursing care needs. A PVS patient should not be maintained in the ICU to the exclusion of a patient who can derive benefit from ICU care."[52]

One may say that these are recommendations *only* for the proper use of limited valuable resources for the benefit of others in need of them, and not for the care of the individual in the persistent vegetative state or coma. And it can be further argued that the recommendations do not address the feelings of the family members.

In practice today, whenever a conflict arises between the medical staff or the hospital administration and the family, the matter is usually referred to the hospital bioethics committee (see Chapter 3). The hope is that the family can obtain further clarification and support by participating in a final decision to stop what is considered futile treatment. Such a decision is not always obtainable, especially when religious views are the main basis for keeping someone alive against all odds. But even then, there are questions that go beyond the considerations of the individual patient. These may involve economic and political issues that will achieve more prominence in the future.

One such consideration that medical providers are increasingly concerned about is the availability of limited valuable medical resources to the rest of society.[53] In his book *Who Lives, Who Dies?*, John F. Kilner, a professor of social and medical ethics at Ashbury Theological Seminary and adjunct professor of medical ethics at the University of Kentucky, analyzed the ethical pros and cons in selecting patients for treatments that are currently limited, such as those who are waiting for organ transplants, intensive care, or newly developed drugs that are available in limited quantity. When selection criteria are used, they are seldom satisfactory to all of those who are waiting for a second change of life. Sometimes, a lottery system may be the only fair method of selection.

Another issue that will assume increasing importance is health care cost. To what degree can a health plan or the government cover the enormous bills incurred for the care of a patient who has no chance of resuming consciousness? Who will pay hundreds of thousands of dollars to care for a patient in a persistent vegetative state who might live for several more years? As in the case of Helga Wanglie, the bill for seventeen months of her care in a comatose state amounted to $800,000. If all of us share the cost of such benefits, how are the recipients of these benefits to be chosen? Can we justify spending large sums of money for treatment that is essentially futile? Can a family impose their wishes on society?

Others might argue in defense of the family that the right to self-determination—that is, the right to autonomy whether the patient is competent or not—should be respected above all, even if it goes against the "rationality of science."[54] No matter how certain the outcome remains in the opinion of the clinicians, if the family sees the outcome as questionable, their decision should be respected. Ethicists make this argument in order to avoid the "slippery slope" that may lead to an abuse of decision-making authority. In the Wanglie case, the court was careful to stay away from the moral dilemma by simply answering the question of who was best qualified to make a particular judgment, not what moral judgment should be rendered.

Controversial cases will continue to challenge ethicists, clinicians, and the courts. In a Boston case that was similar to the Wanglie case, in which the issue was to balance the medical opinion against the family's best interest, a different judge arrived at a different decision, stating that the termination of life support was in the patient's best interest.[55] It is becoming increasingly clear that, when philosophy and science clash, the judicial system takes over. When that occurs, the balance tends to shift in favor of the individual over science or morality.

In this chapter, I have addressed several philosophical issues that arise with the problem of prolonged dying. As we have seen, the problem of dying is also a problem of living, at least of what we perceive as living. Only you alone can decide. And one thing is clear: We are all individuals. Therefore, we must become aware of our own personal philosophy, based on our own personality, our needs, our values, and our goals.

No matter what your perspective turns out to be after you ponder the many issues, it is important for you to retain a sense of humor about the whole matter. Norman Cousins has spent many years writing about the positive influence of humor and laughter on our living and dying. We should not forget his good advice. Echoing Cousin's thoughts, George Burns shared a bit of his own philosophy: "Dying is not popular. It has never caught on. That's understandable. It's bad for the complexion. It also upsets your daily routine and leaves you with too much time on your hands."

NOTES

1. Victor A. Frankl, *Man's Search for Meaning* (New York: Pocket Books, Simon & Schuster, 1984), 131.
2. M. V. Kamath, *Philosophy of Death and Dying* (Honesdale, PA: Himalayan International Institute, 1978), 146.

3. Lisl Marburg Goodman, *Death and the Creative Life* (New York: Springer, 1981), 25.
4. Michael Simpson, *The Facts of Death* (Englewood Cliffs, NJ: Prentice-Hall, 1979), 55.
5. R. Kastenbaum and R. Aisenberg, *The Psychology of Death* (New York: Springer, 1972).
6. T. A. Gonda and J. E. Ruark, *Dying Dignified: The Health Professional's Guide to Care* (Menlo Park, CA: Addison-Wesley, 1984), 30–31.
7. Kamath, 323.
8. Avery D. Weisman, *On Death and Denying: A Psychiatric Study of Terminality* (New York: Behavioral Publications, 1972), 36–41.
9. Frankl, 88.
10. Elizabeth Kubler-Ross, *Death: The Final Stage of Growth* (Englewood Cliffs, NJ: Prentice-Hall, 1975), 167.
11. Simpson, 55–76.
12. P. Aries, *Western Attitudes Toward Death: From the Middle Ages to the Present* (Baltimore: Johns Hopkins University Press, 1974).
13. E. Becker, *The Denial of Death* (New York: The Free Press, 1973).
14. J. D. Morgan, "Living Our Dying: Social and Cultural Considerations," in *Dying: Facing the Facts,* ed. H. Wass, F. M. Berardo, and R. A. Neimeyer (New York: emisphere, 1988), 19–20.
15. Ibid.
16. H. S. Kushner, *When Bad Things Happen to Good People* (New York: Schocken Books, 1981).
17. Morgan, 19–20.
18. Goodman.
19. E. Shneidman, ed., *Death: Current Perspectives* (Palo Alto, CA: Mayfield, 1976), 11–12.
20. Simone de Beauvoir, *A Very Easy Death* (New York: Putnam Sons, Andre Deutsch, and Wiedenfeld & Nicholson, 1966).
21. Miguel de Unamuno, *The Tragic Sense of Life* (New York: Dover, 1954).
22. Shneidman, 12.
23. Robert M. Veatch, *Death, Dying, and the Biological Revolution* (New Haven, CT: Yale University Press, 1989), 234–235, 243.
24. Ibid.
25. Simpson, 55–76.
26. Ibid.
27. E. Heimler, *The Healing Echo* (London: Souvenir Press, 1985).

28. H. Allison, J. Gripton, and M. Rodway, "Social Work Services as a Component of Palliative Care with Terminal Cancer Patients," *Social Work in Health Care* 8 (1983): 29–44.
29. G. M. Burnell, "Research Applications of Human Social Functioning in a Health Care Setting," in *Counseling Diverse Client Groups,* ed. Margaret Rodwa (Lewiston, NY: Edwin Mellen Press, 1989), 139–202.
30. Weisman, 36–41.
31. R. A. Neimeyer, "Death Anxiety," in *Dying: Facing the Facts,* 2nd ed., ed. H. Wass, F. M. Berardo, and R. A. Neimeyer (New York: Hemisphere, 1988), 97–130.
32. Ibid.
33. William J. Mackillop, Brian O'Sullivan, and Glen K. Ward, "Non-Small Cell Lung Cancer: How Oncologists Want to Be Treated," *International Journal of Radiation Oncology, Biology, Physics* 13 (1987): 929–934.
34. Malcolm J. Moore, Brian O'Sullivan, and Ian F. Tannock, "How Expert Physicians Would Wish to Be Treated If They Had Genitourinary Cancer," *Journal of Clinical Oncology* 6 (1988): 1736–1740.
35. L. LeShan and E. LeShan, "Psychotherapy in the Patient with a Limited Life Span," *Psychiatry* 24 (1961): 318–323.
36. "*Schloendorff v. New York Hospital,*" in *Experimentation with Human Beings: The Authority of the Investigator, Subject, Professions, and State in the Human Experimentation Process,* ed. J. Katz (New York: Russell Sage Foundation, 1972), 526.
37. *Natanson v. Kline,* 186 Kan. 393, 350 P. 2nd 1093 (1960).
38. Norman Cousins, *Head First: The Biology of Hope* (New York: E. P. Dutton, 1989), 120, 235, 270–280.
39. Bernie Siegel, *Love, Medicine and Miracles* (New York: Harper & Row, 1986), 51–52.
40. Cousins, 236.
41. Ibid, 120.
42. S. H. Kaplan, S. Greenfield, and J. E. Ware, Jr., "Assessing the Effects of Physician–Patient Interaction on the Outcomes of Chronic Disease," *Journal of Medical Care* 27 (Suppl. 1989): S110–S127.
43. W. M. Buchholz, "The Medical Uses of Hope," *Western Journal of Medicine* 148 (1988): 69.
44. J. R. Calabrese, M. A. Kling, and P. W. Gold, "Alterations in Immunocompetence during Stress, Bereavement, and Depression:

Focus on Neuroendocrine Regulation," *American Journal of Psychiatry* 144 (1987): 1123–1134.

45. S. M. Levy, R. B. Heberman, et al., "Prognostic Risk Assessment in Primary Breast Cancer by Behavioral and Immunological Parameters," *Health Psychology* 4 (1985): 99–113.

46. J. K. Kiecolt-Glaser, R. E. Stephens, P. D. Lipetz, C. E. Speicher, and R. Glaser, "Distress and DNA Repair in Human Lymphocytes," *Journal of Behavioral Medicine* 8 (1985): 311–320.

47. Cousins, 229–242.

48. Kubler-Ross, 167.

49. Derek Humphry, *Final Exit* (Eugene, OR: Hemlock Society, 1991).

50. David Shaffer, personal communication, December 10, 1992.

51. Ronald E. Cranford, "Helga Wanglie's Ventilator," *Hastings Center Report* 21 (July–August 1991): 23–24.

52. Society of Critical Care Medicine, *Consensus Report*, 1990, 1437.

53. John F. Kilner, *Who Lives? Who Dies? Ethical Criteria in Patient Selection* (New Haven, CT: Yale University Press, 1990).

54. D. Callahan, "Medical Futility, Medical Necessity: The Problem without a Name," *Hastings Center Report* 21 (July–August 1991): 30–35.

55. American Health Consultants, "Patient's Death Will Not End Debate Over Wanglie Case Issues, *Medical Ethics Advisor* 7 (1991): 101–102.

CHAPTER 6

How to Talk to Your Family or Friends about Dying or Prolonging Life

The generations need each other.
When death was a family affair,
it brought the generations
together. Now, it seems death
keeps the generations apart.
—Lewis Mumford, Philosopher

DYING IS A FAMILY AFFAIR

Most families today are not well prepared to deal with a sudden death or a terminal illness, perhaps because most people have little experience with or exposure to dying. As we have seen, our society views dying as a phenomenon to be controlled by machines and active interventions. Yet, when someone either is dying slowly or dies suddenly, the impact on family members and friends is very disturbing.[1] Everyone in the family is deeply affected, and major social and psychological changes take place very rapidly.

Jean Quint Benoliel, a professor of nursing at Rutgers University, who wrote extensively on the subject, reported a personal experience as an example. Her sister, four years younger, was in her eighth month of pregnancy with her fourth child, the other children being three, five, and seven years of age. On a Sunday evening, her sister complained of a bad headache and went to the bedroom to rest for a while. Suddenly she cried out in agony. Her husband rushed to the bedroom and observed that she was having a convulsion. She was rushed to the nearest emergency room. While there, she went into respiratory arrest and was immediately put on life-support systems. Soon after, she was taken to the operating room where a caesarean section was performed. Within a short time, a craniotomy (a surgical opening of the skull) was done to relieve the pressure from a cerebral hemorrhage.[2] A few hours later, the attending physician told her husband and her sister that she would remain unconscious and would not be able to breathe. After Jean Benoliel and the husband conferred with the doctor, they all agreed to stop the machine. In a matter of hours, the sister's heart stopped beating.

Benoliel recalled the chaos that followed in the family. The husband, deeply upset by the tremendous impact of the crisis, had to confront the problems of dealing with four children seven years old and under. Major taxing changes took place in this family over the ensuing months. The husband had to rearrange his lifestyle, obtain housekeeping and child-rearing help, and generally adjust to new ways of dealing with the world around him.

While helping her newly bereaved brother-in-law, Benoliel became aware of how important it was to maintain good communication among the surviving family members and friends. A good support system became a crucial factor in planning the future adjustment of her sister's family.[3]

Communication is equally important when someone develops a fatal illness that may last for some time. If the family avoids talking with the patient in the hope of not upsetting him or her, the result is a sense of isolation and a lack of opportunity for the patient to share important feelings and wishes, sometimes with undesirable consequences.

Take the example of a woman dying of advanced cystic fibrosis (an inherited fatal illness of the lungs and the digestive system). The family was intent on protecting her from emotional upset and did not speak to her about her wishes in the event that her illness would require life-support treatment. Once she was hospitalized, the woman was unable to express her wishes. Up to that time, no one in the family had talked openly with her. As a result, she was subjected to intense life-saving efforts that were decided on by strangers.[4] This example illustrates the importance of keeping communication open between the family members and the dying person. Although it is very difficult to talk about dying to the terminally ill, it is worse to avoid the subject.

There are many ways to talk about dying or prolonging life without upsetting anyone, and each family must find its own style. Sometimes, especially when someone is dying in the hospital, organizing a family meeting seems to be the best approach. Each member of the family can bring up specific concerns, such as housekeeping, babysitting, cooking, spending time with the dying person, and arranging transportation. At the meeting people should be allowed to say what they want to do. If the person is dying at home, family members can volunteer to help the patient with basic nursing care. Ideally, such meetings should be regularly scheduled to provide support, sharing of feelings, and coordination of things to be done.

LET YOUR WISHES BE KNOWN

The best time to talk about your wishes concerning life support is when you are in good health. Because people often feel awkward bringing up the subject, they feel unsure about what is the most appropriate time. Many friends who heard that I was writing a book on the subject used that "excuse" to talk to their spouses. Others frequently use an event such as the death or fatal illness of a friend to broach the issue. Another trigger for the conversation might be a visit to a friend in a nursing home or a newspaper article about aging, life support, or the right to die.

The Patient Self-Determination Act passed by Congress in 1990 and enacted in 1991 should effectively bring the topic to the forefront, as it asks people to sign a living will on admission to the hospital.

It is most effective do discuss the circumstances in which you wish to be kept alive with the person closest to you, be it your spouse, one of your siblings, your grown children or your closest friend. You should be specific in stating your preferences about life-support treatments, including the administration of food and water in case you are terminally ill. It is also wise to mention your feelings about being resuscitated so that your family or friends know what to advise your doctor about DNR (do-not-resuscitate) orders. If you take the trouble to do this planning when you are still well, conflicts and disagreements among family members are likely to be avoided. This planning will also facilitate your doctor's ability to care for you.

Talking about your wishes becomes even more important when you are dying. Most seriously ill persons initially opt for aggressive treatment, sometimes under pressure from the family, who tend to favor such treatment.[5] Later, when families decide in favor of nonaggressive treatment, it is usually in the hope that the dying person will gain more comfort. This is also known as "letting go," which I discuss later in this chapter.

It is best for the family to have several meetings to reach a decision about nonaggressive treatment. Patients who have discussed the issue before the illness have a definite advantage in influencing these family discussions. In any case, it is also important to include health personnel in the discussion to prevent conflicts down the line.[6] The decision is easiest if the dying person says, "I'm ready to die." Sometimes the patient says, "Can you do anything to make death come faster?" or "Can you give me some drugs so I can finish it?" This, however, does not always occur.

Betty Rollin, author of the book *Last Wish*, described how her mother spoke to her when she was dying of ovarian cancer. Her mother said, "I've had a wonderful life, but now it's over, or it should be. I'm not afraid to die, but I'm afraid of this illness, what it's doing to me . . . . There's never any relief from it now. Nothing but nausea and this pain . . . . There won't be any more chemotherapy. There's no treatment anymore. So what happens to me now? I know what happens. I'll die slowly . . . . I don't want that . . . . Who does benefit if I die slowly? If it benefits my children I'd be willing. But it's not going to do you any good. There's no point in a slow death, none. I've never liked doing things with no point. I've got to end this."[7] Another time, she told her daughter, "To me, this isn't life. Life is taking a walk, visiting my children, eating! Remember how I loved to eat? The thought of food makes me sick now . . . . If I had life I'd want it. I don't want this."[8] In her book, Rollin describes how she helped her mother die.

Sometimes families find it easier to take a "wait-and-see" attitude, a kind of holding pattern until the fatal prognosis becomes certain. Even physicians often feel more comfortable with this approach, especially when the course of an illness is uncertain and the treatment slow in eliciting a response.[9] In any event, it is important for families to recognize that physicians and nurses tend to favor aggressive treatment because they have an orientation toward curing at all costs, sometimes even in the face of overwhelming evidence that no further treatment will be effective.[10]

You can see why it is also very important for the family to keep the channels of communication constantly open with the treating team in order to avoid conflicts and disagreements. In complicated cases, problems can be presented to the bioethics committee of the hospital for suggestions and support.

For those who have no family or who prefer to rely on close friends to make decisions and provide support, the points made above also apply in discussing preferences about life-support treatments.

TALKING TO A DYING PERSON ABOUT DEATH, DYING OR PROLONGING LIFE

In a previous book, I wrote about how uncomfortable people feel in talking to anyone who has experienced a loss. People often don't know what to say to a recently bereaved person except for the stereotypical clichés.[11] The same holds true when they speak to a dying person. Even doctors and nurses feel uncomfortable talking to a terminally ill patient, and they have been known to avoid not only the subject but, in some cases, even the patient.[12]

In Chapter 1, I discussed why it is difficult in our society to talk about death and why most of us tend to deny death in everyday life. In doing so, we inadvertently isolate the dying person or encourage the terminally ill person to hope for a "miracle cure." Family and friends often find it easier to talk with the dying person in the high-tech environment of the hospital. The implication is that the patient is still in a curable phase and that there is little need for support. But when the high-tech opportunities begin to fade, and when doctors begin gradually to withdraw, personal support becomes very important. Talking and listening to the dying person at an earlier point, however, can be very rewarding to both the talker and the listener.[13]

There are a few simple rules that are obvious and easy to keep in mind. First, talking is still the best way to communicate, but touching, kissing, laughing, and just being there are effective expressions of caring.

Second, talking about distressing feelings may be just as soothing; many of us can attest from our own experiences that we feel better after getting things "off our chest." Being a good listener is all that is required to provide a soothing balm to the dying person. All the listener has to say is an occasional "I see" or "Tell me more." If the dying person poses questions, remember that you don't have to provide the answers. Just continue to listen, because listening will help enough.

Third, it is a misconception of families and friends that talking about fears and death anxiety will create more fear and more worry. For instance, some people believe that bringing up whether the person is worried about chemotherapy or radiation will create even more worry. Studies have shown that the opposite is true. Not talking about the fear tends to exaggerate it. Bottled-up feelings may even cause shame about those feelings of fear and anxiety.[14]

To reach the point of being a good listener, you may need to know what the dying person is really experiencing. This knowledge will reduce your own fear and panic, so that you may be able to think through the situation ahead of time and be prepared to deal with stressful reactions, such as the patient's anger, frustration, and despair. You may then be able to recognize that these feelings are not at all abnormal and that the patient's outbursts are not directed at you. It is important that you try to understand "what is going on" before you engage in active listening. Otherwise, you may become part of the problem.[15]

TALKING TO SOMEONE YOU TRUST

> It takes two to speak the truth—one to
> speak, and another to hear.
> —Henry David Thoreau in "Wednesday,"
> A Week on the Concord and Merrimack Rivers

There are times when dying people pretend to the rest of the family that everything is fine. Sometimes denial is a wonderful thing. It can help maintain a high morale, at least on the surface. But the terminally ill person may also need to speak frankly to someone who can remain objective and supportive. The physician is frequently the person who is chosen for this role. The role is comfortably assumed if the relationship has been of long standing, but for doctors who are busy and have known the patient for only a few hours or days, it may not be comfortable. In such a case, doctors may suggest that the patient speak to another health professional, such as a counselor from the nursing, social work, psychology, psychiatric, or pastoral professions.

Lawrence C. Rainey of the Mason Clinic in Seattle describes in detail the various issues and concerns that counselors must address with families and dying patients. [16] One thing he emphasizes is the importance of working with the families of patients who are dying. He says that the therapist can help facilitate communication and provide support to the family during the

course of the terminal illness. Many hospitals now have professionals on the staff who fulfill that function.

An example of such an intervention is the case of a patient
who just learned that she had widespread metastases of breast
cancer. Her husband had just been transferred to another city,
and she was home alone, with the tasks of selling the home and
organizing the move. She was mainly concerned about how to
break the news to her three children: "I know I'm going to die of
this disease, but I don't want to lay the whole thing on them at
once." The counselor she consulted discussed the questions she
might anticipate from her three children whose ages were seven,
nine, and twelve. She went home, gathered her three children,
and said to them, "Things aren't going very well with my cancer,
and the doctors say I'm going to need more treatment." After
looking her straight in the eye, the seven-year-old asked,
"Mommy, does that mean you're going to die?" The nine-year-
old, always quiet and pensive, said nothing and just looked at
her shoes. The twelve-year-old, "going on twenty," put her hands
on her hips, shook her head, and said, "Mom, does this mean we
can't go to the shopping mall this afternoon to buy my new
swimming suit?" The counselor pointed out that each child in the
family had a particular way of working through feelings about
the impending death of the mother.[17]

Since the early 1970s, counselors from various disciplines
have become very skillful in working with the families of the
terminally ill. They have developed effective counseling approaches
to deal with these families' sensitive problems.[18]

DEALING WITH UNFINISHED BUSINESS

> *A man's dying is more the survivor's affair*
> *than his own.*
>
> —Thomas Mann

Sometimes families have difficulty talking with each other
because of past unresolved conflicts. These are referred to as

unfinished business. In some cases, the conflicts may lead to feelings of guilt and persistent resentment. On occasion, family members who have unfinished business may channel their feelings into insisting that doctors pursue aggressive treatment, which serves to relieve that family member of guilt feelings. This phenomenon is frequently observed when someone in the family has been diagnosed as having advanced cancer.[19]

When unfinished business affects only certain members of the family, it may lead to differences of opinion when the time comes to make a decision about life-support treatment. I am reminded of a woman I saw in counseling who had a long-standing resentment of one of the six sisters in the family. When that sister became terminally ill, my patient insisted more than anyone else in the family that aggressive life-support treatments be continued. I knew that for her to "let go" of her sister would increase her guilt to an intolerable level. For her, insisting on aggressive treatment for her sister would help relieve her own guilt because she would feel that she had "tried everything that could be done." Such feelings may not always be obvious at first, but they should be explored every time there is strong disagreement within a family.

LETTING GO

> *The greatest gift that could be given to me now, or to anyone, would be to allow me to live or die on my own terms.*
> —Arnold R. Beisser, *A Graceful Passage* (1990)

"Letting go" is allowing someone to die peacefully, without guilt, fear, resentment, or regret. For many people, it is very difficult to "let go." David Hendin, author of *Death as a Fact of Life,* describes the case of a man who was dying of stomach cancer. During his wife's visits to the hospital, she continually reminded him of his promise to buy a "retirement" home in the Southwest. Meanwhile, he continued to deteriorate and was in great pain. Yet his family kept reminding him how much he was needed and how they expected him to improve soon. The doctors even talked about the possibility of another operation, and the nurses insisted that he eat more. The poor man felt there was no one he could talk to about the seriousness of his condition.

Finally, the patient asked to speak to the hospital psychiatrist. He spoke about how his waking moments were spent in agony, worrying about how he had failed to fulfill his family's expectations. To the psychiatrist he said, "I want to sleep, sleep, sleep and not wake up. How can a man die in peace when everyone wants him to get well?" The psychiatrist intervened with the family, explaining that the man was facing his impending death courageously, but that their refusal to let go was making it infinitely more difficult. He explained that additional aggressive treatment would only prevent the patient from finding the relief and peace of mind he was seeking. Once the family was able to accept the reality of the situation, they stopped trying to urge him back to health, and the man was able to die in peace.[20]

I recall a case in which a man who was nursing his wife through terminal cancer had set the goal of making sure that she live till their next anniversary. This seemed to be a personal challenge for him, and he felt that he would be better able to "let her go" then. This is another case where a family member's wishes took precedence over the dying patient's desires.

In the following case, disagreements about letting go led to a legal dispute. Thomas Smerdon, age forty-eight, had been comatose since 1981 following surgery for a ruptured blood vessel in his brain. At one time, while watching a man in a wheelchair, he had said in front of his wife, "If I'm ever like that, push me over the Palisades!" His wife, Barbara, took the remark as meaning that, if he were ever seriously disabled, he would not want to live, and therefore she requested the removal of the feeding tube that was keeping him alive. But Smerdon's sister disagreed about his statement, claiming that it did not have anything to do with life-support treatment. She said that the "man in the wheelchair" was a nasty man who was screaming at his wife, and that

Smerdon was referring to his nasty personality, not to his disability. Later, the case was pursued through legal channels. Finally, the appellate division of the New Jersey Superior Court ruled that the feeding tube could be removed. But the decision is being appealed to the state supreme court.[21]

On the other hand, letting go can be a very warm and positive experience. You may recall actor Michael Landon's final battle with cancer. On his last day, he gathered together his inner circle, his wife and nine children. In a calm voice he said to the children, "I love you all very much but would you all go downstairs and give me some time with Cindy?" He died peacefully a few hours later in the company of his wife.[22]

WHEN FAMILIES OR FRIENDS NEED TO DECIDE ABOUT LIFE-SUPPORT AND DO-NOT-RESUSCITATE ORDERS

There is perhaps nothing more difficult in life than having to share the decisions about whether to prolong life or not to prolong dying for a loved one. For example, in the case of DNRs, it has become routine in current medical practice to expect outpatients to express their preferences to their doctors well in advance. In a questionnaire survey done by the Department of Family Practice at the University of Michigan, it was found that although 67 percent of the respondents had given some thought to the question of resuscitation, only 11 percent had mentioned it to their physicians, and only 44 percent had discussed it with a nonprofessional person. Yet an overwhelming 93.9 percent said that a good quality of life was more important to them, even if it meant not living longer. Although most of the people surveyed said that they would select their doctor to discuss this issue with, they felt that their spouse would be the most valued advisor.[23]

In actual practice, however, a substantial number of people suffer irreversible brain damage from resuscitation. The 1981

President's Commission for the Study of Ethical Problems in Medicine and Biomedical and Behavioral Research studied the question and found that, in general hospitals, virtually all deaths were attended by resuscitation efforts. Yet only 3 percent of the attempts had been successful. To make matters worse, 1 in 20 patients who had survived resuscitation efforts had sustained brain damage, and about 1 in 4 had had serious and permanent brain damage. The commission concluded that such efforts are frequently useless, and that they often violate patients' personal control over their lives.[24]

The futility of resuscitation after cardiac arrest was further emphasized by a study featured in the *New England Journal of Medicine*. It reviewed the outcome for 185 patients with cardiac arrest brought to the hospital after unsuccessful efforts in the field by ambulance crews and bystanders. Only 16 of the patients were revived in the emergency room and admitted to the hospital. All but 1 of them were comatose while in the hospital, and none left the hospital alive. Yet they spent anywhere from 1 to 132 days in the hospital at an average cost of $11,307 per patient.[25]

The problem of treating cardiac arrest is being reevaluated. Every year, abut 350,000 Americans suffer cardiac arrest, at least two-thirds of them outside the hospital. It is well known that CPR (cardiopulmonary resuscitation) is successful only if it is given promptly by emergency crews or bystanders. If delay occurs, mild to severe brain damage may result. Even then, the majority of survivors sustain enough brain damage to end up in nursing homes for the rest of their lives.[26]

The question of deciding what is best for a terminally ill patient is even more difficult, especially when the person is incompetent and the decision to withhold or withdraw treatment must be made by the family. As we discussed above, dissension or unfinished business may complicate the decision tremendously.

Sometimes, decisions can be facilitated with the help of the bioethics committee of the hospital. Such was true in the case of

Gloria Simpson, a woman with multiple sclerosis, whose condition had deteriorated and had led to an irreversible coma while she was hospitalized at the Washington Hospital Center in Washington, D.C. Her next of kin was her younger sister, Deborah Langer, who was suddenly faced with having to make one of the most agonizing decisions in her life: the fate of her sister. (Both sister's names have been changed.) Deborah felt totally overwhelmed, saying, "You know, this is somebody I love, somebody I care about. What in the world can you do?" She found help from the hospital bioethics committee, consisting of a staff physician, a social worker, and a minister. With the help of that team, she was able to pull herself together and finally reach the decision to withdraw the life-support systems. Not long after that, her sister died.

Recalling how she had arrived at the decision, Langer said that after the committee told her all the facts, she was asked what her sister would want. She said, "I prayed and prayed and prayed. And the Lord just said to let her go, because she was just being kept artificially alive." After her sister was removed from the respirator, Langer felt that she had made the proper decision, the one that her sister would have wanted.[27]

SHOULD FAMILIES TELL THE TRUTH TO A DYING PERSON?

I have previously discussed the importance of terminally ill patients' knowing the truth about their condition. How the message is conveyed will vary according to the persons involved and the circumstances. The important thing to remember is that it is not helpful to try to conceal the truth from the dying. Keep in mind, however, that there are people who would rather not know that they have a fatal disease.

But if one does try to be "protective" for fear of causing upset, the terminally ill person will eventually feel isolated from the rest of the world. Since the early 1980s, the practice of doctors' not telling patients about their fatal diagnosis has been changing in the direction of increased disclosure.[28] Although situations vary from patient to patient, and many conditions must be evaluated before the doctor decides what to tell, in general, in their own way, doctors will tell patients the potential outcome of their disease.

It has been estimated that about 1.5 percent of the patient population do not want to know about their fatal diagnosis. The situation becomes more complicated when families demand to know the diagnosis but want the patient to be kept in the dark. Doctors then face a real dilemma because the code of medical ethics demands that they respect the confidentiality that their patients expect. Therefore, doctors do not technically have the right to disclose a diagnosis to the family without the patient's knowledge. However, in practice, each situation must be evaluated to meet the particular needs of individual patients and their families.[29]

Patients who are not told the truth are deprived of the opportunity to make decisions about their own health care. This opportunity may be especially crucial for dying patients. The question sometimes remains when and how to tell the truth. Some patients are not ready to hear the truth in so many words. A patient may say, "I know what you are going to say, but don't say it," when learning, for example, that a biopsy came back positive. On some level, most terminally ill patients know the truth without being told directly, or they come to guess it in time. They guess it because they notice a change in their family members' behavior and attitudes toward them. "Why is everybody suddenly being so nice?" asked a woman who began to suspect that something must be unusual about her condition.

Experienced clinicians know that what patients really want to know is not so much "Do I have cancer?" as "How long do I have to live?" and "Will I die a terrible death?"[30] Patients must be told in a way that they can accept, the doctor taking plenty of time and showing care and empathy.

WHAT DO DYING PATIENTS
EXPECT FROM FAMILY AND FRIENDS?

Each person has different expectations, but by and large, most people who have a fatal illness do not want to be pitied or treated as though they are abnormal. Here is what a young woman said after she learned that she had chronic leukemia: "The doctor told me the truth at once because I insisted on knowing. The news came at a crisis time in my life. I had just gone through a divorce and had young children to raise.

"Would you believe I had to move out of town to a larger city because people would not accept me as a normal person? I was devastated, not by the disease, which had been controlled by drugs, but by the way people treated me. Although I could play tennis, ski, dance, hike and take part in community activities, the people at work made my life miserable. One woman refused to use the same washroom! Men wouldn't date me. I was treated like some sort of social outcast—a pathetic hopeless case.

"After I moved to this distant city my life changed dramatically. No one here knows of my illness and I am keeping my mouth shut. I work part time, attend college, have many friends, am involved with community activities and participate in sports. What a pity that I had to move to a town where nobody knew me in order to live a normal life.

"Although I feel well, look fine and am managing beautifully, I know it can't last forever. I dread the day my friends must be told of my illness. I don't want to be pitied. And of course, I fear that I may be deserted as I was once before.

"My purpose is to educate people should they encounter someone who is in the same spot I'm in right now. Here are the ways you can help:

"1. Treat me the same way as a normal person. Don't look at me with pity in your eyes and ask, 'How are you doing?'

"2. Include me in your activities. I need friends just as you do.

"3. Stay off the subject of funeral arrangements and insurance. (Relatives are especially guilty of this.)

"4. Forget my disease. I'll do better if I don't know it's on your mind.

"5. Ask me out. Develop a relationship with me. You can even marry me. I might live another 20 years. (Today that's longer than most couples stay together!)

"6. Hire me. If I'm productive I will live longer. If I'm forced to go on welfare or disability, it will raise your taxes.

"7. Treat me as you would like to be treated under the same circumstances."[31]

Patients do not become different people. Their need for love and respect does not change when they develop a fatal illness. Often, they are puzzled by the change in the behavior of the people around them. That in itself can increase fear and anxiety, even more than the disease itself. This phenomenon was beautifully expressed in the following piece, which was published anonymously in February 1970, probably several years after its author had died. Although the piece is addressed to fellow student nurses, it does apply to all of us dealing with the needs of a dying person. This is what she wrote: "I am a student nurse. I am dying. I write this to you who are, and will become, nurses in the hope that by my sharing my feelings with you, you may someday be better able to help those who share my experience.

"I'm out of the hospital now—perhaps for a month, for six months, perhaps for a year—but no one likes to talk about such things. In fact, no one likes to talk much at all. Nursing must be advancing, but I wish it would hurry. We're taught not to be overly cheery now, to omit the 'everything's fine' routine, and we have done pretty well. But now one is left in a lonely silent void. With the protective 'fine, fine' gone, the staff is left with only their own vulnerability and fear. The dying patient is not yet seen as a person and thus cannot be communicated with as such. He is a symbol of what every human fears and what each know [sic], at least academically, that we too must someday face. What did they say in psychiatric nursing about meeting pathology with pathology to the detriment of both patient and nurse? And there was a lot about knowing one's own feelings before you could help another with his. How true.

"But for me, fear is today and dying is now. You slip in and out of my room, give me medications and check my blood pressure. Is it because I am a student nurse, myself, or just a human being, that I sense your fright? And your fears enhance mine. Why are you afraid? I am the one who is dying!

"I know you feel insecure, don't know what to say, don't know what to do. But please believe me, if you care, you can't go wrong. Just admit that you care. That is really for what we search. We may ask for why's and wherefore's, but we don't really expect answers. Don't run away—wait—all I want to know is that there will be someone to hold my hand when I need it. I am afraid. Death may get to be a routine to you, but it is new to me. You may not see me as unique, but I've never died before. To me, once is pretty unique!

"You whisper about my youth, but when one is dying, is he really so young anymore? I have lots I wish we could talk about. It really would not take much more of your time because you are in here quite a bit anyway.

"If only we could be honest, both admit our fears, touch one another. If you really care, would you lose so much of your valuable professionalism if you even cried with me? Just person to person. Then, it might not be so hard to die—in a hospital— with friends close by."[32]

FAMILY MEMBERS WITH AIDS

The diagnosis of AIDS is particularly stressful for families because the family is often given the simultaneous news of the terminal diagnosis and the homosexual or bisexual activity of the patient. In those cases, the family feels stigmatized and isolated in addition to being shocked.[33] Sometimes the patient feels totally abandoned because of being brought into confrontation with the family about a subject that may have been avoided for years. In many cases, the tension and lack of communication that existed for years benefit from professional counseling. This is particularly true if the patient has adopted a "surrogate family" and may incur society's total rejection of that family. Biological families feel especially stressed because they cannot share their plight with friends in the community. Guilt is one of the most severe emotions experienced because biological families feel that they should have intervened before the disease began.

One additional problem that may arise for families occurs when the patient develops dementia in the late stages of AIDS. The problem is that patients have frequently asked the doctor not to disclose the diagnosis to their family members. Then the question arises of who should be involved in the decision about further life-sustaining treatment. Often, the patient's partner or friend may be totally unknown to the patient's family, yet may want a major part in deciding what is best for the patient. There are no easy answers in this situation. The hospital bioethics committee may be consulted in the hope that conflicts will be resolved between the various parties involved in the decision-making process.

DISCUSSING TREATMENT OPTIONS WITH THE DYING

Families need to know what are the concerns of a dying relative. The dying person often feels that time has become precious, that there is no time to waste, and that it's important to cut through the pretenses. In other words, dying patients demand honesty of those around them.

Dying patients worry about two main things. First, they want to know if they will have a lot of pain and will get help from the doctors or the family in controlling their pain. Second, they want to know if their last moments will be comfortable and not prolonged by extraordinary measures.

Families, however, often have difficulty discussing treatment options and decision making about life-support measures. They will ask, as did the sister of the woman dying of multiple sclerosis, "How could I kill my sister?" In some ways, they feel as though they are "playing God" and have a hard time rationalizing the choices they have to make as time runs out. Families often attempt to buy time, sometimes months or years, still hoping for a miracle.

Aggressive treatment is not for everyone, and some people would prefer a more gentle approach. Having good pain control and enjoying a supportive environment may be far more important to some patients than continuing a fierce battle with risky surgical or medical procedures. They may want to opt for hospice care or for home care (see Chapter 9).

What helps the most is the family's willingness to openly and frankly discuss the options with the dying patient. After having talked about it, they can together follow through with decisions to stop life-support treatments with less anguish, despite their grief and sorrow. Furthermore, the family's guilt is lessened if they have acceded to their loved one's wishes. This is particularly important when the family and the patient disagree on the decision to stop treatments, says Nelson, an ordained minister and clinical psychologist.[34] On the other hand, the sense of guilt may be just as intense if the family wanted to let the patient die, and instead watched her or him linger in pain because she or he insisted on treatment. The only consolation is that they were following the patient's wishes.

Finally, families who live with a dying person must learn to live one day at a time. Chaplain Phillip King, who had been diagnosed with cancer of the colon several years before, learned to follow a friend's advice: "Deny all you can, and hope all you can." He went on to explain, "That does not mean you deny the reality of your illness, that you refuse to consider when you might want treatment stopped. Acceptance doesn't have to mean losing hope, even if that hope is just to enjoy one more meal with your closest friends or family."[35]

QUESTIONS THAT MAY HELP YOU IN CONVERSATIONS WITH YOUR FAMILY OR OTHER SIGNIFICANT ADULTS

It is useful to organize your thoughts before you talk to others about your wishes and preferences in health care decisions. The following list of questions may help you to interact with the people you trust and love.

Write down your answers to the questions, and attach them to your advance directive documents or give them to your physician. Among the preferences you may wish to express are those involving the following medical procedures:

Kidney dialysis
Cardiopulmonary resuscitation (CPR)
Respirator use (breathing assisted through a tube to your lungs)
Artificial nutrition and hydration (tube-feeding)
Organ donation

and any other procedure involving surgery, hospitalization, or antibiotics.

The following questions may help you get started in thinking about your own situation as well as about your conversations with others.

I.   What is your general attitude toward your health?
      A. How would you describe your current health status? How would you describe your current medical problems, if any?
      B. Do any current medical problems affect your ability to function?
      C. How do you feel about your current health status?

D. Do you wish to make any general comments about living with your current health condition?

II.   How are your relationships with your doctor and other caregivers?

A. Do you like and trust your doctors?

B. Would you be comfortable if your doctor made the final decision concerning any treatment you might need? How much do you want to be told? How much do you want and expect to be the decision maker?

C. Are there other caregivers, including nurses, therapists, chaplains, and social workers, whom you have special relationships with or feelings about?

III. What are your thoughts about independence and control?

A. What do independence and self-sufficiency mean to you? To what extent are they important to you?

B. In what ways do you feel independent and in control of your life?

C. If you were to experience decreased physical and mental abilities, how would that decrease affect your attitude toward independence and self-sufficiency?

IV. How are your relationships with the significant people in your life?

A. What part do family and friends play in your life?

B. Do you discuss your health-care decisions with anyone in particular?

C. Do you expect family or others to be involved in health-care decisions that may need to be made for you?

D. Have you made any arrangements for your family or friends to make medical treatment decisions in your behalf? If so, who has agreed to make decisions for you and under what circumstances?

E. Do you expect family, friends, or others to have any difficulty supporting your decisions regarding the medical treatments you may need in the future (e.g., because of personal or religious beliefs, etc.)?

    F. Are there any relationships or pieces of unfinished business from the past that you are concerned about (i.e., personal and family relationships, or business and legal matters)?

V.   What is your general attitude toward life?

    A. Are you happy to be alive and feel that life is worth living?

    B. Do you have any comments about your current living situation?

    C. What do you want most at this time? During the rest of your life?

    D. What do you fear most? What frightens or upsets you?

    E. What plans do you have for the future?

VI. What are your thoughts about finances?

    A. Have you made any arrangements about meeting the costs of your current and future health care?

    B. Do you feel secure and satisfied with the current health insurance you have?

    C. Are you worried about the cost of long-term nursing-home care if you ever need it?

VII. What is your attitude toward illness, death, and dying?

    A. What is the most important issue to you when you are dying (e.g., physical comfort, no pain, or family members present)?

    B. Where or how would you prefer to die?

    C. How do you feel about the use of life-sustaining measures in the face of

        1. Terminal illness?

        2. Permanent coma?

        3. Irreversible chronic illness (e.g., lung disease or Alzheimer's disease)?

    D. Do you want to make any general comments about your attitude toward illness, dying, and death?

As you develop your ideas and participate in discussions, you will notice some topics that inspire different reactions. Continue to expand or revise the questions to suit the situation and the individuals involved.

NOTES

1. J. Q. Benoliel, "Dying Is a Family Affair," in *Home Care: Living with Dying*, ed. E. Pritchard (New York: Columbia University Press, 1979), 17–34.
2. Ibid.
3. Ibid.
4. Ibid.
5. L. F. Degner and J. I. Beaton, *Life-Decisions in Health Care* (New York: Hemisphere, 1987), 67–78.
6. Ibid.
7. Betty Rollin, *Last Wish* (New York: Signet, 1985), 149.
8. Ibid., 150.
9. Degner & Beaton, 67–80.
10. Ibid.
11. G. M. Burnell and A. L. Burnell, *Clinical Management of Bereavement* (New York: Human Sciences Press, 1989), 88–92.
12. Elisabeth Kübler-Ross, *Questions and Answers on Death and Dying* (New York: Macmillan, 1974), 116–141.
13. R. Buckman, R. Gallop, and J. Martin, *I Don't Know What to Say: How to Help and Support Someone Who Is Dying* (Toronto: Key Porter Books, 1988), 3–21.
14. Ibid.
15. Ibid.
16. L. C. Rainey, "The Experience of Dying," in *Dying: Facing the Facts*, 2nd ed., ed. H. Wass, F. M. Berardo, and R. A. Neimeyer. Series in Death Education, Aging and Health Care (New York: Hemisphere Publishing Corporation, 1988), 137–157.
17. Ibid.
18. G. W. Krieger and L. O. Bascue, "Terminal Illness: Counseling with a Family Perspective," *The Family Coordinator* 24 (1975): 351–356.
19. D. V. Schapira, "The Right to Die: Perspectives of the Patient, the Family, and the Health Care Provider," in *To Die or Not To Die:*

Cross-Disciplinary, Cultural, and Legal Perspectives on the Right to Choose Death, ed. A. S. Berger and J. Berger (New York: Praeger, 1990), 5–7.

20. David Hendin, *Death as a Fact of Life* (New York: W. W. Norton, 1973), 96–96.
21. American Health Consultants, "Family Dispute Breaks Out in New Jersey over Withdrawal of Food and Water," *Medical Ethics Advisor* 7 (1991): 94–95.
22. "Goodbye, Little Joe," *People Magazine,* 15 July 1991, 59–62.
23. M. H. Ebell, M. A. Smith, G. Seifert, and K. Polsinelli, "The Do-Not-Resuscitate Order: Outpatient Experience and Decision-making Preferences," *The Journal of Family Practice* 31 (1990): 630–636.
24. J. J. Paris and F. E. Reardon, "The AMA's Guidelines on DNR Policy: Conflict over Patient Autonomy, Family, Consent, and Physician Responsibility," *Clinical Ethics Report* 5 (1991): 1–7.
25. William Gray, et al., "Unsuccessful Emergency Resuscitation: Are Continued Efforts in the Emergency Department Justified?" *New England Journal of Medicine* 325 (14 Nov. 1991),1381–1393.
26. L. B. Becker, et al., "Outcome of CPR in a Large Metropolitan Area: Where Are the Survivors?," *Annals of Emergency Medicine* 201 (1991): 355–361.
27. Don McLeod, "Death in the Family: New Hospital Ethics Committees Help Patients, Families Control Latest Technology," *American Association of Retired Persons Bulletin* (May 1991), 1; 10–11.
28. Robert M. Veatch, *Death, Dying and the Biological Revolution: Our Last Quest for Responsibility* (New Haven: CN: Yale University Press, 1989), 166–196.
29. Ibid.
30. E. Ogg, *Facing Death and Loss* (Lancaster: PA: Technomic, 1985), 21.
31. A. Landers, "She's Dying, but She Still Needs to Be Loved," *Honolulu Advertiser* 26 August 1991, B2.
32. "Death in the First Person," *American Journal of Nursing* 70 (2, Feb. 1970): 36.
33. Burnell and Burnell, 88–92.
34. J. Somerville, "The Final Days," *American Medical News,* 7 January 1991, 10–11.
35. Ibid.

CHAPTER 7

How Does the Law Influence Decisions to End Life Support?

This chapter discusses the legal aspects of life-support measures and the problems patients and families have faced in obtaining permission to discontinue life-sustaining treatments. You might ask, "What does the law have to do with life-support treatment?" The fact is that many situations arise in the course of a terminal illness that can bring about conflict between various parties, including the patient, her or his family, the state, the medical profession, the hospital or nursing home, the appointed surrogates, and even prolife organizations. The conflict may be based on questions of morality, ethics, legality, or liability, but it is usually referred to the judicial system, where the courts are called on to resolve the differences based on existing law. For example, even if your doctor agrees with your feelings and moral reasons for discontinuing life-support measures, the fear of a lawsuit may inhibit her or his action.

That fear of being sued has led doctors to abdicate to hospital administrators, lawyers, and courts their responsibility for medical decisions. The result has been an increase in the bureaucracy of medical practice, to the detriment of both physicians and patients. George Annas, a renowned medical ethicist, has argued that the courts "should not routinely permit themselves to be used by doctors, hospital administrators, and their lawyers to avoid taking professional responsibility for their decisions . . . . Hospital administrators and lawyers often forge 'solutions' to medical practice 'problems' that are disconnected from biological reality and compassionate medical practice."[1] Therefore, there is an urgent need for the general public, and especially health-care and legal professionals to become informed and educated about the ethical and legal aspects of life-sustaining treatment.[2]

The fear of liability or criminality becomes another concern when the attorney general of a particular state raises a question of the legality of stopping life-supporting measures, suspecting that there may be a criminal motive. In order to reach decisions in such matters, the courts have relied on legal precedent, rights or principles of law based on common case law or constitutional law.

The decision to discontinue life-support or life-sustaining treatment is not always your exclusive legal right. That decision may need to be shared by other parties, including the judicial system, especially if you do not have a living will or a durable power of attorney for health care, documents referred to as *advance directives*. There are many situations in which people do not write down such directions, and there are people who are not able to write them, such as juveniles, retarded individuals, and persons who are comatose or in a persistent vegetative state.

Even if you have executed advance directives, there may be a question of whether your appointed surrogate has sufficient authority to act on your behalf. For example, such a person could not authorize active killing for mercy, as that is illegal. Another area of unclear legal policy involves the refusal of hydration and nutrition as life-sustaining treatment. One of the most difficult questions debated in the courts has been whether the next of kin or the surrogate has the right to decide for incompetent individuals. In all of these situations, legislation has been proposed to establish more clearly the authority of the persons involved in making decisions.[3]

It will help you to know about landmark cases that have tested the legal system and brought considerable progress to our current thinking about difficult issues. In virtually every state, appellate courts facing the issue have upheld the right to refuse life-sustaining treatment.

At times, the courts have taken an active part in deciding about forgoing life-support decisions, and at other times, the courts have decided to abstain. Generally, judges believe that these decisions must reside with patients and their doctors. The courts themselves have disagreed, and higher courts have reversed rulings made by lower courts. Some courts focus on different legal principles or tests; others emphasize common law; and some rely more heavily on state or federal constitutional law.

Case law has progressed in three distinctive stages. First, test cases clarified the patient's right to choose based on either the constitutional right to privacy or the doctrine of informed consent, or both. Second, the courts recognized that patients or their surrogates have a right to refuse life-support measures, usually a respirator. Third, the refusal of life-sustaining treatment was expanded to include the refusal of nutrition and hydration through feeding tubes by competent patients or by surrogates in the case of incompetent patients. In general, the courts tend to agree on protecting the individual's autonomy. They differ, however, on the amount of legal intervention required for anyone to exercise the freedom to refuse treatment, especially when this freedom is challenged by others.[4]

At this point, let us briefly review significant pieces of legislation that have had an impact on the issue of life-support measures.

LEGISLATION: THE 1976 CALIFORNIA NATURAL DEATH ACT

California became the first state to pass a law clarifying the rights of persons to write specific instructions about their terminal care.[5] Although the bill was far from perfect, it was a sincere effort championed by Assemblyman Barry Keene, who debated the issue when the decisions to withhold life-sustaining treatment for terminal patients was still a controversial and politically unpopular subject.[6]

California's pioneering legislation focuses primarily on protecting the individual's autonomy and expresses concern about the "loss of patient dignity and unnecessary pain and suffering, while providing nothing medically necessary or beneficial to the patient." It further states that "adult persons have the fundamental right to control decisions relating to the rendering of their own medical care, including the decision to have life-sustaining procedures withheld or withdrawn in instances of a terminal condition."

The right was particularly described as such because of the prevailing beliefs of many in the medical and nursing professions who held that some treatments are "necessary." Whether such treatments were really necessary was based not on medical or scientific evidence, but on the personal ethical judgment of physicians or nurses.

The California legislation provides ways for individuals to exercise their freedom by signing specific directives. The act states that as a matter of "dignity and privacy . . . any adult person may execute a directive directing the withholding or withdrawal of life-sustaining procedures in a terminal condition." Such directives have to be signed in the presence of two witnesses not related to the patient or not entitled to any portion of the patient's estate. Furthermore, the law excludes the attending physician or any employee of the attending physician. The specific form that must be signed says that the individual is of sound mind and does not want life to be artificially prolonged "in the event of incurable injury, disease, or illness certified to be terminal by two physicians, and where the application of life-sustaining procedures would serve only to artificially prolong the moment of my death and where my physician determines that my death is imminent whether or not life-sustaining procedures are utilized." There are conditions, however, that must be carefully considered before the act can be implemented.

First, *the condition must be terminal* before treatment may be stopped. The California law defines *terminal* as "an incurable condition caused by injury, disease, or illness, which, regardless of the application of life-sustaining procedures, would, within reasonable medical judgment, produce death, and where the application of life-sustaining procedures serve [sic] only to postpone the moment of death of the patient." It is easy to see that the definition of *terminal* here is quite limiting. For example, it does not take into account cases of persistent vegetative state or coma, like the cases of Karen Ann Quinlan or Nancy Cruzan. In addition, it does not consider persons afflicted with Alzheimer's disease, strokes, end-stage kidney disease, or advanced cancer, even if life-sustaining treatments will inflict a disproportionate amount of suffering.

Second, the directive, in order to be binding, must be *signed within fourteen days of the patient's being notified and diagnosed that the condition is terminal.* This time limit automatically brings the physician into the decision-making process. Even though the patient's wishes and beliefs, plus the family's feelings are expected to be considered, the doctor may ignore them under certain circumstances if these desires are not clearly enunciated during the fourteen-day period.

Third, treatment may be stopped only *when death is thought to be imminent.* In other words, even if the patient has a "terminal condition" and even if the doctor affirms the directive within fourteen days after the terminal diagnosis, the treatment may not be stopped unless death is imminent. The term *imminent* is not defined by the law. Ironically, if death is really imminent, meaning that it will occur within a very short time, a situation that is medically difficult to predict with any certainty, then it is doubtful that stopping treatment would make any significant difference. Most people afflicted with an incurable illness would probably want to exercise their freedom long before the last few moments.

Fourth, *the directive loses its effect five years from the date of its execution*. This stipulation was included to protect those individuals who might change their minds. The result is that physicians are not obliged to follow directives executed five years ago or longer. If the patient becomes comatose or unable to communicate, however, the directive remains in effect during the duration of the comatose state or until the patient can communicate again.

Fifth, the directive is *not applicable if the patient is pregnant*. The right of a pregnant woman is highly controversial because the right of the fetus must be considered. This issue is still being tested in various courts.

Sixth, *the directive has no effect if signed while the patient is in a skilled-nursing-home facility, unless it is witnessed by a certified patient advocate or ombudsman*. It was felt by the lawmakers that the nursing-home population is very vulnerable and needs special protection against abuses.

Seventh, *physicians and health facilities are guaranteed immunity against any civil or criminal liability and cannot be sued for honoring advance directives*. Despite this guarantee against prosecution, physicians are often reluctant to certify a patient as being in a terminal state. Doctors know that, once the patient is so certified, the patient may want to stop life-sustaining treatment and the outcome will be death. Many physicians, as we have discussed in previous chapters, have difficulty in accepting their proper role as physicians in such situations. The result is that the patient's wishes may not be respected. Incidentally, there was an attempt to revise that aspect of the act, but the attempt was vetoed.

Eighth, *the forgoing of treatment shall not constitute suicide*. This is an important provision that protects the individual who has life insurance, as many policies have exclusion clauses for suicide.

Ninth, the act states that *no other right or authority is superseded*. In other words, other laws, such as common case law addressing the right of stopping life-support procedures, cannot be ignored and are not canceled out by the legislation. As expected, this provision has caused further confusion. On the one hand, it states that the physician must abide by the directive if it has been properly executed by the patient. On the other hand, even if the directive is not proper, the patient still has the right to refuse treatment under common case law. This is a "catch-22."

Another problem arises when patients become comatose or unable to communicate after signing their directives and cannot restate their wishes, a scenario that is not uncommon. For example, healthy persons who make their treatment preferences known clearly in a directive may be kept alive artificially against their will after falling into a coma because of an accident. Furthermore, even those patients who are able to communicate are forced to endure an additional fourteen days of unwanted treatment following the diagnosis of a condition deemed terminal.

The biggest problem in the California legislation is that it provides no guidelines for patients who have never been competent (such as retarded individuals) or for those persons who have failed to prepare a directive while they were still competent (such as individuals with Alzheimer's disease). In this regard, there is still considerable confusion between what common case law says and what the state legislation affirms.[7]

Despite all the qualifiers and limitations, the California legislation has become a blueprint for other state legislation. In the years that followed the passage of the California Act, thirty-nine other states and the District of Columbia passed similar legislation. Many of the limitations in the California Natural Death Act have been corrected and improved. For a detailed discussion of these changes, I refer you to the excellent summary by the Society for the Right to Die.[8] The current status of laws concerning living-will legislation in the United States, of the laws governing durable power of attorney and proxy appointments, and of the laws regulating tube-feeding are given in Appendix A and in charts prepared by the Society for the Right to Die.[9]

LEGISLATION DEALING WITH
DECISIONS FOR INCOMPETENT PERSONS

> *Ordinarily, death will be determined*
> *according to the traditional criteria of*
> *irreversible cardiorespiratory response.*
> *When, however, the respiratory and*
> *circulatory functions are maintained by*
> *mechanical means, their significance, as*
> *signs of life, is at best ambiguous.*
> —Judge Lawrence H. Cooke,
> New York State Court of Appeals
> (October 30, 1984)

In the 1970s, several states passed legislation that gave various rights to incompetent patients and their surrogates to limit life-supporting measures.[10] It is beyond the scope of this book to analyze the detailed provisions and limitations of state laws with regard to withholding or withdrawing life-support treatments.

In the 1980s, a group of states passed new legislation granting family surrogates additional decision-making power that extends beyond the cases of comatose patients. By 1992, twenty states and the District of Columbia passed such laws.

Among these twenty states, Virginia seems to have the best statute.[11] It provides authorization for surrogates to make decisions in cases of patients who are comatose, incompetent, or otherwise physically or mentally unable to communicate and who have not prepared any advance directives. Eligible surrogates in order of priority are (1) a guardian or committee appointed by the court; (2) a person or persons designated in writing by the patient to make treatment decisions; (3) a spouse; (4) an adult child of the patient or a majority of the children; (5) the parents of the patient; and (6) the nearest living relative.[12]

Still, no legislation is entirely adequate to cover all situations that may arise in terminal care. In his book *Death, Dying and the Biological Revolution*, Veatch has suggested the following improvements for future legislation:

1. The decision to withhold or withdraw treatment should be made in more general terms, not just limited to patients who have terminal illnesses or whose death is imminent.

2. Persons who are competent should have the right to refuse any treatment, based on their values and beliefs that the treatment may be useless or burdensome.

3. Surrogates should be able to determine what treatments the patient would have wanted. The surrogates' decision should be respected as long as it is within reason. If the surrogates' decision appears to be beyond reason, a judicial review should be required.

4. The presumed surrogate for incompetent patients should be a court-appointed guardian. If no guardian has been appointed, the surrogate should be someone who was designated while the patient was still competent. If no one was designated, then the surrogate should be the next of kin according to normal orders of degree of kinship in the state.

5. No private person or persons (such as an attending physician or an ethics committee) should ever be given authority to make life-and-death decisions for patients.

6. Patients should be permitted to refuse all disproportionately burdensome treatment, regardless of how simple or common, including the administration of fluid and nutrition.

7. Advance directive documents should be recognized in all jurisdictions across the nation.

8. An explicit provision should be made for naming a proxy (a durable power of attorney).

9. Any model declaration should be prepared with the recognition that alternative model forms may coexist. The reason is that people's views on life-sustaining treatments may vary, and it would be difficult to develop a form that would be universally accepted by patients.

Therefore, various options for refusing treatment should be offered.

10. People should be assured that they will be adequately informed about their medical condition in order to make choices based on their personal beliefs and values.[13]

WHAT ARE THE PRINCIPLES AND RIGHTS USED BY OUR CURRENT LEGAL SYSTEM?

> *Every human being of adult years and*
> *sound mind has a right to determine*
> *what shall be done with his own body.*
> —Justice Benjamin N. Cardoza, U.S. Supreme Court (1914)

Currently legislation uses a piecemeal approach to dealing with the terminally ill. It relies on a set of principles based partly on Anglo-American common law and partly on American constitutional law. To understand the decisions in the landmark cases we shall discuss later, it is important to know a few of the basic principles and rights invoked under these two bodies of law.

The Principle of Self-Determination

The principle of self-determination is based on a fundamental right of Anglo-American law that goes back to the earliest period of English history. It was reaffirmed in 1960 by Kansas Supreme Court Justice Alfred Schroeder and states, in essence, that all individuals are masters of their bodies and, if of sound mind, have the right to decide what will be done with their bodies and what medical treatment they will authorize or prohibit.[14]

The best illustration of the principle is the case of Karen Ann Quinlan, a twenty-two-year-old woman who became comatose in April 1975 after an alleged overdose of drugs and alcohol. She remained in a persistent vegetative state, being kept alive by a respirator because physicians and the hospital refused the pleas of the family to stop the respirator. This was the first case to decide the question of withdrawing life-sustaining support when the refusal of treatment would result in death.

The Right to Privacy

The right to privacy is recognized by the U.S. Supreme Court as a basic fundamental right, even though it is not explicitly enunciated in the U.S. Constitution. By saying that anyone has a right to be left alone, this right gives the individual free choice even in the matter of refusing treatment, as in the *Quinlan* case. The Supreme Court has interpreted the First, Fourth, and Fifth Amendments in the Bill of Rights as creating the right to privacy.

The principle of privacy became better known by all of us when in 1973, the U.S. Supreme Court invoked that right to permit women to obtain abortions in its decision in the case of *Roe v. Wade*. The same issues have once again inspired heated debate as a result of some state legislation and recent decisions in some state courts.

On questions involving the right to refuse treatment, the privacy right is often confused with the right to self-determination or autonomy, according to Veatch.[15] Some argue that the value of life is decreased by the individual's wish to refuse treatment, but the Court has argued that, on the contrary, the value of life is lessened by not allowing a mentally sound person to exercise freedom of choice. This kind of reasoning has been further supported by seven jurisdictions: California, Colorado, the District of Columbia, Florida, Hawaii, Massachusetts, and New York.[16]

The Doctrine of Informed Consent

Related to the right to refuse treatment is the common law doctrine of informed consent. It goes back to 1891 when the U.S. Supreme Court, in the case of *Union Pacific Railway Co. v. Botsford*, stated: "No right is held more sacred, or is more carefully guarded, by the common law, than the right of every individual to the possession and control of his own person, free from all restraint or interference of others, unless by clear and unquestionable authority of law."[17]

This doctrine says that, before anyone touches your body, you must be given information about the proposed touching. In current medical practice, this means that a physician must obtain consent from a patient before starting any procedure or treatment. But for a consent to be valid, the physician must explain and provide information about the proposed course of treatment or procedure, the risks of death or harm that may result from the treatment, alternate therapies, and the complications that may arise during the recovery process.

Providing information to help patients make decisions about treatment implies that they have the capacity to do so. The law presumes competency. In the real world, however, physicians often have to decide whether the patient has enough knowledge to make such decisions. Not infrequently, the physician finds reasons to question the patient's judgment and ability to make proper decisions when there is disagreement about the proposed course of action.[18]

The Principle of Beneficence

The principle of beneficence is well known to ethicists and clinicians, and it is frequently applied in medical practice. This principle says that you should not receive a treatment that has less potential benefit than any potential risks incurred during diagnosis or treatment. Sometimes, the principle is referred to as the *principle of nonmaleficence*, which literally means "the doing of no harm." But there are ethical shadings of difference between "doing good" and "doing no harm." Another related principle is that of *proportionality*. This principle takes into account two things: first, the fact that the treatment may be worse than the condition being treated, and second, the patient's overall medical condition and personal values, religious convictions, and psychological resources.

The Doctrine of Best Interest

The doctrine of best interest implies that others will be making a decision on behalf of the patient, assuming that the patient is unable to do so. It says that others will decide on the basis of what they believe is "best" for the patient. In spite of the clearly subjective aspect of substituted judgment, it is often described as an "objective standard."

The State Interest

Whether we like it or not, the state has some say over right-to-die decisions. It will weigh your right to refuse treatment against four categories of interest. It can therefore override your right to refuse treatment. In other words, if you decide to refuse treatment, the state has the right to see that your decision does not conflict with the following four interests:

1. *The preservation of life.* The state considers life sacred; therefore, it has a compelling interest in preserving life. That position is based on an abstract concern that we should respect the sanctity of life. There is also an assumption that you as an individual have some contribution to make to society that should not be ignored because you decide to refuse treatment, particularly if you have a curable condition. Generally, however, the courts have not taken action against anyone who has an incurable condition and who wishes to discontinue treatment. Usually, the right of self-determination outweighs the interest of the state. The *Cruzan* case, however, was an exception: the Missouri Supreme Court held that the state's interest in preserving life was absolute and therefore could intrude on an individual's right to accept or refuse treatment. The *Brophy* case illustrates the court's position of deciding in favor of the patient's right over the state's interest. Let's briefly review that case.

Paul Brophy, a forty-five-year-old firefighter and emergency room technician, suffered a brain hemorrhage from a ruptured aneurysm on March 22, 1983. He lost consciousness and was taken to a hospital. Surgery was performed a few days later but was unsuccessful. Brophy never regained consciousness and remained in a persistent vegetative state. Because of his inability to swallow, he received nutrition and hydration through a gastrostomy tube, which was inserted through the abdominal wall into his stomach. In December 1984, Patricia Brophy, his wife, as legal guardian, asked the doctors and the hospital to remove the gastrostomy tube, but they refused.

In February 1985, Mrs. Brophy petitioned the probate court to authorize her to withdraw and withhold all treatments from her husband. But even though Brophy's wife, his guardian *ad litem*, his seven brothers and sisters, and his five adult children all agreed that Brophy would have wanted treatment withheld, the court concluded that the state interest in preserving life outweighed Brophy's right to choose his own treatment. The court wrote, "The proper focus should be on the quality of treatment, i.e., the invasiveness of treatment, furnished to Brophy, and not on the quality of Brophy's life. Otherwise, the Court is pronouncing judgment that Brophy's life is not worth preserving."

Patricia Brophy appealed the decision directly to the Massachusetts Supreme Judicial Court. On September 11, 1986, the court reversed the lower court's decision by a decision of 4 to 3 that held that Brophy's right to discontinue treatment overrode the state's interest in preserving life, even though Brophy was not "terminally ill" in the traditional sense. It stressed that the "State's interest in life encompasses a broader interest than mere corporeal existence." It went on to say, "In certain . . . circumstances the burden of maintaining the corporeal existence degrades the very humanity it was meant to serve. The law recognizes the individual's right to preserve his humanity, even if to preserve his humanity means to allow the natural processes of a disease or affliction to bring about a death with dignity."[19]

2. *The prevention of suicide.* The interest of suicide prevention does not apply in cases where life-support measures are involved because death usually results from natural causes and not from

actions taken by the patient. However, in the *Brophy* case, the Massachusetts Supreme Judicial Court did address the question. It rejected the contention by the medical authorities that the removal of the feeding tube would constitute suicide. It affirmed that the cause of death would be the underlying condition (Brophy's persistent vegetative state) that prevented him from swallowing, not the removal of the G-tube.

3. *The protection of innocent third parties.* This interest takes into account the protection of minors. For example, in the case of a patient who is competent and wishes to die but is pregnant or has minor children, the state may intervene to protect the rights of the child or children. However, in the case of a terminally ill patient, it is hard to see how the interests of his or her children would be served. In the *Brophy* case, this interest did not apply, but in the rare situation in which a competent patient chooses to die and the family objects, one wonders if the state would move in to protect the family members from the sorrow and suffering inflicted on them by the patient's death. At this writing, that question has not been addressed.[20]

4. *The safeguarding of the integrity of the medical profession.* This issue is not usually a problem except when the physician's duty to sustain life conflicts with the duty to relieve suffering or with the wishes of the patient or the family. In the *Brophy* case, the medical profession refused to remove the artificial feeding tube. One has to wonder why the medical profession took such a stand when the entire Brophy family was in agreement about removal of life-support measures. The grounds for such refusals are usually based primarily on the fear of being sued, and then on medical ethics. But it is interesting to note that both the lower and the appellate courts were careful not to offend the moral and ethical principles of the hospital community and the medical profession, agreeing instead to the transfer of the patient to another hospital (Emerson Hospital in Concord, Massachusetts), where the gastrostomy tube was finally removed. Brophy died peacefully of pneumonia eight days later, on October 23, 1986.[21]

The Doctrine of Substitutive Judgment

The doctrine of substitutive judgment says that another person has the right to make a choice for the patient when the patient is unable to make that choice. In other words, the decision maker stands in the patient's shoes and makes the decision as if the patient were deciding. This is sometimes referred to as a *subjective standard*. This doctrine typically comes into play in cases of incompetent patients who are in a persistent vegetative state or a coma.

In the *Brophy* case, the court relied on several statements that Brophy had made before his illness. Although he had never specifically discussed with his wife the issue of having a feeding tube removed if he were in a persistent vegetative state, he did at one time discuss the Karen Ann Quinlan case with her. In that context, he had stated: "I don't ever want to be on a life-support system. No way do I want to live like that; that is not living." At a later time, when Brophy had rescued a man from a burning truck who died a few months later of extensive burns, Brophy stated to his brother "If I'm ever like that, just shoot me; pull the plug." About twelve hours after being transported to the hospital, while still conscious, he said to one of his daughters, "If I can't sit up to kiss one of my beautiful daughters, I may as well be six feet under."

With that kind of evidence, sometimes referred to as *clear and convincing evidence*, the court held that Brophy's substituted judgment would be honored, and that if the hospital refused to honor it, Brophy's guardian would transfer him to the care of other physicians in another hospital. As mentioned above, this is what was done.

The Test of Clear and Convincing Evidence

This test of clear and convincing evidence is another form of substantiating substitutive judgment. What the patient would want must be based on clear and convincing evidence of the patient's intent, derived from the patient's explicit expressions of intent or from knowledge of the patient's personal value system.

The definition of clear and convincing evidence, however, varies according to the interpretation by the court that reviews the facts in the case. Hence, what constitutes clear and convincing evidence in one court may not be sufficient evidence in another court.

In the *Brophy* case, the patient had made several statements about his values in similar situations. But in the *Cruzan* case, mentioned in Chapter 1, the Missouri State Supreme Court reversed a state trial court decision and ruled against the parents' and coguardians' wishes to discontinue artificial feeding of food and water. The court rejected the evidence that a roommate had heard from Nancy a year earlier that she would not want to continue her life unless she could live "halfway normally." The court argued that this was not "clear and convincing evidence." In 1990, when the case was heard by the U.S. Supreme Court, the decision was split in a 5–4 vote, demonstrating once more the lack of judicial unanimity in cases involving life-support measures.

On November 1, 1990, the Cruzans returned to the trial court in Missouri with additional evidence from three new witnesses, who testified that Nancy had said that she did not want to be force-fed or dependent on machines, or to exist "like a vegetable." At that point, the office of the state attorney general stopped opposing the request, saying that the state was now satisfied, through the Supreme Court's clarification, that a state could require "clear and convincing evidence." On December 14, 1990, Judge Teel of the probate court found that the statements made by the new witnesses were "clear and convincing evidence" that Nancy would have wanted the removal of the feeding tube. Her feeding tube was removed two hours later, and Nancy died peacefully on December 26, 1990.

The Principle of Familial Autonomy

The principle of familial autonomy is considered weak and not well articulated. Yet it recognizes that the family is a fundamental unit within our society. Just as individuals are entitled to personal autonomy, families are entitled to some limited autonomy based on their values, beliefs, and commitments.[22] This principle is usually invoked in cases where the patient is incompetent. Even then, familial autonomy is applicable only if the decision about treatment choices is made "within the limits of reason."

LIVING-WILL STATUTES IN THE UNITED STATES

Since the early 1980s, the courts have pressured state legislatures to take steps to clarify and protect the right to refuse life-sustaining treatments. On the one hand, this clarification ensures that the wishes of patients will be carried out by physicians; on the other hand, it protects physicians from civil and criminal liability for acceding to a patient's wishes.

The first living-will statute was enacted in California in 1976, just before the *Quinlan* case. To date, forty-two states and the District of Columbia have passed laws that permit people to refuse medical treatment if they become unable to speak for themselves.

The California Natural Death Act states that any adult may execute a living will, which is called a *directive*. In such a directive, one may state one's wishes that life-sustaining procedures be withheld or withdrawn in the event of a terminal condition. In some states, *terminal condition* refers to illness or disease, but in California, it includes injuries.

As in California, most other states contain an exclusion for pregnant women. This means that if a patient who has signed a directive becomes pregnant, the document cannot be honored as long as the patient is pregnant, although some states limit this exclusion to cases in which the fetus will remain viable to the point of live birth with the continuation of life support to the mother.[23]

Like all living-will laws in the country, the California act assures that physicians who comply with the directive will not be subject to civil or criminal liability.

One major problem as in the California Natural Death Act is that physicians may not always comply, because in order for them to comply, the patient must already have been diagnosed as terminally ill when the directive is signed. If the individual is well when signing, the directive is only advisory and need not be followed. In such a case, the document must be reexecuted after the diagnosis of terminal illness. Unfortunately, the person often becomes comatose or unable to communicate after signing the directive and therefore cannot restate his or her wishes. This is what may happen, for example, when a person who has signed such a directive becomes comatose following an automobile accident.

Another problem with living-will legislation as with the California act is that physicians may be reluctant to certify a patient as terminally ill because they know that this certification may result in the withdrawal of life-sustaining treatment and the eventual death of the patient. The physician's reluctance is usually based on the fear of being sued, even though the statute guarantees immunity from civil or criminal liability. As a result, there is no guarantee that the patient's wishes will be honored, and most statutes do not hold the physician liable for not respecting the living-will directive. Noncompliance is not considered unprofessional conduct. All that most statutes require is that, if physicians are not willing to comply with a living will, they must take reasonable steps to transfer the patient to the care of another physician.

It should be noted that all of the existing statutes exclude people who are not diagnosed as terminally ill. Many of these statutes are not as restrictive as the California act and will allow an individual to execute a binding directive before becoming terminally ill, but the directive becomes effective only after a doctor has certified that the patient is terminally ill and unable to make decisions.

A serious problem that may arise if the patient is not terminally ill is illustrated by the case of *Bartling v. Superior Court.* William Bartling, a competent seventy-year-old man who was not terminally ill, executed a living will that did not comply with the California act. In April 1984, he was admitted to Glendale Adventist Hospital in California for treatment of depression. He was also suffering from emphysema, arteriosclerosis, and an abdominal aneurysm. On Bartling's admission, the doctor also found a malignant lung tumor. A lung biopsy was performed, but because of the emphysema, the lung collapsed and failed to reinflate. A tracheotomy was done, and Bartling was put on a respirator.

While in the hospital intensive-care unit, Bartling tried to remove the respirator, so his wrists were put in restraints. Both he and his wife made repeated requests that the respirator be stopped, but the hospital and the treating physicians refused. In June 1984, Bartling sought an injunction to prohibit the hospital and the physicians from giving any further treatment. He also filed a complaint in court seeking damages from the physicians and the hospital for treatment given without consent and violation of his constitutional rights.[24]

Bartling had executed a nonstatutory living will, a document in which he stated that he did not want to continue to live under such circumstances, as well as a California durable power of attorney for health care decisions, designating his wife as his proxy. In addition, he and his wife had signed documents releasing the hospital and his physicians from all liability if they complied.[25] Bartling's physicians, however, felt that his condition was not terminal and that he could live for another year. They questioned his judgment and his ability to make a meaningful decision, even though they admitted that he was legally "competent." The doctors maintained that it would be unethical to discontinue life-support measures, and furthermore that they were concerned about civil and criminal liability if they acceded to Bartling's wishes.

The trial court ruled that Bartling's life support could not be removed because he was not terminally ill or comatose. Bartling appealed the decision, but he died the day before the court of appeals heard the case. Interestingly, the court of appeals reversed the trial court's decision and held that the right to disconnect life support was not limited to terminally ill or comatose patients, or their representatives. The decision stated that written expressions of competent patients without a diagnosis of terminal illness—not necessarily on the official directive form—could be recognized. It also stated that such written expressions should be followed by hospitals and physicians and would be sufficient to provide them legal immunity if hey complied with the patient's wishes. The court also held that Bartling had a constitutional right to refuse treatment, that such a right predated any statute, and that signing a directive was not the only way to exercise this right of refusal.

As you can see, a legislature can confuse the issue by drafting statutes that are limited to terminally ill patients, and that, at the same time, ignore prior constitutional rights to refuse treatment.

Sometimes the confusion is compounded by the way the statute is drafted. In some states, the drafted living will may even undermine the right of a terminally ill patient to refuse treatment. For example, the Indiana Living Wills and Life-Prolonging Act of 1985, in Section 11, states that "a living will declaration . . . does not obligate the physician to use, withhold, or withdraw life-prolonging procedures." In other words, living wills do protect the hospital and physicians from liability, but they do not necessarily guarantee that the patient's wishes will be honored. The living will may serve as "presumptive evidence" only if the doctor chooses to give it "great weight."[26]

STATUTES IN THE UNITED STATES ON DURABLE POWER OF ATTORNEY FOR HEALTH CARE

A durable power of attorney for health care is a document that gives decision-making power in health care decisions to the person designated by an individual incapable of expressing (or interpreting) wishes. Unlike the living will, it is a binding instrument. States began in the 1980s to pass laws governing durable power of attorney, and by 1991, twenty-eight states and the District of Columbia had such a device available (see Appendix A). Such a power of attorney can be given to a family member or to a trusted friend and is valid for seven years.

The document can be signed and executed while one is still in good health. Also, it allows the person with the power of attorney to make decisions about any treatment, not just life-supporting measures like a respirator. In fact, the document may mention specific treatments that would be unwanted by the person signing the power of attorney. The law then requires the designated person to act in accordance with the desires expressed in the document.

The thing to remember about a durable power of attorney for health care is that it extends beyond the living will in that it is binding, extending treatment decisions beyond the case of terminal illness. The only problem may be that some people do not know someone they trust enough to respect their wishes. Of course, the same problem would apply to appointing a proxy under a living will.[27]

WHY IS THERE SO MUCH CONFUSION IN THE LEGAL SYSTEM?

> *Let us ask . . . what is it about our thinking that has got us into trouble. The fault lies in our unreasonable wish to have simple rules for our conduct in a complex world. We are on a wild goose chase if we are looking for a set of a few simple rules, without exceptions, which will give us the right answer to all moral questions. Life is too complicated for that. There is no substitute for careful thought about particular cases.*
> —R. M. Hare, *Applications of Moral Philosophy*, (1972)[28]

It is clear from the above examples that legislatures are inconsistent and often confused in applying legal tests or preexisting laws. Ever since the *Quinlan* case in 1976, legislators and judges, as well as medical ethicists, physicians, nurses, philosophers, and theologians, have been unable to cope with this dilemma.[29] The search for simple and universal rules goes on in the hope that we will find an answer for the majority of people facing a difficult death. Later, I shall discuss various proposals for model legislation.

We have seen how confusing living wills appear to the courts, especially when they apply to artificial feeding. We have seen how differently the courts have applied various doctrines and legal tests to competent and incompetent patients. Meanwhile, the psychological trauma experienced in these cases cannot be overestimated. To make matters worse, the tremendous burden of legal costs thrust upon families represents an additional stress. Litigation can cost over $50,000 in some cases. Incidentally, this was a major consideration in my giving up on my mother's case, described in Chapter 4. The opposing party, a lawyer, did not have the financial problem because he intended to represent himself in the matter.

Another source of stress is the suffering due to enormous delays in reaching legal decisions. Sometimes decisions cannot be reached till after the patient has died.

So, you may be wondering, "What is the answer?" The answer lies in greater education of the public and greater awareness in the health-care community, which is the purpose of this book. Decisions pertaining to health care should be private decisions between the patient, the family, and the doctor. No one else should be involved. The decisions do not belong to the legislatures or the courts.[30]

Generally, the courts do not get involved unless a conflict arises between the physicians, the hospital, the nursing staff, the patients, or their families. Sometimes disagreements occur among physicians or between physicians and nurses.

Whenever the physician cannot agree with the patient or the patient's surrogates on the course of action, such as discontinuing life-support measures, including hydration and nutrition, the matter becomes one for the courts to decide. The *Quinlan* and *Brophy* cases are excellent examples.

Physicians' fear of litigation is tremendous, and it leads to extreme positions before agreement to withhold or withdraw treatment. Physicians and hospitals seek legal immunity from civil and criminal liability, and the result is that patients and families are often forced into time-consuming, costly, and otherwise burdensome litigation.

Doctors need to be reassured that their fears are exaggerated, and that the living will does protect them from liability. Even in states without living-will statutes, not one doctor has ever been convicted of murder for withholding or withdrawing life-sustaining treatments. Even in the only case in which murder charges were brought against the treating doctors for withholding or withdrawing treatment, the court dismissed the charges. Let us briefly review that case, *Barber v. Superior Court*.[31]

The patient, Clarence Herbert, had cancer and had undergone surgery to close an opening in the bowel. In the recovery room, he suffered a cardiac arrest, and after resuscitation, he was left severely brain-damaged and in a vegetative state. Because of the extremely poor prognosis, the family drafted a written request stating that they wanted "all machines taken off that are sustaining life." The doctors ordered the removal of the respirator and other life-sustaining equipment. Two days later, they discontinued intravenous hydration and nourishment. Herbert died a few days later.

Someone brought the matter to the attention of the state, and the state pressed murder charges against Drs. Neil Barber and Robert Nejdl. Later, the matter went from the superior court to the California Court of Appeals. The latter overturned the superior court's ruling and dismissed the murder charges. In this case, the doctors were in agreement with the patient's family, and the matter would not have proceeded to litigation without interference by a third party, who complained to the state, which then felt obligated to pursue the matter.

Even an extreme case, such as the one reported in Chapter 4

involving the Florida physician Rosier, who was charged with murdering his wife with morphine injections, did not lead to conviction.

Physicians should know that the danger of liability is greater today if they do *not* accede to a patient's wishes to reject treatment. In the *Bartling* case mentioned above, the patient filed a complaint seeking damages from the physicians and the hospital for treatment without consent and violation of his constitutional rights. As it turned out, the California Court of Appeals based its decision to recognize the right to refuse treatment not only on the federal and California constitutions, but also on the law of actionable battery. In other words, the hospital and the physicians could be held liable for assault and battery. In October 1987, a trial court ordered the hospital and the doctors to pay Bartling's representatives $160,000 in attorneys' fees.[32]

THE PATIENT HAD A LIVING WILL, BUT THE HOSPITAL WOULDN'T LET HIM DIE

The first case in which the living will was not honored by physicians will illustrate the point that health-care professionals may be liable if they do not follow the instructions of the living will. This Florida case involved Francis B. Landy, who was admitted to the John F. Kennedy Memorial Hospital in April 1981. Within two days, he stopped breathing and was placed on a respirator. Examination revealed that he suffered from respiratory failure, lung disease, and gastrointestinal bleeding. He was declared incompetent, and his wife was appointed his guardian. Fortunately, Landy had executed a living will, and he had asked that it be made a part of the hospital record if he were to be admitted in the future. As his guardian, Mrs. Landy had done this, and she requested that all "extraordinary life-support systems" be discontinued.

The hospital, concerned about civil and criminal liability, asked the court to rule on its rights and liabilities. Even though

Mr. Landy died before the hearing, the matter was continued because the court felt it was particularly important to reach a decision. After several hearings by the trial court (the district court of appeals), the matter went on to the Florida Supreme Court, which upheld the family's right to refuse extraordinary life-saving measures. This was the first time that the highest court in any state had recognized the validity of a living will as the significant factor in making decisions for an incompetent patient.[33]

Again, this case would never have proceeded to litigation if it had not been for the hospital's undue fear of liability. Ironically, as it now stands, fear should arise over failure to comply with advance directives.

But where does this all leave us, people like you and me, who come under the care of hospitals and health-care professionals? Arthur S. Berger, author, attorney, and director of the International Institute for the Study of Death, writes, "We should know what our last rights are: that we have the right to be free from non-consensual bodily invasions, that we can refuse to submit to medical treatment; that we have a cause for damages on the ground of battery against doctors and hospitals for treatment we do not want; and we have the right to discharge paternalistic physicians and replace them with doctors who will accord these rights the respect that they deserve. We should also know that we have the right to leave or be removed from uncompromising hospitals or nursing homes to other more cooperative institutions where our rights will be honored!"[34]

OTHER LANDMARK CASES OF SPECIAL INTEREST

Case law has provided the courts with much of the background and justification for decisions concerning life-support problems. Since the very first case, involving Karen Ann Quinlan, considerable progress has been made in understanding the subtleties and complexities of the issues encountered in each case. So far, fifty-five cases have been decided in thirty-one states between 1976 and 1990. In advancing the right to die, these cases have all proved major points based on well-established legal and social principles. They have shown that each citizen has a basic right to be free of interference in matters of health care and, at the same time, have safeguarded our rights to maintain integrity over our bodies. And they have led to new legislation.

I describe here only a few of these cases that may be of special interest to the general reader. Excellent detailed summaries covering all cases from 1976 to 1990 have been published in three volumes by the Society for the Right to Die. Discussing in detail the legal implications of each case, these volumes can be obtained by writing to Choice in Dying, Inc. (See Appendix F).

Case of a Retarded Adult Dying of Leukemia

Joseph Saikewicz, a sixty-seven-year-old Massachusetts mental health patient, was diagnosed as having an acute and rare fatal form of leukemia. With an IQ of 10 and a mental age of two, he could not communicate verbally. The facility superintendent petitioned the probate court to make treatment decisions, specifically to decide whether he should receive chemotherapy, with all of its painful side effects. A guardian *ad litem* and two physicians testified against administering chemotherapy because the pain and fear that Saikewicz would endure would outweigh the possibility of some "uncertain but limited extension of life." The probate court accepted the recommendation, and upon appeal, the Massachusetts Supreme Judicial Court affirmed the lower court's decision. Saikewicz died fourteen months later, in November 1977, of bronchial pneumonia as a complication of the leukemia.

In reviewing the decision, the Supreme Court of Massachusetts held that a patient has the right to privacy "against unwanted infringements of bodily integrity in appropriate circumstances": "The constitutional right to privacy . . . is an expression of the sanctity of individual free choice and self-determination as fundamental constituents of life. The value of life as so perceived is lessened not by a decision to refuse treatment, but by the failure to allow a competent human being the right of choice." Subsequently, the Massachusetts Supreme Judicial Court examined the four state interests we discussed above: (1) the preservation of life; (2) the protection of innocent parties; (3) the prevention of suicide; and (4) the safeguarding of the ethical integrity of the medical profession. It found only the first to be applicable, and after balancing it against the individual's right to reject any bodily intrusions, it affirmed the lower court's decision. It also held that the ethical integrity of the medical profession was not offended by the withholding of treatment.

One major difference from the *Quinlan* case is that the court did not want to leave future similar cases in the hands of the guardian, the family, the attending doctors, or hospital ethics committees. It ruled instead that future cases should be brought to the probate court for an adversarial hearing in which the probate judge would appoint a special guardian to represent the patient and to present the judge with all reasonable arguments in favor of treatment to prolong life.[35]

Case of a Patient with Alzheimer's Disease and Medical Complications Needing a "No Code Order"

In 1978, Shirley Dinnerstein, a sixty-seven-year-old patient with advanced Alzheimer's disease and a coronary condition, suffered a stroke. An adult son and daughter sought legal support to obtain a "no code order," so that their mother would not be resuscitated in case of cardiac arrest. The probate court deferred to the Massachusetts Court of Appeals for a decision.

The court of appeals differentiated the medical circumstances heard six months previously in the *Saikewicz* case, stating that because this present case did not present the possibility of "a permanent or even temporary cure of or relief from the illness," the question was medical rather than judicial. This opinion was welcomed by the medical community, which had feared liability for withholding and withdrawing treatment from an incompetent patient, as in the *Saikewicz* case. Ronald Schram and his colleagues wrote in the New England Journal of Medicine, "The clarifications brought about by Dinnerstein should encourage physicians to discuss the 'no code' decision openly with patients if they are competent or with their families or guardians if they are not competent. The attending physician should document in the patient's chart his opinion of the patient's competence, his opinion that the patient meets the medical criteria for a 'no code' order and the nature of his discussion with the patient, his family or guardian and their wishes. Any 'no code' order should be clearly and prominently marked in the chart."[36]

The *Dinnerstein* case was the first one to uphold the validity of the "no code orders" directing that resuscitation measures be withheld from an incompetent, irreversibly terminally ill patient in the event of cardiac or respiratory failure.[37]

Case of a Patient with Lou Gehrig's Disease (Amyotrophic Lateral Sclerosis) Who Wanted to Get Off the Respirator

Abe Perlmutter, a seventy-three-year-old suffering from Lou Gehrig's disease and bedridden in a Florida hospital, was told by his doctors that he would probably die within a few months. Although he was conscious, he could speak only with great difficulty and pain. On several occasions, he had told his family of his intense suffering, and he had tried to rip off the attachment to the respirator. Each time, the respirator had been reattached when the alarm sounded. He finally retained an attorney, who petitioned the Broward County Circuit Court to have the respirator removed. At the bedside hearing, the judge approved the request. However, the state attorney general got involved and argued that anyone who helped to disconnect the respirator would be guilty of assisting a suicide. The case was sent to the district court of appeals.[38]

That court observed that the family was supportive of the patient's wishes: "Abe Perlmutter should be allowed to make his

choice to die with dignity, notwithstanding over a dozen legislative failures in this state to adopt suitable legislation in this field.
It is all very convenient to insist on continuing Mr. Perlmutter's
life so that there can be no question of foul play, no resulting civil
liability and no possible trespass on medical ethics. However, it
is quite another matter to do so at the patient's sole expense and
against his competent will, thus inflicting never ending physical
torture on his body until the inevitable, but artificially suspended,
moment of death. Such a course of conduct invades the patient's
constitutional right of privacy, removes his freedom of choice
and invades his right to self-determination."[39]

Case of a Patient with Severe Cerebral Palsy, Competent and Not Terminally Ill, Who Wanted to Forgo Food and Water

Remember the history of Elizabeth Bouvia from Chapter 4.
Her case is one of the most significant since the *Quinlan* case
because it was the first case (1983) in the United States to allow
the removal of food and water from a patient who was neither
terminally ill nor incompetent.

Afflicted with cerebral palsy since birth, at age twenty-eight
she was bedridden, in acute pain, quadriplegic, helpless, financially insolvent, and in a public hospital. Totally dependent on
others for care, she also suffered from degenerative and severely
crippling arthritis, and she was receiving morphine through a
tube attached to her chest to relieve some of the pain and discomfort. She was intelligent and competent. Forced by mounting
expenses to accept public assistance, on several occasions she
had expressed a desire to die. She was being spoon-fed in the
hospital, and her weight had dropped to sixty-five pounds, so
tube-feeding was imposed against her will and against her written instructions.

The appeals court affirmed that everyone in California has a
right to refuse medical treatment, including artificial feeding, and
the right not to be kept alive against his or her will. The court
further affirmed that it was her right to die if that was her wish,

and that the forceful placement of tubes in her body was a violation of her constitutional rights.

The court stated: "Here, if force-fed, petitioner faces 15 to 20 years of a painful existence, endurable only by the constant administration of morphine. Her condition is irreversible. There is no cure for her palsy or arthritis. Petitioner would have to be fed, cleaned, turned, bedded, toileted, by others for 15 to 20 years! Although alert, bright, sensitive, perhaps even brace and feisty, she must lie immobile, unable to exist except through physical acts of others. Her mind and spirit may be free to take great flights, but she herself is imprisoned and must lie physically helpless subject to the ignominy, embarrassment, humiliation and dehumanizing aspects created by her helplessness. We do not believe it is the policy of this state that all and every life must be preserved against the will of the sufferer. It is incongruous, if not monstrous, for medical practitioners to assert their right to preserve a life that someone else must live, or, more accurately, 'endure for 15 to 20 years.' "[40]

Another point of litigation developed later when it was discovered that Bouvia was not receiving sufficient morphine at the High Desert Hospital. The judge ordered that she be given morphine at its former dosage and that she be transferred to another facility.

It is true that, between 1983 and 1986, her condition improved and she was no longer requesting assistance in starving herself to death, but she was asking to be able to reject the tubal feeding of the supplemental food she could not ingest orally.

Despite recognition of this landmark case, new cases continue to appear in court each year with slightly different twists. On June 24, 1987, three "right-to-die" cases were decided simultaneously by the New Jersey Supreme Court. They were about three women in their twenties, thirties, and sixties, with different medical conditions and different treatment situations in nursing homes and at home. Providing important guidance for the future, the analysis made in these three cases represents the most comprehensive and thoughtful coverage of a person's right to refuse medical treatment, including artificial feeding, whether that person is about to die or may be maintained indefinitely if treatment is continued.

The main thrust of these three court decisions is that medical decisions should be made not by the court, but by the patient or by the family, close friends, and doctors. As long as good-faith actions are carried out, the New Jersey Supreme Court has declared that no civil or criminal liabilities will ensue.[41] Let us briefly review these three landmark cases.

Case of a Nursing-Home Patient in a Persistent Vegetative State Who Had Signed a Power of Attorney

Hilda Peter, a sixty-five-year-old former hospital worker, collapsed in her kitchen in October 1984. Her friend, Eberhard Johanning, called the paramedics, who resuscitated her, but she remained in a persistent vegetative state. In a nursing home from January 1985, she was kept alive by nasogastric feeding. In 1983, she had executed a power of attorney specifically authorizing Johanning to make all health-care decisions on her behalf, having clearly expressed to her friends, "Under no circumstances would I want to be kept alive on a life-support system. I've seen too much of this at the hospital, and that's not for me." On another occasion, she had said, "When it's time to die and God wants to take me, I never want to linger around like my mother."

The court rejected the argument that the mere withdrawal of food and water causes death directly: "Withdrawal of the nasogastric tube, like discontinuance of other kinds of artificial treatment, merely acquiesces in the natural cessation of a critical bodily function."[42] In other words, the court made no distinction between artificial feeding and other life-sustaining treatments, and it affirmed that the withdrawal itself is not what causes death.

Then the court established a set of guidelines. First, the surrogate decision maker should inform the state's Ombudsman for the Institutionalized Elderly that a decision has been made to forgo treatment. The ombudsman then should obtain two independent medical opinions to confirm the patient's medical condition, the alternatives available, the risks involved, the likely outcome if medical treatment is discontinued, and assurance that recovery to a cognitive, sapient state cannot be reasonably expected. Then, if there is "clear and convincing evidence" that the patient has designated a family member or a surrogate to make decisions concerning life support, the ombudsman should defer to this designated person. If there is no designated person, a guardian must be appointed.

One of the issues brought out by the ombudsman was that Hilda Peter, unlike other patients in similar cases, was not expected to die within a year with the tube in place, but the court said the ombudsman was mistaken and should consider the *Quinlan* case for comparison. The court held that the test to be applied was whether there was a reasonable possibility that the patient would return to a cognitive and sapient state, which was not the case. Hilda Peter died on November 23, 1987, a few days after removal of the feeding tube.

Case of a Young Woman with Lou Gehrig's Disease Wanting to Get Off a Respirator in Her Own Home

Kathleen Farrell began to experience symptoms of amyotrophic lateral sclerosis in her early thirties. The disease typically destroys muscles, but it does not affect mental functioning. Eventually, she was admitted to a Philadelphia hospital, where she underwent a tracheotomy and was later connected to a respirator. A few months later, she was discharged and sent home with the respirator to live with her husband and her two teenage sons.

While at home, she required around-the-clock nursing care because she was totally paralyzed. Two years later, in November 1985, after an experimental program that her husband had labeled "their last hope," Mrs. Farrell asked to be disconnected from the respirator. Her doctor asked to consult a psychologist to determine whether she was clinically depressed. The psychologist concluded that Mrs. Farrell was not depressed, did not need psychiatric treatment, and furthermore was informed, voluntary, and competent.

On June 13, 1986, Mr. Farrell applied to the court to become special guardian for medical decisions concerning his wife, with specific authority to disconnect her respirator. He also asked for a declaratory judgment stating that he or anyone helping him in disconnecting the respirator would be immune from civil or criminal liability. At one of the hearings, when asked why she wanted to disconnect the respirator and let nature take its course, Mrs. Farrell answered, "I'm tired of suffering." After the closing arguments, the trial court granted all the relief Mrs. Farrell had asked for, but it decided to postpone the order pending further review by the appellate court. Meanwhile, Kathleen died while still connected to the respirator.

Because this case was so important, because of the inevitability of cases like this one arising in the future, and because of urging by Mr. Farrell and the children's guardian *ad litem*, the New Jersey Supreme Court agreed to render a decision. In a unanimous decision, the court reaffirmed that a patient's right to refuse medical treatment, even at the risk of personal injury or death, is protected by the common law and the federal and state constitutional rights of privacy.

This case is particularly important because it represents a cornerstone in legal thinking on the subject of life support. The court concluded that (1) as a general rule, the patient, the family, and the doctors, not the courts are most properly involved in medical decisions; (2) in the case of a competent adult, it is primarily that person who should make the decisions; and (3) no civil or criminal liability can attach to good-faith actions in accordance with the patient's decision. This was the first time that a court had provided a kind of judicial deregulation, while providing some boundaries within which patients and families can act in privacy without court involvement.[43]

Case of a Young Pregnant Woman, Unconscious after an Auto Accident, Who Was Maintained by Tube-Feeding

Nancy Ellen Jobes was twenty-five and was four-and-a-half months pregnant when she was involved in an automobile accident in March 1980. During an operation to remove the fetus, which did not survive, she suffered severe loss of oxygen to the brain and irreversible brain damage. In July 1980, she was moved to a nursing home, and artificial feeding was provided, first by nasogastric tube, and later through a J-tube inserted through the abdominal wall into her small intestine (jejunostomy). In addition, she needed a tracheotomy to breathe, and she was receiving antibiotics and antiseizure medicines.

After five years, Nancy Jobes's husband and her parents requested the removal of the J-tube, which provided hydration and nutrition. The nursing home made several legal motions to resist the removal of the tube, finally appealing the trial court's decision approving removal to the New Jersey Supreme Court. The Society for the Right to Die and several other organizations filed a brief as *amicis curiae.*

On June 24, 1987, over a year after the trial court had authorized the removal of the tube, the New Jersey Supreme Court approved discontinuation of the tube-feeding by a 6–1 decision. Meanwhile, the nursing home had continued to challenge earlier decisions by asking several courts to postpone the removal of the tube pending further review, but all the courts denied the request. In the interim, Nancy Jobes was moved to Morristown Memorial Hospital, where all life support was withdrawn. She died a few days later.[44]

Because Nancy Jobes had never clearly made her views known to anyone regarding life-support measures, the court decided that there was insufficient evidence to meet the clear and convincing standard of the subjective test. Therefore, the court deferred the judgment to the family members, unless a health professional had doubts about whether the family had the patient's best interest at heart. Another major breakthrough in the *Jobes* decision was that institutions now must honor treatment refusals by patients or their surrogates, and that institutions must inform patients upon admission about their policies regarding forgoing treatment.

Case of a Teenager in a Persistent Vegetative State after an Auto Accident, Whose Parents Wanted Removal of Life Support

Chad Eric Swan was just over seventeen years old when he was in a car accident on January 20, 1989. Suffering severe facial and head injuries that led to unconsciousness, he was diagnosed as being in a persistent vegetative state with no chance of recovery.

On September 5, 1989, his father, his mother, and his older brother asked the court for permission to remove the gastrostomy tube providing him with food and nourishment without incurring civil and criminal liability of the family, the attending physician, and the hospital. The guardian *ad litem* who was appointed supported the family, as did the State Department of Human Services. But the district attorney disagreed with the plan. Because Chad had developed serious complications in the form of wound infections around the gastrostomy tube, and because a major surgical procedure would be required to correct the situation, the attending physician recommended that Chad be allowed to die. The parents and coguardians agreed.

On January 10, 1990, the trial court approved the order for the removal of Chad's tube with the consent of his guardians, stating that the decision resided with the family, the guardian, and the attending physician. Meanwhile, a central venous tube had been inserted to maintain hydration until the final legal decision was obtained.

The Maine Supreme Court was unanimous in its decision to affirm the lower court's recommendation to remove the feeding tube. It stated, "When an individual has clearly and convincingly in advance of treatment expressed his decision not to be maintained by life sustaining procedures in a vegetative state, health care professionals must respect that decision." Furthermore, the court ruled that Chad's age was not significant: "Capacity exists when the minor has the ability of the average person to understand and weigh the risks and benefits."

The decision was based on previous statements that Chad had made to his parents when speaking about the *Gardner* case, which had been publicized in the area where he lived. It was the case of a twenty-two-year-old who, after he fell from the back of a moving pickup truck, never regained consciousness. Referring to that case, Chad had wondered why Joseph Gardner was not allowed to die, and he said to his mother, "If I can't be myself . . . no way . . . let me go to sleep." In another conversation with his brother a week before the accident, after visiting a comatose friend in the hospital, he said, "I don't ever want to get like that. I would want somebody to let me leave—to go in peace."[45] Relying on clear and convincing evidence to allow the parents to proceed with the decision, as in the *Gardner* case, the court did not have to rely on the principle of substitutive judgment.[46]

Case of a Woman Who Suffered Severe Brain Damage after a Hiking Accident and Received Tube-Feeding in a Nursing Home

Shirley Crabtree fell while hiking on the island of Oahu on January 5, 1986, and suffered severe brain damage. She could not care for herself or manage her physical, mental, and personal needs, so she was taken to a nursing home, where she was maintained on a nasogastric feeding tube.

Two years later, her husband died, and her son, an attorney, was appointed successor guardian on December 1, 1988. As an attorney, he appeared as his own lawyer as well as the guardian of the person of Shirley Crabtree on behalf of his mother, his sister, and himself. At the hearing, there were representatives of the Hawaii Office of the Public Guardian, but representatives of the City and County of Honolulu, the State of Hawaii, and the

Island Nursing Home waived the right to appear and declined to take any position on the issues.

This case was unusual in that Shirley Crabtree could not be clearly diagnosed as being in a persistent vegetative state. There were differing medical opinions about her level of awareness and ability to communicate. It was agreed, however, that she was in a "pervasive, irreversible, and deteriorating physical and mental condition." The court acknowledged that the medical opinions varied, but it also recognized that Mrs. Crabtree would not oppose the petition requesting the discontinuation of tube-feeding.

To support the petition, the son recalled that she had made statements to friends and family that, if she were ever to become "totally and permanently disabled, she would not want to be kept alive." The court also noted that, although there was no advance directive, the Hawaii living-will statute explicitly states, "In the absence of a declaration, ordinary standards of current medical practice will be followed." In this case, the court concluded that withdrawal of the feeding tube was "accepted as ordinary, current medical practice in Hawaii under the facts of this case if that is the decision of the attending physician and family members." Furthermore, the court also recognized that artificial feeding was not a procedure meant to provide comfort and relief in this case and therefore could be withdrawn without detriment to the patient.[47]

Shirley Crabtree died on May 8, 1990, four years after her accident, and six days after the feeding tube was removed.[48]

This case is different in that it is one of the few cases in which the patient had severe brain damage but was not in a persistent vegetative state. The final decision was based essentially on the principle of substitutive judgment. The reasoning in the case also took into account the current Hawaii living-will statute, which, when there is no living will, gives great flexibility to the decision makers, namely, the family and the physicians. It also cited the Hawaii Constitution's right to privacy, thus creating an important precedent.

LEGAL IMPLICATIONS OF THE *CRUZAN* CASE

In the *Cruzan* case, discussed in Chapter 1, the U.S. Supreme Court affirmed constitutional support for the right to die, but varying interpretations of the decision have been confusing to many, including health-care professionals. To clarify the implications of the *Cruzan* decision, a group of bioethicists published a statement in the *New England Journal of Medicine* summarizing the major points of that decision.[49]

First, the Supreme Court affirmed the right of competent patients to refuse life-sustaining treatment.

Second, the Court did not see any difference between the forgoing of artificial nutrition and hydration and the forgoing of other forms of medical treatment.

Third, the only reservation held in the *Cruzan* case was that the State of Missouri could require the continued treatment of a patient in a persistent vegetative state unless there was "clear and convincing evidence" that she had explicitly authorized the termination of treatment before losing the capacity to make decisions for herself.

Fourth, the Court did not require that other states adopt Missouri's rigorous standard of proof, nor did it preclude Missouri from adopting a different standard of evidence in the future.

Fifth, the Court did not attempt in the *Cruzan* decision to change any of the laws, ethical standards, or clinical practices allowing the forgoing of life-sustaining treatment that have evolved in the United States since the *Quinlan* case in 1976.

The bioethicists recommended that physicians continue to follow the guidelines of the medical profession and current practices concerning life-support measures, keeping in mind the particular laws of their own states. They urged all doctors to discuss the use of life-sustaining treatments with all of their patients so as to learn the patient's preferences and values. They stressed that it is important for patients to discuss their preferences with their families and close friends and to prepare advance directives.

There is not much question that the *Cruzan* decision will have a profound impact on future legislation throughout the country. Lawmakers will now be urged to develop right-to-die legislation rather than continue to proceed on a case-by-case basis.[50] Already five states (Montana, Georgia, Tennessee, North Dakota, and West Virginia) have expanded the rights of patients to refuse unwanted life-sustaining treatment.

But some legal experts feel that the ruling, which allows some states to require a "clear and convincing evidence" standard, is unfortunate. Attorney Susan M. Wolf, associate for law at the Hastings Center, a bioethics think tank in Briarcliff Manor, New York, fears that the ruling will be misunderstood by doctors, who may think that this ruling applies in all states. In actuality, at this writing, the standard of clear and convincing evidence applies only in the states of Missouri, New York, and Maine. On the other hand, most states will apply the tests of substitutive judgment and the "best interest" standard.[51]

The main problem, according to some ethicists, is that there is a mythology among caregivers that the rights of patients and doctors are extremely limited when it comes to making decisions about life-support measures. Wolf claims that this is simply not true, and therefore doctors should not shy away from discussing this issue with patients and their families.

The *Cruzan* decision may have appeared complicated in the way it was presented. Stuart Westbury, president of the American College of Healthcare Executives, says "The Supreme Court always has a way of not answering the whole question." However, the Court did say, according to him, that "individuals have the 'liberty' to reject treatment, and that they had better do it clearly and explicitly." The solution, he says, is to encourage people to develop a living will and a durable power of attorney with very explicit statements.

NEW LEGISLATION:
THE PATIENT SELF-DETERMINATION ACT

In its 1990 session, Congress passed new legislation known as the Patient Self-Determination Act, which took effect on December 1, 1990. The law requires hospitals, skilled-nursing facilities, home health agencies, and hospice programs that receive Medicare and Medicaid patients to maintain certain policies and procedures. To comply with this law, these institutions must provide each patient with written information describing her or his rights under the state law. This information must describe the right to refuse treatment and the types of advance directives available, including the living will and the durable power of attorney (DPA). The law also requires that these documents be entered into the patient's medical record, along with a statement on whether the patient has a durable power of attorney. The law also mandates the formation of ethics committees in all institutions qualifying for Medicare and Medicaid.

As you might expect, this law has stirred debate among practitioners and ethicists. John Fletcher, former director of the Center for Biomedical Ethics at the University of Virginia, thought that the act would be very helpful.[52] He believed that the law has the following three main goals.

The first goal is to give every adult an opportunity to learn about end-of-life choices during a hospital or nursing-home admission. It will provide the newly admitted patient with information about the option to sign an advance directive and a durable power of attorney in case the patient should become incapable after admission.

The second goal is to provide a supportive climate within the institution so that the first goal can be implemented. This means that hospitals will have to establish ethics committees, which will help educate health-care providers and facilitate the decision-making process in complex cases.

The third goal is to require all the remaining states that have not yet enacted a natural death act to do so.

Fletcher believed that the mandate for hospitals to develop hospital committees has some merit. Even though hospital ethics committees grew rapidly in the 1980s, many hospitals still do not have them.[53] Only 30 percent of hospitals in Virginia, for example, have an ethics committee, even though the 1983 President's Commission actively recommended the establishment of such committees in the hope that they would help competent patients in their decision making.

The law also has its critics. Alexander Capron, a professor of law and medicine at UCLA, believes that there are several problems.[54] First, there will be considerable difficulty in implementing the giving of information to the patient on admission to the hospital. The admitting clerk, who is usually charged with asking the patient to sign various forms, is not the right person to discuss this delicate issue and to explain the documents to the patient. Nor is it the best time to bring up such issues in a formalistic approach.

Second, the statute will give the wrong message to physicians about who should discuss the directives and when. The implication is that the federal government has mandated that it is the job of hospitals to confer with patients about their living wills and durable powers of attorney. Capron feels that discussion about advance directives belongs in the routine care that physicians give to their patients.

Because the law is already in effect, it is all the more important that both health professionals and the public become better informed, which is the basic purpose of this book.

PROPOSED LEGISLATION

Since 1990, several proposals for new legislation have been made to provide some uniformity of rules and guidelines throughout the country. The following acts are in the process of being studied by legislative committees and bodies.

Uniform Rights of the Terminally Ill Act

Most states have a patchwork of statutes and court decisions, none of which provide a safe form of protection for patients who wish to refuse life-support treatments. The National Conference of Commissioners on Uniform Laws has issued a model of legislation designed to improve this situation.[55] The newly proposed document is a revised version of a 1985 proposal and is intended to make state laws similar to one another.

One of the advantages of the newly proposed act is that it combines three of the basic statutory provisions that protect the individual patient's right to die: the living will, the durable power of attorney, and the provision for surrogate decision making. Rose Gasner, a staff attorney for the Society for the Right to Die, says, "We think it's the best draft legislation to date. It has all three major features and it's in very straightforward language. It's simple."[56]

Despite its relative simplicity and attempt to be concise, the act still includes some definitions that may cause confusion. For example, the act defines *terminal condition* as an "incurable and irreversible condition that, without the administration of life-sustaining treatment, will, in the opinion of the attending physician, result in death within a relatively short time." But certain statutes and health providers prefer to use the more specific term *terminal illness* because it implies a disease process that will lead to death, whereas *terminal condition* is not limited to disease. Yet the act requires that the "terminal condition" be "incurable and irreversible," and there is no mention of the possibility of reversibility.

Some statutes have related the terminal condition to patients whose death is "imminent," a term whose meaning can range from a few hours to a year. Others say that if death is really imminent, there is little point in having a statute that permits the withdrawal of life-sustaining treatment, which is "any procedure or intervention that, when administered to a qualified patient, will serve only to prolong the process of dying." Therefore the two terms *terminal condition* and *life-sustaining treatment* cannot be taken individually because they are really interdependent and "must be read together."[57]

Finally, like other statutes, the Uniform Rights of the Terminally Ill Act would provide legal immunity to physicians and other health-care providers when they act according to the patient's instructions, even though the act does not compel them to perform actions against their own ethical standards. However if the physician or the hospital has ethical objections that prohibit them from acceding to the patient's wishes, they should take reasonable steps to transfer the care of the patient to another doctor or hospital. In fact, doctors who do not comply with the act's requirements might incur penalties, which have yet to be determined.[58]

The Death with Dignity Act

The Death with Dignity Act was drafted by several attorneys headed by Robert Risley, a Los Angeles lawyer. Risley became personally involved in the right-to-die issue after his wife died of cancer in the Bahamas in December 1984. With some colleagues, he founded an organization called Americans against Human Suffering, dedicated to enacting state laws that permit, on request, physician aid in dying for the terminally ill. The organization has 27,000 supporters throughout the United States, Canada, Australia, and Europe.

The main thrust of the act is that it involves "love and caring enough to permit dying people to end their suffering with the help of a physician rather than being forced to endure the agony of the dying process to the bitter end."[59] According to Risley, it involves letting patients or loved ones go when they are ready.

The basic and fundamental right incorporated in this act is that everyone should have the freedom to choose the time and place of her or his own death at the end of life. This right is based on the fundamental belief that all of us should have control over our own destiny. This freedom is being equated with the freedom of worship, the freedom to express oneself, the freedom to petition the government for redress, and the freedom to choose the school for our children.

The Death with Dignity Act (DDA) was the first attempt in this country to propose an "active euthanasia" alternative by petition in California on the November 1988 ballot. It did not qualify because of failure to get the required number of signatures. Washington State presented Initiative 119 to its voters in November 1991 to provide physicians' aid in dying. It was narrowly defeated by a 54 percent to 46 percent vote after very active anti-initiative campaigns led by the Catholic Church and right-to-life organizations. The Hemlock Society of Oregon is actively campaigning to get an Oregon version of the DDA passed.

The proponents of the DDA argue that, although current legislative efforts aim at supporting the right to refuse treatments such as being on a respirator or the artificial tube-feeding of water and nourishment, these withdrawals are not without considerable discomfort and needless suffering. For example, if the patient is on a respirator, removing it will cause death by suffocation. If the patient is on artificial feeding, the patient will probably die of starvation or dehydration when the tubes are removed. The removal of these life supports are permitted under the law, but they are not very appealing. In fact, to some people, they might even be frightening. In many cases, the dying process is not made easy by the withdrawal of these supports.

The DDA aims at providing a more humane way for patients to die by permitting physicians to use analgesics, sedatives, and anesthetics. In this way, patients would die in the dignified and peaceful manner requested. When used in proper dosages, these medications completely and painlessly suppress respiration, thus allowing the patient to die a "good death" without pain or turmoil.

The DDA would not be limited to patients on life support, but would also apply to any patient who is terminally ill. Even the legal profession is providing support for this idea. Judge Lynn Comptom, who decided the *Bouvia* case, stated, "The right to die is an integral part of our right to control our destinies so long as the rights of others are not affected. *The right should, in my opinion, include the ability to enlist assistance from others, including the medical profession, in making death as painless and quick as possible* . . . If there is a time when we ought to be able to get the government off our backs, it is when we face death—either by choice or otherwise."

This freedom, Risley asserts, is not suicide. It is not blind, irrational self-destruction. It is one way to take a rational approach to ending life when all hope is lost in end-stage disease.

The DDA would confer on all competent terminally ill adults the right to request and to receive a physician's aid in dying, carefully defined circumstances. Combining the two previous California laws (the California Natural Death Act and the Durable Power of Attorney for Health Care Decisions Act), the DDA states that adults can declare their desire not to be kept alive artificially by life-support systems and that they can appoint an attorney-in-fact or a surrogate decision maker to make health care decisions, including withholding or withdrawing life support, if as patients they become incompetent. The DDA adds the provision that all competent terminally ill adult patients have the right to request and to receive aid in dying from a physician. This provision would immunize physicians and health-care workers from liability in responding to a patient's request for aid in dying, provided the request is in writing and conforms to the strict rules spelled out in the act.

Let us briefly review the directive and the conditions that must be satisfied according to the Death with Dignity Act.

First, competent patients must sign a DDA directive in the presence of two disinterested witnesses. Witnesses cannot be beneficiaries, heirs, or creditors of the patient, nor can they be health-care providers. The patients must designate someone to act for them if they become incompetent. They must specify that they request that their lives not be prolonged artificially and/or that their lives be ended, on request, with the help of a physician. Also, if patients so desire, they can also empower the surrogate decision maker to make the request for aid in dying. Second, patients must inform their families and show that they have discussed the matter with them. Although a patient may have heard opposing opinions from family members, the final decision will rest with the patient as long as she or he is competent. The directive will be valid for seven years, although it can be extended indefinitely if the patient becomes incompetent during that period.

Several conditions must be met before the physician may legally comply with the patient's directive:

1. The DDA directive must be properly signed by a competent adult and by two appropriate witnesses (see above).
2. It must be in effect and not revoked. The directive may be revoked by being canceled, defaced, burned, torn, or destroyed by the signer or the signer's designate.
3. The directive is valid for only seven years.
4. Two physicians must certify that the patient is terminally ill and that death is likely to occur within six months.
5. One of the certifying physicians must be the treating physician, but the two physicians must be independent of each other; that is, they cannot be partners in the same medical practice.
6. If the patient becomes incompetent after the physicians' certification, and if the final decision is made by a surrogate, the decision must be reviewed by a three-person ethics committee.
7. The treating physician, with the patient's consent, may order a psychiatric or psychological consultation if the physician is uncertain about the patient's competence to make the request for the physician's aid in dying.[60]

As you would expect, there are many opponents to the Death with Dignity Act, including many from the medical profession. In the spring of 1990, I attended a conference where Risley was the main speaker and where he presented his views and the various points of the DDA. During the question-and-answer period, the debate became heated between the audience of health professionals and the panel members, who also represented strongly held views. For a detailed commentary on the Death with Dignity Act, please refer to Appendix G.

As the DDA introduces the topic of active euthanasia, I deal with euthanasia in the next chapter.

NOTES

1. George J. Annas, "At Law: Brain, Death and Organ Donation: You Can Have One without the Other," *Hastings Center Report* 18 (1988): 28–30.
2. Arthur S. Berger and Joyce Berger, ed., *To Die or Not to Die: Cross-Disciplinary, Cultural, and Legal Perspectives on the Right to Choose Death* (New York: Praeger, 1990), 37.
3. Robert M. Veatch, *Death, Dying and the Biological Revolution: Our Last Quest for Responsibility* (New Haven, CN: Yale University Press, 1989), 158–165.
4. Robert L. Risley, *Death with Dignity: A New Law Permitting Physician Aid-in-Dying* (Eugene, OR: Hemlock Society, 1989), 11–12.
5. California Natural Death Act. (1976) Chapter 1439, Code Health and Safety Sections: sections 7185–95.
6. Veatch, 158.
7. Ibid., 158–162.
8. Society for the Right to Die, *The Physician and the Hopelessly Ill Patient: Legal, Medical and Ethical Guidelines* (New York: Society for the Right to Die, 1985).
9. Society for the Right to Die, "Geographical Charts of State Laws Governing Durable Power of Attorney, Health Care Agents, Proxy Appointments: Tubefeeding Law in the U.S. Living Will Legislation," 5 June 1991.
10. Barbara Mishkin, *A Matter of Choice: Planning Ahead for Health Care Decisions* (Washington, DC: American Association of Retired Persons, 1986).
11. Veatch, 163.
12. State of Virginia, "Virginia Natural Death Act," *Va. Code Ann. Stat.* 2 (1984), 54-325.
13. Veatch, 164–165.
14. *Nathanson v. Kline*, 186 Kan. 350 P. 2nd 1093 (1960).
15. Veatch, 94.

16. Berger and Berger, 132–135.
17. Union Pacific Railway Co. v. Botsford, 141 U.S. 350, U.S. Supreme Court.
18. Berger and Berger, 132–135.
19. *Brophy v. New England Sinai Hospital, Inc.,* 398 Mass. 417, 497 N.E. 2nd 626 (1986).
20. Berger and Berger, 144.
21. Society for the Right to Die, *Right-to-Die Decisions,* Vol. 1 (New York: Society for the Right to Die, 1976–1990), MA-7.
22. Veatch, 118.
23. Risley, 31–35.
24. *Bartling v. Superior Court,* 163 Cal. App. 3rd 186, 209 Cal. Rptr. 220 (1984).
25. Society for the Right to Die, 1976–1986, *Right to Die Court Decisions,* vol. 1, CA-3.
26. Berger and Berger, 140–141.
27. Ibid., 142–143.
28. R.M. Hare, *Applications of Moral Philosophy* (Berkeley, University of California Press, 1972), 68.
29. Berger and Berger, 143–144.
30. Ibid.
31. *Barber v. Superior Court,* 2nd District 147 Cal. App. 3rd 1006, 195 Cal. Rptr. 484 (1983).
32. Society for the Right to Die. *Right to Die Court Decisions,* vol. 1, CA-3, Bartling v. Superior Court, 163 Cal. App. 3rd 186, 209 Cal. Rptr. 220 (Ct. App. 1984).
33. *John F. Kennedy Memorial Hospital, Inc. v. Bludworth,* 452 So. 2nd 921 (Fla. 1984) (1984).
34. Berger and Berger, 145.
35. Society for the Right to Die. *Right to Die Court Decisions,* vol. 1, MA-1, 1977. Superintendent of Belchertown State School v. Saikewicz, 373 Mass. 728, 370 N.E. 2nd 417 (1977).
36. Ronald B. Schram et al., " 'No Code' Orders: Clarification in the Aftermath of Saikewicz," *New England Journal of Medicine* 299 (1978): 875.
37. Society for the Right to Die. *Right to Die Court Decisions,* vol. 1, MA-3, 1976–1986. In re Dinnerstein, 6 Mass. App. 466 380 N.E. 2nd 134 (Ct. App. 1978).
38. Society for the Right to Die. *Right to Die Court Decisions,* vol. 1, FL-1,

1976–1986. Satz v. Perlmutter, 362 So. 2nd 160 (Fla. Ct. App. 1978) aff'd 379 So. 2nd 359 (Fla. 1980).

39. *Satz v. Perlmutter,* 379 So. 2nd 359 (Fla. 1980) (1978).
40. Risley, 22–23.
41. Society for the Right to Die. *Right to Die Court Decisions,* vol. 2, NJ-1, NJ-4, NJ-8. In re Farrell, 108 N.J. 335, 529 A. 2nd 404 (1987). In re Peter, 108 N.J. 365, 529 A. 2nd 419 (1987). In re Jobes, 108 N.J. 394, 529 A. 2nd 434 (1987).
42. Risley, 24–25.
43. Society for the Right to Die, vol. 2; NJ-I, 1987.
44. Society for the Right to Die, vol. 2; NJ-8 1987.
45. Society for the Right to Die. *Right to Die Court Decisions,* vol. 3, ME-1, 1990. In re Chad Eric Swan, 569 A.2nd 1202 (Me. 1990).
46. Ibid.
47. Society for the Right to Die. *Right to Die Court Decisions,* vol. 3, 1990. In re Guardianship of Crabtree Ne 86-0031 (Hawaii, Farn, Ct.) 1st Circ. April 26, 1990 (Heeley, J.).
48. Society for the Right to Die, (vol. 3; H-I, 1990).
49. G. J. Annas et. al., "Bioethicists' Statement on the U.S. Supreme Court's Cruzan Decision," *New England Journal of Medicine* 323 (1990): 686–687.
50. American Health Consultants, "New Right to Die Laws Reflect Aftermath of Cruzan Decision," *Medical Ethics Advisor* 7 (June 1991): 78–79.
51. American Health Consultants, "U.S. Supreme Court Recognizes Constitutional Right to Die," *Medical Ethics Advisor* 6 (July 1991): 85–89.
52. J. C. Fletcher, "The Patient's Self Determination Act: Yes," *Hastings Center Report* (Sept./Oct. 1990) 33–36.
53. Ibid.
54. A. M. Capron, "The Patient Self-Determination Act: Not Now," *Hastings Center Report* (Sept./Oct. 1990): 35–36.
55. American Health Consultants, "Uniform Laws Commission Issues Model 'Right-to-Die' Legislation," *Medical Ethics Advisor* 6(July 1990): 91–94.
56. Ibid.
57. Ibid.
58. Ibid.
59. Risley, vii.
60. Ibid., 48–49.

CHAPTER 8

The Right-to-Die
Movement and Euthanasia

> *When life is so burdensome, death has become for man a sought-after refuge.*
>
> —Herodotus (485–425 B.C.)

Euthanasia, like abortion, capital punishment, suicide, and animal experimentation, raises in people intense emotional reactions and strong convictions. It is the purpose of this chapter and this book not to change people's opinions, but simply to inform and educate. Those who have opinions both for or against euthanasia will find material here to substantiate their beliefs. My purpose is mainly to provide you with background information that will prepare you and your family to make educated and intelligent choices when the time comes to meet the challenge of life's ending.

WHAT IS EUTHANASIA?

The word *euthanasia* comes from the Greek words *eu* ("well") and *thanatos* ("death"). It means a painless and gentle death. But in modern usage, it has come to imply that someone's life is ended for compassionate reasons by some passive or active steps taken by another person. The word has acquired a very bad connotation ever since the Nazis ordered so-called euthanasia to exterminate specific groups of people, such as Jews, communists, and nonaryans. Their acts were in fact the murder of helpless victims and hated enemies because it was perpetrated without the consent of the individuals.

Because of this unfortunate connotation, we need to define euthanasia as it is understood by the modern community in the free world. Today, euthanasia is referred to as either passive or active, even though many feel that the distinction is arbitrary and reflects an attitude rather than a real difference. Nevertheless, active and passive euthanasia are differentiated on the basis of the behavior and the intent of the person who helps another person die.

Passive euthanasia refers to someone's helping another person to die by withholding or withdrawing life-sustaining treatment, including the administration of food and water. It is also known as *euthanasia by omission*. As you recall, we discussed the various legal, moral, and philosophical aspects of this practice in previous chapters. Thus, passive euthanasia is usually requested by the person dying, either verbally or through a written document such as a living will. In passive euthanasia, by withholding intravenous feedings, medications, surgery, a pacemaker, or a respirator, the doctor can let the patient die of the underlying disease.

Active euthanasia, on the other hand, refers to someone's taking active steps to give a dying person, *on his or her request*, a lethal dosage of drugs in order to hasten death. The press frequently refers to "mercy killings" as being synonymous with euthanasia. Technically, that is incorrect, as *mercy killing* is a term reserved for shooting or strangulation only, methods not approved by people who want euthanasia. It is unfortunate that these two terms are sometimes used interchangeably.

The debate over the moral, ethical, and legal bases for euthanasia has spilled considerable ink since the early 1970s and will probably continue to do so into the twenty-first century. Before I mention the major points usually made for or against euthanasia, let me briefly give some historical background. Because many of the arguments and reasonings for passive euthanasia were discussed in the last chapter, I focus primarily on active euthanasia in the next sections. At times, however, you should note that the arguments for or against active euthanasia have been raised about passive euthanasia as well.

Discussions about euthanasia tend to be generalized and not to take into account the fact that it encompasses several acts that are vastly different. Among these acts are so-called mercy killings, the act of allowing a person to die, carrying out decisions to stop treatment, administering treatments that are risky to life, and exercising the right to refuse treatment. It is of utmost importance that these distinctions be made before public policies are instituted.[1]

HISTORICAL PERSPECTIVE ON THE RIGHT TO DIE

The Romans and the Greeks believed that it was important for individuals to be able to die decently and rationally and to experience a dignified death. In Athens, magistrates kept a supply of poison on hand for anyone who wished to die by poison. Even though official permission was required, it was not difficult to get.

In the second and third centuries, A.D., Stoicism was denounced under Christian rule. Anyone taking her or his life was denied a Christian burial, and it became impossible for anyone to gain any kind of merciful relief from an affliction, no matter how painful or horrible.

During the Renaissance, educated people began to move away from the condemnation of suicide. In Europe, and later in America, the right-to-die movement began to gain momentum. Since the early 1960s, legislatures have struggled with laws relating to living wills, aid in dying, and power of attorney.

The modern euthanasia movement began in England in 1935, when notables such as George Bernard Shaw and H. G. Wells started a Voluntary Euthanasia Society. Later, the society became known by the name Exit. In the United States, the movement was begun by a Unitarian minister, Charles Potter, under the name Society for the Right to Die. In the early 1970s, other voluntary euthanasia societies were formed in the Netherlands and in Australia as the two-edged blade of modern medical technology became obvious.

The major turning point in the United States occurred when the tragic 1976 case of Karen Ann Quinlan became known to everyone as she was kept alive for eight years after slipping into a coma from an overdose of medication. As worldwide attention raised the public's awareness of the need to think about such matters in advance, the reaction eventually led to the passage of the first living-will law in California. That law enables people to state that they do not wish to be kept alive on artificial life support if their prognosis is hopeless and if they are terminally ill. To anyone interested in a detailed history of the evolution of the right-to-die movement throughout the centuries, I recommend *The Right to Die* by Derek Humphry and Ann Wickett, published in 1986.[2]

In the 1970s, a whole field of study called *bioethics* evolved from the narrower subject of medical ethics, developing a vast scholarly literature by experts known as *ethicists*. This new field has involved scholars from the fields of philosophy, theology, medicine, and law. Judges have become increasingly involved in cases that have been challenged in courts of various jurisdictions and at various levels. Many examples of case law and constitutional law were discussed in the last chapter.

The law is intimately involved in right-to-die issues in many different ways. Suicide, for example, is not illegal in the United States today, although that was not always so, but helping someone to commit suicide is against the law, although several states have introduced legislation to deal directly with aid in dying. Instances of active euthanasia, in which a person or a doctor actively helped someone in the dying process often have led to charges of murder, although in most cases, the charges have been dismissed or the defendant has merely been put on probation. Yet the problems surrounding the right to die are particularly difficult when they involve incompetent persons, children severely handicapped at birth, or demented individuals.

WHY WOULD ANYONE
WANT EUTHANASIA TODAY?

There are at least three major reasons why people may request euthanasia when they are competent, terminally ill or not.

First, people may wish to *avoid or end unbearable pain* during a terminal illness. Opponents of the euthanasia movement argue that most patients can get adequate relief of pain with appropriate analgesics. In fact, the National Institute of Aging studied the deaths of 1,227 selected residents of Fairfield County, Connecticut, randomly chosen from a list of all those who died in 1984–1985. The researchers reported that 53 percent of the people died in their sleep, and that 80 percent of the people were free of pain the day before they died. Dwight Brock, principal investigator in the survey, concluded, "Not all older persons should necessarily expect to experience a slow, painful or lingering period of dying accompanied by disabilities."[3] Nonetheless, it is well known that 10 to 15 percent of patients experience slow and painful dying in the last few weeks of life.

I have heard from several of my colleagues that physicians, other than those practicing in hospices, are relatively untrained in good pain management.[4] In general, pain management is not practiced by enough physicians in any part of the world, including England, Canada, and the United States.[5]

Second, people may wish to have *a better quality of life*. Of course, defining quality of life is very difficult and highly individual. What may be a miserable quality of life for one person may not be for another. My friend, Bob, whom I discussed in Chapter 1, did not find any reason to continue his life for another few months, knowing that he could no longer be of any use to anyone and that he could no longer enjoy the activities that meant so much to him. Others, however, would find some meaning, as Frankl put it, in the experience of dying itself, even if they are bedridden, terminally ill, and totally dependent on others.

Third, some people may want to hasten death through euthanasia to *prevent unnecessary financial burden on their families.*

When death is inevitable, lingering for many months in a nursing home or in an intensive-care unit at great cost may be a source of realistic concern for some responsible individuals. There is no question that the cost of dying in the United States may be very high and is ruinous for some families: in the Wanglie case discussed in Chapter 5, the cost of care in the hospital and the nursing facility amounted to $800,000 over a period of five months.

Several books have been written on the subject of cost, and the public is generally aware of the problem. Studies have shown that 80 percent of the American health-care budget is spent in the last months of life, usually to provide extraordinary treatments for people who have incurable illnesses.[6] Therefore, some people have argued, euthanasia would allow such individuals to die before the horrendous costs of prolonging life bankrupt their families. Others would say that, this is a sad commentary on our society, which is unable to deal with the basic problem of the economics of health care.

Euthanasia remains an ethical, legal, and philosophical issue for all concerned with health care or health policies. Nevertheless, some people do not want to wait for legislation. They plan for an escape by saving prescription medications in the hope of using them for suicide if they ever become terminally ill. They believe that they can retain a feeling of control over their lives and prevent a painful and undignified death or old age. There are no studies of how many of these people do succeed in taking their own lives. In Chapter 5, we mentioned a few anecdotal reports of well-known people who chose death to avoid suffering or the infirmities of old age. The important recurring element in those decisions was the desire to retain a feeling of control and a sense of dignity in their lives.

In the United States, the subject of euthanasia became reignited when a relatively obscure pathologist from Detroit acceded to a patient's request for active euthanasia. Janet Adkins was a fifty-four-year-old teacher from Oregon, the mother of three grown sons, who had allegedly been diagnosed a year earlier as having Alzheimer's disease, a degenerative disease of the brain. She had always been physically and intellectually active and on learning of the diagnosis, she was devastated. As she slowly became aware that the illness was affecting her ability to function, Mrs. Adkins resolved that she did not want to continue living through a steady deterioration of her abilities and personality. She had already received experimental treatment, but there is still no known cure for Alzheimer's disease. After consulting with several doctors in her area, she resolved that she would end her life.

Mrs. Adkins grew increasingly fearful of the consequences of the disease, and having seen Dr. Jack Kevorkian and his suicide assistance device on television in late 1989, she decided that she would go to meet him in Michigan, where she had heard the legality of assisted suicide described as "murky" and therefore, in her mind, possible.

After confirming the diagnosis of Alzheimer's disease and the fact that Mrs. Adkins was competent, that is, that she understood what she was doing and the nature of her decision and her request, Kevorkian placed an intravenous line in her arm. He explained to her that she would first receive an intravenous injection of saline solution, then a second solution with Pentothal, and finally a solution of potassium chloride and succinylcholine. She was then instructed that she could push a red button on the front of the device, which would release the lethal solution of potassium chloride. Six minutes later, she died.

Shortly thereafter, Kevorkian notified the coroner's office, Mr. Adkins, and the *New York Times*, which printed the story on its front page the next day. On learning of the event, Michigan authorities moved very quickly to stop Kevorkian from the further practice of aid in dying. They asked the courts for a temporary restraining order, so that they could impound his car, which contained the device and the drugs. The court also issued an order restraining him from helping anyone else.

Approximately two months after Janet Adkins's death, there was another case in which euthanasia was performed by a man named Robert Bertram Harper. He too had flown to Michigan because of his belief that it would not be illegal there to help his wife, Virginia, commit suicide, as she was dying of widespread cancer. He informed the authorities on his wife's death and was immediately arrested and charged with murder.

Six months later, Kevorkian was also charged with murder. But ten days later, a judge dismissed the case.[7] Much of the controversy centered on the fact that Janet Adkins was not terminal at the time of her suicide. People thought that she had acted prematurely, just as in the case of Jo Roman described in Chapter 4. Much discussion followed about whether Alzheimer's disease can be considered a fatal disease. In one sense, the disease does not kill directly. Patients deteriorate slowly over a period of five to ten years before they develop complications from other diseases, such as heart or lung conditions. Alzheimer's, however, can be viewed as a sort of "partial brain death" in the sense that the person remains conscious although unaware of any meaningful interaction with the environment. The illness may have devastating emotional and financial effects on the family.

In drawing considerable fire in lay and professional circles, the Kevorkian–Adkins case heightened the controversy over euthanasia. Some ethicists, like Arthur Caplan, director of the University of Minnesota Center for Biomedical Ethics, felt that Kevorkian's actions had caused "significant harm to discussions of both active and passive euthanasia." He said, "It will play on the fear many Americans have that doctors might be led to do away with their patients in circumstances where cost and convenience make that seem attractive."[8] Others, like James Bopp, general counsel for the National Right to Life Committee, felt that the Kevorkian type of case illustrates the "slippery slope" problem that euthanasia may bring about. Yet it is interesting that the general public was much more sympathetic with Janet Adkins and Kevorkian. Adkins has become a symbol of patients who vow to maintain their dignity despite a fatal disease.

At a conference I attended on the topic of euthanasia, I heard the following statement made by a layperson who was sharing a personal experience during the question-and-answer period: "Dying is a private and individual experience. My father, who was eighty-seven when he died, had an enormous amount of pain and indignity toward the end. By contrast, my dog, at about the same time, developed an incurable illness. I took my dog to the vet, and the vet said that he didn't have a chance. So I agreed to the dog's being put to sleep. Well, judging from this experience, if I ever get the same illness as my father's, I guess I'll go to a vet, not a doctor."

Meanwhile, experts continue to devote much time to proposing arguments for or against euthanasia in order to defeat or gain legal support. If you are going to follow the continuing debate on euthanasia in the press and on television, you should become familiar with the arguments that are usually brought forth in the debates.

At the same conference I just mentioned, ethicist Edmund Pellegrino of Georgetown University said that he had at least forty-nine reasons why euthanasia was not a good idea. Experts seem to go on endlessly about the reasons that support their own biases, and I do not intend to give you their long list of arguments for or against euthanasia. But if you are interested in an in-depth study of the rationale offered in the debate on euthanasia, I refer you to the reading list at the end of this book. For now, I shall review only the salient points made in these arguments.

WHAT ARE THE ARGUMENTS FOR OR AGAINST EUTHANASIA?

In the following discussion, I first present the arguments in favor of euthanasia, then the arguments against euthanasia, addressing the major points debated by experts.

1. *The relief of suffering and pain.* As mentioned above, 10 to 15 percent of cancer patients suffer significant pain and troublesome symptoms (constipation, nausea, and vomiting) in the last few weeks of life. Although many patients obtain significant relief from their pain with adequate medication and psychologi-

cal support, many do not achieve pain control because physicians tend to underuse analgesia.

Others, however, prefer to hasten death rather than go through deterioration of their physical and mental abilities. They say that euthanasia is more humane than forcing a person into unmitigated suffering. According to this view, there is no moral difference in some circumstances between active euthanasia and the withholding of life-sustaining treatment. In both situations, the eventual result is death, except that the withholding of treatment entails more pain and suffering.[9]

Opponents of euthanasia stress the point that most physical pain can be relieved by analgesic medication.[10,11] This is especially true today, says John Lewin, director of the Department of Health in Hawaii, as patients can regulate morphine in their own home. Nevertheless, the fact that patients may or may not accept the responsibility for that approach should be recognized. Opponents also say that although many physicians get poor training in the management of pain,[12] that is not a valid reason to favor euthanasia.

2. *The sanctity of life.* Although it is true that some people who have strong religious orientation do not want euthanasia, others believe in God and still approve of euthanasia. Even people with a theological background have chosen death over a course of incurable illness or infirmity in old age (see the case of the Van Dusens mentioned in Chapter 4). Gerald A. Larue, emeritus professor of religion and adjunct professor of gerontology at the University of Southern California, and a former president of the Hemlock Society, made a detailed study of the attitudes and views of the world religions on euthanasia.[13]

Religions have views that might be surprising to some. The Catholic view expressed by Pope Pius XII, for example, distinguished between ordinary and extraordinary measures in prolonging life. Ordinary measures are any treatments that patients can obtain or undergo without an excessive burden to themselves or to others. Therefore, the pope concluded, under some circumstances, passive euthanasia through the omission of treatment is theologically acceptable to the Roman Catholic Church.

On the other hand, opponents feel that people, including doctors, do not have the right "to play God." They feel that life is sacred, that "God alone is the author of life and that whatever other rights we may have, the right to take or destroy our own life is not one of them. It expresses a belief that our life is simply not our own, but God's."[14]

3. *The risk of the "slippery slope."* The analogy is often made between euthanasia and the actions of the Nazis. Will the legalization of euthanasia lead to a spreading of the practice to the point of abuse, so that old people, the retarded and demented, the severely handicapped, and all of those who are no longer useful, will be killed for the good of society? Would legalization open the door to genocide, as was practiced in Nazi Germany? Would it not lead to a devaluation of life? The Nazi practices are only partially relevant. The Nazis did not try legal voluntary euthanasia. What they did was to go straight to involuntary killing. Proponents of euthanasia bring out the following major differences.

First, killing in Germany never occurred with the consent of the persons being killed, who in most cases were not dying. Second, unlike ours, Nazi Germany was a homogeneous society. Any move toward active killing in our society would meet with strong political opposition. Third, genocide in Germany was based on racial, political, and cultural bias, and it was based on the beliefs of the officials, not the individuals involved.

Euthanasia supporters believe that individuals themselves should decide what is best for them. Therefore, the proponents support carefully drafted and monitored legislative measures.

The opponents emphasize the possible harmful effects of legalizing euthanasia, such as abuse by the political or judicial system. Thus, the devaluation of life would be selective because euthanasia might be applied to certain groups of people. The practice of euthanasia might be abused not only by society at large, but by individuals as well. For example, it is easy to imagine the ne'er-do-well nephew persuading his rich old uncle to request euthanasia.[15]

4. *The problem that people may be emotionally depressed.* Euthanasia supporters agree that emotionally disturbed people should be screened, carefully evaluated, and referred for treatment. The request to end one's life should be made in writing and over a significant period of time. Legal documents should be carefully prepared, validated, and properly notarized. The decision to request euthanasia should never been supported when someone is in a state of depression or despair. Such a person should be appropriately referred for psychiatric treatment. The degree of pain and the presence of severe symptoms should be checked for the role they may play in the decision. The family of the dying patient should be asked if they understand and support the wishes of the terminally ill person.

But opponents say that many people who opt for euthanasia may be suicidally depressed. Furthermore, they may not be loved by family members who wish to inherit the estate and may encourage the terminally ill member to decide on euthanasia "for the good of the family."[16]

5. *The issue that doctors may be wrong in their diagnosis or prognosis.* Those who favor euthanasia agree that any prognosis of terminal illness should be confirmed by a second or third opinion. Mistakes do occur, and anecdotal reports occasionally surface about patients diagnosed as comatose or terminally ill who have recovered. Cures can be found, but before they can be used by patients, they must usually go through years of testing, analysis, government approval, and acceptance by the medical community. Doctors do know what curative treatment will be available during the remaining life span of the patient. However, skeptics about euthanasia believe that a life may be ended prematurely if the doctors are wrong in their diagnosis or prognosis.

6. *The issue that euthanasia is illegal.* Passive euthanasia has received considerable legal support in the United States (see Chapter 7 for case law and state and federal legislation). Living-will statutes have been passed in almost every state, and new

initiatives are being introduced in several states for aid-in-dying legislation. Laws change because they reflect the people's current will. The Judicial Council of the American Medical Association issued an official statement in March 1986, affirming that it is ethically permissible for physicians to withhold all life-promoting treatment, including nutrition and hydration, from patients who are in irreversible coma or who are terminally ill.

7. *The issue that doctors should not be expected to do such work and that it is against the Hippocratic oath.* Those who argue in favor of euthanasia point out that the Hippocratic oath was modified in 1948 by the General Assembly of World Medical Associations and in 1949 in the International Code of Medical Ethics.[17] In 1991, surveys of physicians indicated that nearly 50 percent have deliberately taken steps that would indirectly cause a patient's death, that 3.7 percent have provided patients or their next of kin with information to be used for suicide, and that 30 percent agreed that there are circumstances in which a physician would be justified in causing a patient's death.[18]

Those physicians who practiced in Hippocratic times never had to worry about having machines that could prolong life indefinitely. They also had to gain the confidence of the population by not being connected with governmental officials.

Those who argue against euthanasia quote the famous phrase, "I will neither give a deadly drug to anyone, if asked for, nor will I make a suggestion to this effect." Nevertheless, depending on the type of case, anywhere from 10 to 88 percent of physicians would accede to patients' requests for death if all liability for civil or criminal liability were removed.

In a mail survey of 676 San Francisco Bay Area physicians, the local medical society found that 70 percent of the doctors supported the right of patients to active euthanasia; only 23 percent opposed, and 7 percent were unsure. If active euthanasia were to become legal, 45 percent said they would actively participate in euthanasia; 35 percent said they would not.

In another survey by the Hemlock Society, 79 physicians who responded to an anonymous questionnaire said that they had already actively assisted in the dying of terminally ill patients, and 29 said that they had done it three or more times. Yet, despite increasing acceptance by physicians, the American Medical Association has consistently opposed active euthanasia.[19] Nonetheless, a group of twelve eminent doctors published an article in the *New England Journal of Medicine* urging colleagues to reexamine their attitudes and responsibilities toward hopelessly ill patients. They not only recommended a large program of education for physicians on the issues of terminal care, but ten of the twelve stated that they "believe that it is not immoral for a physician to assist in the rational suicide of a terminally ill person."[20]

Others argue that doctors should not be expected to perform actions that go against their own conscience. However, they should be able to transfer the care of a patient requesting euthanasia (or self-deliverance, as it is also called by proponents) to another physician or to another facility. This position is substantiated by the belief that the physician may feel that there is something morally wrong in giving a lethal injection to a patient, even if it has been requested.

8. *The fact that people can make a lack of productivity the reason to choose death.* Proponents believe that a person who is no longer able to function and to be productive should have the right to choose to die. Although this is a very utilitarian viewpoint, it is one that is held by many individuals.

Those with opposing views say that even people who suffer can be very productive and share their insights with the rest of us. They also claim that effective pain and symptom control can extend the time of being useful and productive to the end. Also, the time gained in terminal illness may allow the survivors to share precious moments together to provide memories that will later help with their grieving.[21]

9. *Euthanasia used for the problems of aging.* Some people suffer from major losses due to aging, such as increasing blindness, becoming bedridden, and losing the ability to speak or to eat. They should have the right to choose whether they wish to

prolong what they consider a meaningless and demeaning existence. Many have lived long, productive, and full lives, and they should have the right to decide, based on their acquired wisdom, whether they want to endure the infirmities and indignities of advanced age.

Set against this argument is the fact that our society does not give proper recognition to the elderly's potential contribution. Opponents claim that euthanasia is not the way to deal with the indignities suffered by the aged. They claim that it is society's duty to change and to give the respect and recognition due to senior citizens for their wisdom and insights.

10. *The difference between passive and active euthanasia.* Once the decision to end life has been made, what difference does it make whether one withholds treatment or gives a lethal injection? Some argue that there is basically no moral difference. Others strongly disagree with active killing because they believe that it is inherently wrong. They say that the *active killing of a human being is a* prima facie *wrong-making characteristic of actions* compared to letting a person die. In other words, no matter what the circumstances, they feel that *prima facie* wrong-making actions violate fundamental principles of morality.[22] On the other hand, they do not feel that *letting* a person die, even by withholding treatment, violates that same *prima facie* wrong-making principle.

11. *Legalizing euthanasia.* Some people would like to legalize euthanasia and develop safe guidelines. They say that it is not easy for most people who wish to die to commit suicide or even to refuse treatment, especially if they meet with the resistance of hospital staff. Furthermore, if they are unable to communicate, they are incapable of requesting that life-support systems be turned off.

Others say that there is no need to legalize euthanasia because people today can refuse any treatment, even life-saving treatment. One exception, I have learned from my colleagues, is that persons will invariably be resuscitated if they call an ambulance. The paramedics, no matter what the patient or the family says, will always resuscitate the patient en route to the hospital.

It is possible that legalizing active killing would lead to abuses. The law is at best such a crude instrument that it might not be used effectively in many cases. Opponents cite the "red light rule," which says that it is better and safer for every car to stop at every red light, no matter what the conditions are, rather than to allow some cars to continue through the light even with caution. The "proceed-with-caution rule," has some risks in that mistakes are likely to be made. Therefore, in the final analysis, opponents say, it is better to keep euthanasia illegal so as not to have to deal with exceptional cases that can be reviewed carefully and thoroughly.[23]

Finally, arguments pro and con have taken into account the principles we discussed in Chapter 3, such as the principle of autonomy and the principle of proportionality. You may recall that these principles refer to patients' rights to decide for themselves what is in their best interest.

Although not everyone agrees with the concept of active euthanasia, it is nonetheless endorsed by thousands of people in the United States and elsewhere. Periodically, public opinion is tested by polls. In May 1991, the Roper Organization of New York City conducted a poll of 1,500 people in California, Oregon, and Washington. About 500 people in each state were asked what they thought about the practicalities and law reforms on euthanasia. Of those polled, 60 percent thought that the law should be changed to allow doctors to help a suffering person end his or her life; 32 percent believed that the law should remain unchanged; and 8 percent had no opinion.[24] The poll also showed that more Californians than Oregonians and Washingtonians favored changes in the law. Also, more men than women wanted changes in the law; and younger people favored the reforms.

Other poll results showed that more people preferred receiving a prescription for a lethal drug to take their life (60 percent) to receiving a lethal injection from a doctor (54 percent). A much higher percentage of people favored the use of a power of attorney to authorize the administration of drugs to end the lives of patients who are incompetent (as in the *Cruzan* case).[25] The practice of a physician's providing aid in dying was favored by 72 percent of the people questioned; 67 percent of Protestants and 66 percent of Catholics favored the practice. In general, people with higher education and higher income levels tended to favor euthanasia.

To complete our discussion on euthanasia, let us review briefly the practice of euthanasia in the Netherlands.

EUTHANASIA IN THE NETHERLANDS

> *Death is perhaps nothing, dying is everything.*
> —E. du Perron, Dutch writer (1926)

One common misconception is that euthanasia has been legalized by statute in Holland. It has not. The procedure of euthanasia, however, has been legalized by case law; that is, each case has been judged on its own appropriateness and special circumstances. All euthanasia cases are brought to the regional prosecutor. The public prosecutor's office is in charge of prosecuting criminal cases and has the freedom to pursue or drop the case if it is considered to be in the public interest. The prosecutor's office receives recommendations from the Netherlands Office of Medical Inspectors about whether the act was appropriate according to current ethical medical practice.[26]

Active euthanasia in the Netherlands can take place only by the patient's voluntary decision.[27] Patients must give unequivocal instructions in writing before the procedure can take place, and the patient's wishes are usually expressed in the context of a terminal illness. Pieter Admiraal, who has been practicing euthanasia in a Dutch hospital, says that physicians will, in hopeless cases, suggest various alternatives to the patient, including euthanasia. Patients often make that choice and seem grateful for the opportunity. This decision is usually the result of careful deliberation.[28]

How did euthanasia come about in the Netherlands? The *Schoonheim* decision was the first case, named after an elderly woman treated by Dr. Schoonheim. Marie Barendregt was a strong-willed eighty-nine-year-old woman who had moved into a home for the aged in 1976. Recognizing her increasing disability and dependence on others, she signed an advance directive after four years in the home, asking Schoonheim to avoid using extraordinary measures to keep her alive. Some time later, she fell and broker her hip. She refused surgery unless the surgeons could assure her that she would die on the operating table. They refused to operate.

After the patient's transfer to a critical-care unit in a hospital, where her condition continued to deteriorate, during periods of alertness and coherence she repeatedly asked her doctor to perform active euthanasia. She also pleaded with her son, the other doctors, and the nurses. Finally, Schoonheim called in two independent physicians and the nursing staff. After they had reached a consensus, Schoonheim agreed to proceed with her request. Mrs. Barendregt said good-bye to her son and her daughter-in-law, expressing her gratitude for their willingness to comply with her wishes.

Several days later, Schoonheim and his assistants again asked her if her decision was still to die. She reiterated, "If it can be done, please, do it at once, doctor, quickly, not one night more." After the family said good-bye one last time, the doctor returned and gave Mrs. Barendregt an injection that put her into an immediate sleep and coma. About eight minutes later, he repeated the injection. Five minutes later, she stopped breathing and died.

The case would have been routine had the certificate of death indicated that the patient died of "natural causes." However, because Schoonheim informed the medical examiner of the lethal injection, he was charged with murder. The district court found him innocent and acquitted him on the grounds that he had acted honestly in his duty to his patient and that he had not acted with criminal intent. The prosecutor appealed, and the court of appeals reversed the previous decision. Schoonheim was found guilty under the Homicide Act of the Netherlands.

Schoonheim then appealed his case to the Dutch Supreme Court. In turn, the Supreme Court decided that the Appeals Court had failed to recognize that Schoonheim had been subject to a conflict in his duties: being expected to obey the law of the land as a good citizen and also recognizing his duty to his patient. It ruled that, given the current standards of medical ethics and expertise, the court of appeals should have weighed the conflicting duties and interests. It thus concluded that Schoonheim was not guilty of a crime. Later, when the case was referred back to the court of appeals, this court decided that Schoonheim had acted within "current ethical practice." Finally, Schoonheim was acquitted.[29]

This case provided the basis for the current guidelines on whether active euthanasia is legal or illegal. According to the new guidelines, the following conditions have to be met before an active euthanasia request can be considered:

1. There must be clear and convincing evidence that the patient has made repeated and well-considered requests.
2. There must be a thorough understanding that the patient has enough information to justify the decision to request euthanasia.
3. The patient must be undergoing intolerable and irreversible suffering.
4. There must be a lack of reasonable alternatives *from the patient's point of view.*
5. The procedure of euthanasia can be carried out only by a qualified physician, and only after consultation with another physician, who must concur with the decision.
6. The physician must exercise due care and responsibility in the exercise of the guidelines and in the performance of the act of euthanasia itself.[30]

APPLICATION OF THE DUTCH GUIDELINES

Since the early 1970s, the subject of euthanasia has been hotly debated in the Netherlands. After many exchanges, opponents and supporters agreed on a definition used by the State Commission on Euthanasia in 1985, which defined euthanasia as "the deliberate action to terminate life, by someone other than, and on request of, the patient concerned." The meaning of *euthanasia* in the Dutch interpretation was narrowed down to active euthanasia only. It excluded the old concept of passive euthanasia, which is associated with a request for nontreatment or the withholding or withdrawing of life-sustaining treatments.

The decision-making process, as in the *Schoonheim* case, rests with the patient and the physician. It also leaves the decision within the medical community, taking into account current ethical practice and recognizing the impact of modern technology on medical care. The commission had become aware of the conflict between the ethics of medical practice and the legal statutes, and thus acknowledged that euthanasia may be justifiable according to medical practice even though it is in conflict with the law.

It is interesting that, in the guidelines, terminal illness is not a prerequisite for active euthanasia. Another notable point is that the courts considered physical deterioration a form of pain and also considered death with dignity important. Another major provision is that substitutive judgment is not acceptable. Only the patient can decide.

Following the *Schoonheim* case, all physicians who followed the Schooheim guidelines were acquitted by the district courts. Marvin E. Newman, professor of legal studies at Rollins College, had this to say when asked if active euthanasia would be subject to abuse if legalized: "The experience that I have witnessed in the Netherlands leads me to conclude that that is improbable. I have never met a medical doctor in the Netherlands who after performing the act ever appeared indifferent to it. It is a very emotional experience for all concerned and especially for the medical staff and the physician. Medical doctors who have performed the act may remain depressed for days after the action is taken.[31]

The leading advocate of euthanasia in the Netherlands is Pieter V. Admiraal, an oncologist and anesthesiologist at a Catholic hospital in Delft. It is his conviction that, over time, the Netherlands will demonstrate to the world that euthanasia can be "the last dignified act in the health care process."[32] He believes that only a physician should perform euthanasia under controlled conditions. He recommends that the patient be given an initial injection of barbiturates, which produce unconsciousness, to be followed by an injection of curare, which stops the heart and lungs. After death, the physician notifies the coroner, who in turn notifies the prosecutor's office. Unless the prosecutor finds something improper, no further inquiry takes place.[33]

UNIQUE ASPECTS OF THE DUTCH CLIMATE

Although there are many similarities between the Dutch and American courts in how they look at euthanasia cases, the rationale applied in the United States for passive euthanasia is, in the Netherlands, extended to cases of voluntary active euthanasia as well. American doctors fear criminal prosecution if they openly assist patients with suicide because the right to privacy in the United States protects the individual and the doctor only in cases of refusal of treatment in terminal illnesses, where the patient's interests are presumed to outweigh those of the state.

The extent of euthanasia in the Netherlands is not known. Generally, 150 cases are reported each year. Admiraal says that many cases are not reported to the legal system because of unfamiliarity with and unease about the legal process.[34] Estimates of actual cases vary widely but one commonly cited figure is three thousand a year, or about 2 percent of all deaths occurring annually among Holland's fifteen million people.[35] If one were to extrapolate this figure to the United States, assuming that euthanasia were legal, it would account for approximately fifty thousand deaths per year.

Another important factor that makes the climate more receptive in the Netherlands is the fact that physicians are rarely, if ever, the subject of malpractice actions by their patients. In fact, there has been considerable public concern for the physicians who have had to stand trial. Even the Royal Medical Association has given its support to the accused physicians, thus joining forces with patients' rights groups in asserting support of voluntary active euthanasia.

The doctor–patient relationship in the Netherlands is uniquely strong and is based on a deep mutual trust. The practice of defensive medicine is unknown, and the concept of liability is rarely mentioned in the context of medical practice. This, as we know, is not the case in the United States. Therefore, it is easy to see why the process is evolving along a different path in the United States. We discussed that development in the last chapter and shall not repeat it here.

Some of us may ask the question: What makes Dutch doctors accept the alternative of active euthanasia over passive euthanasia? Some physicians feel that the restriction to passive euthanasia may lead to dangerous results with less control and supervision. By contrast, as active euthanasia is such an extreme act, it is undoubtedly much more controlled than passive euthanasia. Doctors also recognize that despite advances in pain control and management, there are still cases in terminal illnesses in which pain cannot be controlled or even reduced. Pain and suffering occur even in cases of passive euthanasia.

Despite a relatively more accepting climate in the Netherlands, there is still some opposition. Richard Fenigsen, a cardiologist in 's-Hertogenbosch, says that Holland is not setting a good example for the rest of the world. He contends that the slippery-slope problem is real, and that the practice of euthanasia may lead to the murder of those who are judged to be mentally or physically inferior and a burden to society, much as in the Holocaust.

Fenigsen has brought his message to the United States by publishing articles in the *Wall Street Journal* and in the *Hastings Center Report,* the authoritative journal of bioethics. He also visited Washington State to raise opposition to Initiative 119. One of his critics, Theresa A. Takken, an ethicist and a Catholic nun, describes him as "a wonderful Jewish Pole who went through hell during WWII, but who exaggerates." Nonetheless, she admits that abuses could occur in the United States unless health care and housing become available for all citizens.[36] The central issue is one of control, according to Margaret P. Battin, a philosopher at the University of Utah who also studied euthanasia in Holland. She believes that a person should have the right to determine the manner of his or her death and to avoid pain and suffering.[37]

There are those who argue that active euthanasia should be performed by patients themselves. But it is well known that this act is not easy to perform and that it can lead to disastrous complications and failures (see the case of Patty described in Chapter 4). The process of active euthanasia is difficult and takes much energy, both physical and mental, and many people cannot do it safely alone. It is best performed when many people are involved in it, for physical and emotional reasons.[38] Of particular interest is the fact that, in 1991, the Dutch Ministry of Health sent a letter to all physicians, informing them that mental suffering was not sufficient reason for assisting patients with suicide. This letter obviously aimed at protecting psychiatric patients who may not be able to make an informed choice if they are suffering from a suicidal depression.[39]

RECENT SURVEY FINDINGS ON EUTHANASIA IN THE NETHERLANDS

Although euthanasia has been practiced for almost two decades in the Netherlands, there is little knowledge about who has requested euthanasia, what some of the justifications have been, and who has been involved in practicing the procedure. In 1991, a group of four researchers published their findings in the weekly *Netherlands Journal of Medicine*. The major findings were reported in the *New York Times*.[40]

I present here only some of the highlights of the study. One of the major findings is that typical patients who request euthanasia are persons in their early sixties who have advanced cancer, and who fear becoming dependent and losing dignity through pain and humiliation. Most of them rely on their family doctor and prefer dying at home.

To do the survey, the researchers mailed anonymous questionnaires to 1,042 physicians, obtaining 676 responses, among which 388 provided detailed information about case histories.

Euthanasia was performed on a voluntary basis. Typically, the physician injected a large dose of barbiturates to produce a coma, and then injected curare to stop the breathing and the heartbeat. In cases where assistance with suicide was requested, the physician would give a prescription for a large dose of barbiturates, which the patient could take at home or in the presence of the doctor.

The study revealed that 85 percent of the patients were cancer patients in their last weeks of life. The remaining 15 percent included patients with AIDS (about 3 percent), multiple sclerosis, and other neurological diseases that cause paralysis. There were very few cases involving cardiovascular disease. In general, the requestors tended to be younger, with an average age of sixty-three for men and sixty-six for women. Very few requests for euthanasia were made by people over age seventy-five and were very rare over age eighty-five, an unexpected finding. The researchers speculated that the reason could have been a lack of information and assertiveness by older people or their better adjustment to their infirmities. Two-thirds of the people requesting to die were thought to have only two weeks to live, and approximately one-tenth had three or more months of life expectancy. The request was made by the patients themselves in 83 percent of the cases; in

10 percent of the cases, the suggestion was made by the physician, and in 7 percent by the family. In 75 percent of the cases, less than one month passed between the first and the final request made by patients.[41]

THE RIGHT-TO-DIE
SOCIETIES IN THE UNITED STATES

Several organizations have taken up the cause of the right to die from different vantage points, some working to propose new laws or modify current legislation, others offering counseling services and information to the public. The following are brief descriptions of the main ones in the United States today.

Choice In Dying, Inc.

With headquarters in New York and originally called the Society for the Right to Die, this organization aims at disseminating information nationwide. It seeks to protect the individual's right to control treatment decisions at the end of life, including the right to refuse unwanted medical procedures that can only prolong the dying process.

The organization lists the following as its purposes and functions.

- To inform people of their rights to refuse treatment under state statutes, and constitutional and common law.
- To work with the general public in support of living-will and related legislation.
- To distribute living-will declarations and the other appropriate documents authorized in each state.
- To offer right-to-die legal counseling as needed by patients, their families, their caregivers, and their attorneys.
- To serve as a clearinghouse for lawyers on right-to-die law.

Americans against Human Suffering

This national political-action organization is dedicated to enacting state laws that permit aid in dying by physicians for the terminally ill on request. The organization has about 27,000 supporters throughout the United States, Canada, Australia, and Europe. Its offices are located in Washington, D.C., and in California. Robert Risley, an attorney and the organization's past president, along with colleagues, drafted the Death with Dignity Act (formerly called the Humane and Dignified Death Act), which is a model piece of legislation being proposed in California.

The National Hemlock Society

The National Hemlock Society was founded by Gerald A. Larue, former professor of religion and archaeology at the University of Southern California and currently an adjunct professor at the Andrus Gerontological Institute in Los Angeles. Currently, the thirty-thousand-member society, in Eugene, Oregon, has cofounder author and journalist Derek Humphry as its director and Larue as its president. It derives its name from the root plant hemlock, which was used in ancient Rome and Athens for rational suicide in certain situations. The death of Socrates is the most famous example of death by hemlock. In Western literature, the phrase 'drink the cup of hemlock' has become known through Shakespeare and others as the way to a rational suicide.

The society is dedicated to exploring and promoting the option of active voluntary euthanasia for the terminally ill. It believes that in certain compassionate and justified cases, there is an obligation, if one is asked, to assist a dying person wanting to end life with dignity. However, the society makes clear that it will not offer personal counseling or advice to anyone. It gives three reasons for the policy:

1. Any direct form of assistance in suicide, no matter how humanitarian, is now illegal.

2. The society has neither the required skills nor the staff to assess individuals in need.
3. The society believes that such acts are essentially private and a matter for the family, and that outsiders should not be involved in the personal decisions of others.

Although at the present time, the practice of active euthanasia is against the law, the organization is working toward introducing initiatives that would permit physicians to aid in dying without fear of prosecution.

Derek Humphry is the author of the book *Final Exit*, which offers explicit instructions on how to commit suicide with barbiturates and other medications. The book was published by the National Hemlock Society and is protected by the First Amendment.

World Federation of Right to Die Societies

This organization, consisting of thirty right-to-die societies from nineteen countries, believes that patients have a right to die with dignity, which includes the right to refuse life-sustaining treatment and the right to painless dying. Although some countries and some states in the United States have enacted legislation protecting patients' rights, there are still many countries and states that do not have such legislation. The federation considers this right so important that it has urged the United Nations Organization to deal with it under the Human Rights Commission. The organization is encouraging other countries to introduce suitable reforms into their laws to affirm patients' right to die with dignity.

WASHINGTON STATE'S INITIATIVE 119

As mentioned in Chapter 7, an initiative that would allow physicians to perform active euthanasia legally was introduced to Washington voters on November 5, 1991. Some doctors felt that this initiative was a step toward more compassionate care. Others felt it was equivalent to condoning murder. The bill, if passed in its original form, would have given doctors immunity from legal prosecution if they give aid in dying to terminally ill patients. Although that choice would not be for everyone, having that option would provide relief to some patients. "I would want it for myself," said Robert W. Wood, director of the AIDS Control Program and an associate professor of medicine at the University of Washington.[42]

Public support for the initiative was polled at 94 percent wanting doctors to honor the request of a dying patient to be taken off life support, with over 61 percent saying that they would vote for the initiative.[43] There was a group called Interfaith Clergy for Yes on Initiative 119, a committee of 236 ordained clergy representing most mainstream Protestant denominations and including four Jewish rabbis and a Mormon bishop. Some Roman Catholic clerics gave financial support but stopped short of listing their names in public endorsement. A group of doctors formed a support group called Physicians for Yes on Initiative 119.

The initiative was defeated by the narrow margin of 54 percent to 46 percent. Opposition came from the Washington State Medical Association, even though a substantial number of physicians favored the bill. Significant opposition also came from the state chapter of the National Right to Life Committee and the Catholic Church.[44]

In spite of its defeat, Initiative 119 represented the growing interest in proposing legislation concerning aid in dying. New laws are being proposed in several states, heralding important changes in attitudes and laws as public interest increases and technology advances.

NOTES

1. Robert M. Veatch, *Death, Dying and the Biological Revolution* (New Haven, CN: Yale University Press, 1989), 59.
2. Derek Humphry and Ann Wickett, *The Right to Die* (New York: Harper & Row, 1986).

3. "Most Die Free of Pain, Says Survey," *Hemlock Quarterly* 42 (1991): 2.
4. Edward W. Keyserlingk, "Relating the Right to Die and the Need to Bereave" (London, Ontario: King's College, 1991).
5. Harry van Bommel, *Choices: For People Who Have a Terminal Illness, Their Families and Their Caregivers*, 2nd rev. ed. (Toronto: NC Press, 1987), 83.
6. J. Q. Benoliel, "Institutional Dying: A Convergence of Cultural Values, Technology, and Social Organization," in *Dying: Facing the Facts*, 2nd ed., ed. H. Wass, F. M. Berardo, and R. A. Neimeyer (New York: Hemisphere, 1988), 180–181.
7. Derek Humphry, *Final Exit* (Portland, OR: Hemlock Society, 1991), 131–140.
8. American Health Consultants, "Will Suicide Machine Case Affect the Right-to-Die Movement?" *Medical Ethics Advisor* 6 (July 1990): 89–91.
9. M. Angell, "Euthanasia," *New England Journal of Medicine* 319 (1988): 1348–1350.
10. K. M. Foley, "The Treatment of Cancer Pain," *New England Journal of Medicine* 313 (1985): 84–95.
11. Robert I. Misbin, "Physicians' Aid in Dying," *New England Journal of Medicine* 325 (1991): 1307–1311.
12. Beverly Merz, "Will Doctors Hear the Wake-Up Call? Pain Control Experts Say Surge in Euthanasia Interest Is Sending a Message," *American Medical News* (1991): 9, 35.
13. G. A. Larue, *Euthanasia and Religion: A Survey of the Attitudes of World Religions to the Right to Die* (Los Angeles: Hemlock Society, 1985).
14. D. Callahan, "Can We Return Death to Disease?" *Hastings Center Report* (Special Suppl., Jan./Feb. 1989): 4.
15. Angell, 1348–1350.
16. van Bommel, 120–123.
17. Ibid.
18. Mac Overmyer, "National Survey: Physicians' Views on the Right to Die," *Physician's Management* 31 (1991): 40–76.
19. A. Parachini, "The California Humane and Dignified Death Initiative," *Hasting Center Report* (Special Suppl., Jan./Feb. 1989): 12.
20. S. H. Wanzer, D. D. Federman, S. J. Adelstein, et al., "The Physician's Responsibility toward Hopelessly Ill Patients," *New England Journal of Medicine* 320 (1989): 844–849.
21. van Bommel, 120–123.

22. Veatch, 70.
23. Ibid, 74–75.
24. "1991 Roper Poll of the West Coast," *Hemlock Quarterly* 44 (July 1991): 9.
25. Ibid.
26. M. E. Newman, "Active Euthanasia in the Netherlands," in *To Die or Not to Die? Cross-Disciplinary, Cultural, and Legal Perspectives on the Right to Choose Death* (New York: Praeger, 1990), 117–128.
27. Ibid., 119.
28. P. V. Admiraal, "Euthanasia Applied at a General Hospital," *The Euthanasia Review* 97 (1986): 1.
29. Newman, 117–128.
30. Ibid.
31. Ibid.
32. J. Horgan, "Death with Dignity: The Dutch Explore the Limits of a Patient's Right to Die," *Scientific American* (March 1991): 17.
33. Ibid.
34. H. Rigter, "Euthanasia in the Netherlands: Distinguishing Facts from Fiction," *Hastings Center Report* (Special Suppl., Jan./Feb. 1989): 31–32.
35. Horgan, 20.
36. Ibid.
37. Ibid.
38. Newman, 117–128.
39. M. Simons, "Dutch Survey Casts New Light on Patients Who Choose to Die," *The New York Times*, 11 September 1991, 2.
40. Ibid.
41. Ibid.
42. "Should Physicians Perform Euthanasia?" *American Medical News*, 7 January 1991, 12.
43. American Health Consultants, "Euthanasia Drive in Washington Claims Enough Signatures for Vote," *Medical Ethics Advisor*, 7 (July 1991): 4–6.
44. American Health Consultants, "Euthanasia Wins Place on Washington Ballot, Picks Up Support of Many Physicians," *Medical Ethics Advisor*, 7 (June 1991): 75.

CHAPTER 9

The Hospice Movement and Alternative Solutions to Incurable Illness

THE HOSPICE AND HOME CARE

> *You matter because you are you. You matter to the last moment of your life, and we will do all we can not only to help you die peacefully, but also to live until you die.*
>
> —Cicely Saunders

Neither aggressive treatment nor euthanasia is for everyone afflicted with a terminal illness. Some people would prefer to elect a more natural course of action and a gentler adjustment to the last stages of life. Those people often choose hospice care.

Before discussing the types of care that can be expected in a hospice program, let me give you a bit of historical background.

HISTORY OF THE HOSPICE MOVEMENT

Hospice is basically a concept of medical, nursing, and spiritual care for the terminally ill. Its basic purpose is to provide patients and families a comfortable and supportive environment to ease the period of illness before death.

The concept is not new in the sense that as far back as the fifth century, one could find types of way stations where terminally ill, dying, or merely exhausted pilgrims on their way to the Holy Land could get care and attention as needed.

The modern concept of hospice began in 1967 with St. Christopher's Hospice in the London suburb of Sydenham. In the United States, the first hospice appeared in Branford, New Haven, Connecticut in 1974. This hospice was created by Dr. Sylvia Lack with the help of the National Cancer Institute and generous donations from the community, and it opened an inpatient facility in 1978 to supplement its home care program.

In the 1970s, the hospice movement grew steadily despite some initial resistance from and indifference of the medical profession. In 1978, the National Hospice Organization was formed, and by the mid-1980s, there were over 30 hospice programs in Britain and over 1,345 in the United States. Today, hospice programs exist in every American state.[1]

PHILOSOPHY OF THE HOSPICE

Hospice care is centered on the philosophy of humanistic medicine, which cares for the whole person, including the family. It aims at preparing the terminally ill person to die with dignity.

The hospice tries to answer the question: What does each individual need? The answer lies in providing each patient and family with whatever they need to cope with the physical and psychological stresses of the terminal illness. In practice, the patient and the family are treated as one unit because of a belief that the problems of the dying patient and of her or his family are inevitably intertwined. If the family is going to be involved in the care, the members must be supported with services, education, counseling, and whatever else they need. The better informed family members are, the less anxiety exists.

Studies have shown that patients in a hospice program experience less anxiety, helplessness, inadequacy, and guilt than patients who receive care in an acute-care general hospital.[2] The hospice staff helps families and patients with the psychological problems that develop during the patient's illness and during the period of bereavement.

Hospice care is viewed as an alternative in care of the dying. The National Hospice Organization defines its philosophy this way: "Hospice is a medically directed multidisciplinary program providing skilled care of an appropriate nature for terminally ill patients and their families to allow the patient to live as fully as possible until the time of death. Hospice helps relieve symptoms during the distress (physical, psychological, spiritual, social, economic) that may occur during the course of the disease, dying, and bereavement."[3]

For those patients who do not have any family or anyone else to help as a primary-care person, and for those who need more medical care than can be offered in the home, inpatient care is coordinated under the hospice program.

The cornerstone of the hospice philosophy is the belief that the patient is unique and comes first in considerations of how to meet her or his individual needs. This philosophy was inspired by Cicely Saunders, the dean of the hospice movement, who stressed the importance of emotional support and pain and symptom control. This help includes effective pain and symptom control, emotional support, and "bringing the family together" in the dying process. Thus, the dying patient will not feel alone and abandoned, and the family will not feel guilty or inadequate during the course of the terminal illness. The focus is on the quality of life and on helping families optimize the time remaining with the dying member. Considerable emphasis in put on pain control, because the control of pain and other symptoms can help the dying patient and the family gain a sense of peace and relaxation. When the patient finally approaches death, the family and the staff all feel that they have done everything they could for the patient's comfort, and in the end, nothing matters more.

Comfort is the mainstay of patient care in a hospice program. That is why hospice is becoming increasingly popular with patients and families. It is also slowly gaining acceptance among the new generation of physicians, who have benefited from their rotations through hospice programs.

MEETING THE NEEDS OF
PATIENTS AND FAMILIES

One major goal of a hospice in making patients and families comfortable is to help them live as fully as possible.[4] With the emphasis on pain control as a central part of the program, hospice physicians and nurses are well trained in the dosages of morphine required for the management of pain and other symptoms. This training contrasts with that of hospital staff, who tend to be hesitant about the liberal use of pain medications.

I discussed the issues of pain control in Chapter 1, so at this point I want only to point out that hospice personnel are extremely sensitive to pain and other symptoms of the terminally ill. They know how to evaluate the relationship between physical symptoms and depression; therefore, they can provide medications in adequate doses, along with the necessary emotional and spiritual support. Most of all, a top priority of the hospice staff is to be available at all times.

Another goal is to help families accomplish the tasks of everyday living while having the patient at home. A corps of volunteers is usually available to help families with household responsibilities, or with shopping, driving, and babysitting. They also arrange for getting clergy to come to provide spiritual support.

The hospice staff is acutely aware of how disturbing the illness is to the family members. One of the most helpful things the staff does is to facilitate the interaction between the dying patient and her or his family. They want to make the last few months as comfortable, peaceful, and meaningful as possible. It is not unusual for the family to be as upset as the patient by the terminal illness. In that charged atmosphere, it is difficult for families and patients to speak easily and meaningfully. This is where the hospice staff provide the needed emotional support.

Even after a death, the hospice staff continues to provide support and assistance in arranging the funeral. Counseling and support during bereavement are also available for a period of at least one year following the loss.

ORGANIZATION OF THE HOSPICE

Hospices are usually private, nonprofit organizations with a community board of directors and an advisory committee. Services to patients are provided in a variety of ways, primarily through home care, but also in institutional settings such as nursing homes, freestanding facilities, or even palliative-care units in general hospitals.[5]

In home care, sometimes referred to as *hospice without walls*, the program is affiliated with a hospital or a health-care agency. The patient remains at home and receives all kinds of care from a team of professionals including physicians, nurses, social workers, volunteer caregivers, and ministers who come into the home.

Freestanding facilities (St. Christopher's Hospice in England is the prototype) provide the care and atmosphere needed for comfort and pain control, but no facilities for acute medical care.

Freestanding hospital-affiliated units exist as a separate building but are affiliated with a specific hospital, usually a teaching hospital.

Hospital-based units, usually called palliative-care units (PCUs) are separate units within a general hospital. The prototype is the PCU at Montreal's Royal Victoria Hospital, McGill's teaching hospital, established in 1976 by surgeon Balfour Mount. It is a ward dedicated to the care of the terminally ill with severe pain and special problems. The ward consists of cheerfully decorated rooms that provide privacy for family discussions and where family members can stay overnight if they wish. Children and pets are welcome visitors. The atmosphere is free and relaxed, and the emphasis is on providing emotional and physical comfort.

Finally, there is the hospital-based hospice team, caregivers who go to the various wards of the hospital and in some cases to nursing homes or chronic-care hospitals. Typically, the hospice staff provides coordination of various services, such as social services, homemaking, visiting nurses and physicians, volunteers, and ministers.

The emphasis remains on making patients and families as comfortable as possible during the patient's last few weeks or months. Patients are admitted only after a diagnosis of terminal illness with a short prognosis, usually less than six months. Patients can be admitted to a hospice program only after the patient, the family, and the attending physician have agreed to such care.

Although no aggressive treatment is given in a hospice, an open relationship with the hospital is maintained in case its services are needed.

CURRENT STATUS OF HOSPICE CARE

As hospices multiplied in the 1970s, it became necessary to develop standards of care. To meet that need, the National Hospice Organization (NHO) was founded in the United States to act as a guide and pacesetter. After setting some definitions and standards of care, it now serves as a clearinghouse for information and deals with the federal government on questions of reimbursement for hospice care through Medicare.

Currently, the law allows a Medicare Part A beneficiary to use the benefit if the attending physician and hospice director certify that the patient is terminally ill and has a six-month expectancy. The only reservation is that the services must be provided in a Medicare-certified hospice program.

In 1983, before care was covered as a benefit, about 101,000 people received care in hospice programs in the United States. In 1989, it is estimated that 200,000 patients received such care, among whom 73,000 were Medicare recipients.[7]

Yet, despite these remarkable advances, there is still a need to integrate the hospice program into the mainstream of medicine.[8] Michael Levy, director of the Palliative Care Service at the Fox Chase Cancer Center in Philadelphia, believes that all physicians should have training in hospice care and that all hospitals should have hospice programs; this view would have been totally unacceptable two decades ago. Traditionally, "physicians are trained to cure disease and prolong life, whereas a hospice is the opposite of that," says Josefina B. Magno, director of the hospice program at the Henry Ford Hospital in Detroit.[9]

For a more detailed history and discussion of hospice care and philosophy, I refer the reader to *The Hospice Movement: A Better Way of Caring for the Dying* (1978), by Sandol Stoddard,[10] *Hospice: Complete Care for the Terminally Ill* (1986), by J. M. Zimmerman,[11] and *The Complete Hospice Guide* (1983), by Robert Buckinham.[12]

SUICIDE AS A SOLUTION TO TERMINAL ILLNESS

Sometimes, people choose suicide as a solution to terminal illness. I am referring specifically to so-called rational suicide and not to suicide that is associated with the various psychological motives and disorders well known to psychiatric professionals. It is not my purpose to review the multiple motives behind suicides. Such a review would be beyond the scope of this book, and many books have been written on the subject. Here, I discuss strictly the suicide of persons who do not suffer from depression or psychosis, even though the reality of such a possibility is questioned by some authorities.

In recent years, because of the increasing complexity associated with terminal illness and the convincing arguments presented by the Hemlock Society, rational suicide came to be thought of by many as a desirable choice for certain terminally ill individuals. The Hemlock Society argues that common-sense suicide has a rational basis because the right to end one's life is a final right to choose a painless over a tortured, pain-racked death.

Leo Rangell, a psychoanalyst in Los Angeles who has been in clinical practice for over fifty years, has admitted that suicide is not proof of a mental disorder and that it may have a place in today's agonizing dilemmas about the termination of life.[13]

In her book *Common Sense Suicide: The Final Right*, Doris Portwood, a freelance writer and editor, writes about the various aspects of arguments for rational suicide. She cites the famous case of feminist Charlotte Perkins Gilman, who committed suicide in 1935 while dying of advanced cancer at the age of seventy-five. Mrs. Gilman explained her actions in a note: "Believing the choice to be of social service in promoting wiser views on this question, I have preferred chloroform to cancer."[14]

As I explained in Chapter 4, some people justify rational suicide by analyzing the benefits against the burdens of living with a terminal condition. When pain and discomfort become intolerable, a competent person may conclude that death will be a relief and a more desirable choice.

Even Elizabeth Kübler-Ross, the psychiatrist who has worked with thousands of dying patients, made the following remark about the choice of suicide in terminal illness. "I don't think suicide is always abnormal behavior. We have heard of patients who have completed their unfinished business, who have put their houses in order, have reached a stage of peace and acceptance, and have then terminated their lives, perhaps to leave a home and some money for a wife and children, or because they could not see any sense in prolongation of the dying process when they were ready to die."[15]

Who else chooses suicide? As a psychiatrist I see suicidal patients everyday. I am acutely aware of the need to distinguish patients who are clinically depressed from those who are not when they contemplate suicide. Many psychiatrists and researchers question the rationality of any suicide. Edwin Schneidman put it succinctly: "Never kill yourself when you are suicidal."[16]

Others have warned against the problem of missing the diagnosis of depression in the terminally ill or in geriatric patients.[17] I agree that physicians often overlook depression, and therefore, I would urge that any patient asking for assistance with suicide be seen in a psychiatric consultation. Nevertheless, I have seen patients who were not clinically depressed and typically suicidal, who after careful consideration of their situation and illness, preferred not to prolong their misery for themselves or their family. At present, we do not have any data or statistics on such patients because they are not usually reported as suicides.

Because there are no accurate statistics, we have only impressions offered by clinicians who work with dying patients. Kübler-Ross says that suicides tend to be people with advanced stages of cancer or AIDS, patients on kidney dialysis or awaiting organ transplants, or people who are neglected, isolated, and deserted. They are also people who are not conventionally religious; they have accepted their finiteness and would rather shorten the process of dying than linger on for another few weeks or months in what they regard as useless suffering.[18]

Public opinion on the acceptance of suicide in terminal illness seems to have been changing since 1975, when a Gallup poll was taken on the subject. Then, 40 percent of the public felt that suicide was a "moral right" for persons afflicted with an incurable illness. In 1990, 49 percent of those polled by the Times Mirror Center for the People and the Press approved of suicide for the terminally ill. The 1975 poll also showed that 41 percent of those surveyed favored suicide for patients with intractable pain, whereas the figure was 55 percent in 1900.[19]

Rational suicide, aggressive treatment, the forgoing of life-sustaining treatments, and hospice care represent only some of the many choices individuals make for facing the challenges of terminal illness.

ALTERNATIVE THERAPIES FOR INCURABLE ILLNESSES

Since the early 1970s, a number of nontraditional therapies have appeared to answer the needs of some terminally ill patients and their families. Before considering such therapies, it is advisable to consult the attending physician, who may be informative about the pros and cons of such therapies. In the event that the physician does not believe in any form of alternative therapy, the patient should research the therapy in question through a library, through medical reports, or by writing to the organization supporting the therapy. Regardless of the alternative therapy chosen, however, one's physician should be informed about any new therapies being tried.

The decision to try an alternative therapy is a personal one. One should be careful to choose a therapy that is appropriate; that is, the therapy should not be harmful or expensive (many fraudulent therapies are expensive) and should have some proof of efficacy.

Some alternative therapies are known by the term *holistic health* or *holistic medicine*, which refers to a system of care that emphasizes the whole person, that is, her or his physical, nutritional, environmental, emotional, spiritual, and lifestyle aspects.[20] The holistic approach encourages the patient to take a more active role in the management of illness.

Part of the holistic philosophy is to

1. Maintain a positive attitude toward living to the fullest with hope, inner peace, and humor.
2. Reduce environmental and emotional stress through relaxation exercises and recreation.
3. Encourage activities like nature or beach walks, sex, music, and art.
4. Practice good nutrition.
5. Nurture good relationships with loved ones and provide support to others.
6. Use prayer, meditation, and visual imagery to promote healing and peace.

It is beyond the scope of this book to list all of the alternative therapies available. Only a few are mentioned here. Keep in mind that most of them are not accepted by mainstream medicine. The important thing to remember is that an alternative therapy must remain a personal choice and that it should be discussed with one's attending physician. Here are a few examples.

Acupuncture

Acupuncture is an ancient Chinese technique using sterile needles that are inserted through the skin at predetermined points on the body, often removed from the original site of the symptom. It is used primarily to control pain.

Biofeedback

Biofeedback is a technique using electronic equipment to relay information about the patient's pulse rate, body temperature, or muscle tension. People with high blood pressure, neck and back pain, muscle spasms, and generalized tension have used it to reduce tension and stress.

Chiropractic Care

It is claimed that chiropractic care can relieve back and neck pain through manipulation of the spine and vertebrae.

Autosuggestion

Autosuggestion is a form of self-hypnosis that uses meditative and relaxation exercises. It is becoming more popular as a stress management technique rather than as a treatment approach.

Herbal Therapy

In herbal therapy various herbs from native American, Chinese, and Eastern prescriptions are used instead of vitamins and minerals; thus, danger of side effects are avoided.

Therapeutic Touch

Therapeutic touch is a simple technique that is based on the belief that the lay-on-of-hands uses the energy in one person's hands to help balance the energy in someone else's body and will produce healing. In some American universities, it is taught to student nurses, although with the modification that it relies not on actual touching of the patient, but on passing one's hands over the patient's body.[21]

Will to Live and Power of Love and Hope

Other alternative approaches have emphasized the will to live and the power of hope. In the 1970s, physician O. Carl Simonton and his psychotherapist wife, Stephanie, both working at the Cancer Counseling and Research Center in Fort Worth, Texas, offered a systematic way to bolster the will to live. In the workshops they conducted around the country, they suggested various exercises, sensible nutrition, and plans for positive changes in the participants' lives. For some people, that meant being more assertive and learning to say no; for others, it meant setting new goals. But the mainstay of their approach is the meditation–visualization technique offered as an adjunct to standard cancer treatment, whether surgery, radiation, or chemotherapy.[22]

The idea that a positive frame of mind may help in the course of cancer was further supported by the observation that despair depresses the body's immune system, thus rendering it incapable of defending itself against cancer cells. Studies have shown that bereaved people, for example, have a lower count of white blood cells (lymphocytes). Clinical psychologist Lawrence LeShan reported his observations in a book entitled *You Can Fight for Your Life: Emotional Factors in the Causation of Cancer*.[23] He found that cancer patients had a long-standing pattern of hopelessness that predated the onset of the cancer. He also found that they had incurred many losses and had not been able to replace these losses.

Hopelessness, however, need not be an irreversible condition. The Simontons claim that, by interpreting the drawings of their patients, they have been able to change patterns of behavior as well as the course of disease in some of their patients. However, they are careful to make appropriate disclaimers. In their book *Getting Well Again*, they say, "The course of cancer differs so dramatically from person to person that we would not presume to offer guarantees. There is always uncertainty, as there is with standard medical procedures, but hope, we feel, is an appropriate stance to take toward uncertainty."[24]

Bernie Siegel, a surgeon who teaches at Yale University and a former president of the American Holistic Medical Association, has promoted the power of unconditional love as a stimulant for the immune system. In his book *Love, Medicine and Miracles*, he offers inspirational lessons for cancer patients, whom he calls "exceptional patients."[25] He, too, promotes love, understanding, the use of humor, and self-healing. He believes that people who have learned to give love can achieve a feeling of inner peace and can die peacefully. He even sees death as a form of healing for some people whose bodies are tired and sore. But sometimes they have "a little miracle" and go on living for a while, "because there is so much peace that some healing does occur."[26]

Norman Cousins, author of the bestseller *Anatomy of an Illness*, has written several books in which he recorded his battle against life-threatening illnesses. He personally experienced the power of creativity, the importance of having a sense of purpose, and later the use of humor in maintaining the body's immune system in the fight against fatal illnesses. He gave numerous examples of people he knew who, despite bad hearts, emphysema, arthritis, or other diseases, lived into their eighties and nineties. He believed that they lived longer because they had a sense of purpose and that they had things to do; they had no reason to die. They had an appointment with life instead of with death.[27] In his book *Head First*, Cousins further elaborated on the power of hope in a patient's fight against cancer cells and the importance of a strong, trusting relationship with the treating doctor.[28] In the same book, he also stressed the power of laughter and the usefulness of humor in reducing stress and boosting the immune system.

CONCLUDING REMARKS

As a psychiatrist who has worked with cancer patients and with other dying patients, I have reached several conclusions that I would like to share with you.

First, I have become convinced that emotional states in dying patients can change the type of dying experience they will have. There is no question in my mind that the control of pain remains the single dominant preoccupation of patients facing imminent death in terminal illness. But it is also clear that the amount of pain a dying patient experiences depends on his or her mood level. If one's mood can be changed by some means, whether with the help of antidepressant medications, the use of support, or the giving of hope, one's tolerance of pain can be significantly increased. In any case, the problem of pain should never be underestimated or ignored in terminally ill persons.

Second, it is of utmost importance for patients to have trust in those who treat them and care for them. If you trust someone, you also gain hope, and many medical authorities agree that hope has tremendous impact on the course of illness and the well-being of seriously ill persons.

Third, emotional support cannot be overestimated. One should never feel that "there is nothing more that can be done," because as long as there is life, something can be done, if only to make the individual feel comfortable and at peace. We have reached such a stage of specialization in today's society that caring for a dying patient has also become a specialized matter. Physicians have become highly trained technicians in particular specialties, and in many cases, they have little time to see a patient through the end of an illness. One has to recognize this reality in the present world of medicine.

Fourth, it is not for us to judge whether the decisions made by a terminally ill person are right or wrong. Only that person knows what is the correct solution and what feels right for her or him. It is easy for theorists to debate the issues from academic viewpoints or for health professionals to cling to their own values, but in the last analysis, the dying person must face the ultimate truth of being and not being in this world. Ultimately, that truth is unique to each dying person, and it should not be challenged by those who view life from another perspective.

Finally, we can often determine the course of our illness in some ways if we choose to take some responsibility for making treatment decisions in cooperation with our doctor. The physician can advise, suggest, recommend and support, but the decisions about treatment should ultimately rest with us alone.

NOTES

1. Elizabeth Ogg, *Facing Death and Loss* (Lancaster, PA: Technomic, 1985), 31–53.
2. Robert W. Buckingham, *The Complete Hospice Guide* (New York: Harper & Row, 1983), 1–30.
3. Ibid.
4. T. A. Gonda and J. E. Ruark, *Dying Dignified: The Health Professional's Guide to Care* (Menlo Park, CA: Addison-Wesley, 1984), 205–213.
5. G. W. Davidson, ed., *The Hospice: Development and Administration* (Washington, D.C.: Hemisphere, 1985).
6. C. Saunders, ed., *The Management of Terminal Disease* (London: Edward Arnold, 1978).
7. L. Jones, "Hospice's Next Step: Moving into Mainstream of Medicine," *American Medical News,* 7 January 1991, 17–19.
8. Ibid.
9. Ibid.
10. Sandol Stoddard, *The Hospice Movement: A Better Way of Caring for the Dying* (New York: Vintage Books, 1978).
11. J. M. Zimmerman, *Hospice: Complete Care for the Terminally Ill* (Baltimore: Urban Schwarzenburg, 1986).

12. Robert Buckinham, *The Complete Hospice Guide* (New York: Harper & Row, 1983).

13. Leo Rangell, ed. *The Decision to Terminate One's Life: Psychoanalytic Thoughts on Suicide* (The American Association of Suicidology), 18 (1, 1988): 28–46.

14. Doris Portwood, *Common Sense Suicide: The Final Right* (Los Angeles: Hemlock Society, 1980), 29–33.

15. Elisabeth Kübler-Ross, *Questions and Answers on Death and Dying* (New York: Macmillan, 1974) 58.

16. Edwin Shneidman, "Some Essentials of Suicide and Some Implications for Response," in *Suicide,* ed. A. Roy. (Baltimore, Williams & Wilkins, 1986), 8.

17. Y. Conwell and E. D. Caine, "Rational Suicide and the Right to Die," *New England Journal of Medicine* 325 (1991): 1100–1103.

18. Kübler-Ross, 52–53.

19. American Health Consultants, "Polls Show Public Acceptance for Rational Suicide by Patients," *Medical Ethics Advisor* 6 (1991): 107–109.

20. Harry van Bommel, *Choices: For People Who Have a Terminal Illness, Their Families and Their Caregivers,* 2nd rev. ed. (Toronto: NC Press, 1987), 27–29.

21. Ibid.

22. Ogg, 31–53.

23. Lawrence LeShan, *You Can Fight for Your Life: Emotional Factors in the Causation of Cancer* (New York: M. Evans, 1977).

24. O. Carl Simonton, Stephanie Matthews-Simonton, and James Creighton, *Getting Well Again* (Los Angeles: J. P. Archer, Inc., 1978), 12.

25. Bernie Siegel, *Love, Medicine and Miracles* (New York: Harper & Row, 1986), 51–52.

26. Ibid.

27. Norman Cousins, *Anatomy of an Illness* (New York: W. W. Norton, 1979).

28. Norman Cousins, *Head First: The Biology of Hope* (New York: E. P. Dutton, 1989).

CHAPTER 10

Practical Steps to Gain Peace of Mind

In previous chapters, I prepared you to understand the complexities of the issues involved in decisions concerning life-sustaining treatments. Now you are ready to take some steps to gain peace of mind. This means that you should get ready to sign a few legal documents that will ensure that your wishes will be respected and that your family will be protected from the unexpected. These legal documents are called *advance directives.* Since December 1, 1991, federal law has required that all health-care institutions and agencies provide you with information regarding these advance directives.

It is best to prepare these documents before you become ill or incapacitated. Once you are in a hospital or in an institution, it may be more difficult for you or your family to deal with the completion of the advance directives.

I shall not discuss the preparation of a regular will, which is concerned with the transfer of assets and property. I will refer only to documents pertaining to medical decision making, especially those involving terminal illness.

HOW TO MAKE A LIVING WILL

A living will is a written document that states your wishes regarding the use of any medical treatment you choose to have in the event of terminal illness, a persistent vegetative state, or any condition in which you are unable to communicate. It tells the physician that, if you are in one of those conditions, you want to be allowed to die naturally, without receiving life-sustaining treatments, including food and water, except for measures that may be necessary to provide comfort and relief from pain.

The living will provides a way to limit the extent of the medical care and treatment that you will receive when you are no longer able to make these decisions and when death will occur within a relatively short time. You do not need a lawyer to make a living will, but you may want to consult a lawyer to check the validity of your living will and whether it satisfies your personal situation.

Your living will must be signed by you in front of two witnesses who are at least eighteen years old and who are not related to you. The witnesses cannot be employees of the facility where you are a patient, employees of your doctor, or your doctor or your beneficiaries. Finally, the living will must be notarized.

If you change your mind about your decision on life-sustaining treatment, you can revoke your living will by orally stating your intention to revoke it in front of two adult witnesses or by making a written statement, which must be signed and dated.

The living will is valid in most states whether you are competent or incompetent. You should consult the map in Appendix A for the current living-will statute in your state. In some states, the living will is not accepted by statute. In those states, the court will be satisfied with "clear and convincing evidence" that you have indicated to others your wish not to be kept alive under certain circumstances. If you want updated information on your state, you may call or write to Choice In Dying, Inc. (see Appendix F).

It is of utmost importance to have a living will, especially if you should become unable to speak for yourself while in the hospital. If you do not have a living will, decisions will be made by others, such as your family, the health personnel, or a court-appointed guardian (see Appendix H).

The living will should be updated periodically. The time period during which the living will is valid varies in each jurisdiction, so you should find out what is the law in your state. For a generic sample of a living will, please refer to Appendix B.

HOW TO APPOINT SOMEONE TO MAKE MEDICAL DECISIONS ON YOUR BEHALF

You can designate someone to make health care decisions for you in three ways.

First, you can appoint a person or agent by establishing a durable power of attorney for health care or medical treatment decisions. In some states, that document is made under a state statute. In other states, the declaration is made under case law based on previous court decisions. The document becomes effective only when the patient is incapable of making medical decisions (see Appendixes B and C). The forms differ from state to state, and they can be obtained from Choice in Dying, Inc.

Second, you can name a "proxy" in the text of your living will. Again you should be aware that conditions vary from state to state (see Appendix A).

Third, you can appoint an agent under a general-durable-power-of-attorney statute. Usually, a general power of attorney applies to property and money matters; it does not make specific mention of medical matters. This document may be usable in states where laws covering a proxy appointment or a durable power of attorney for health care do not exist (see Appendix A).

Next, I review the specific ways of appointing an agent for your health care decisions.

HOW TO OBTAIN A MEDICAL DURABLE POWER OF ATTORNEY

A medical durable power of attorney (or health care power of attorney, or health care proxy) is a written document that authorizes someone you name (your "agent" or "attorney-in-fact") to make medical decisions for you if you become unable to speak or to decide for yourself. The document outlines specific instructions that you wish your agent to follow.

Such a document is useful only if you are unable to communicate your wishes while you are in the hospital because of a temporary or permanent illness or injury. This document is particularly important in the event of terminal illness and when life support may be used. The document helps you retain some control over medical decisions so that you do not have to rely on others to guess about or interpret your wishes.

If you have not designated an agent (proxy), a court-appointed guardian may be appointed to make decisions for you, especially if money must be spent for your care. Such an appointed guardian may make decisions that do not agree with your values or your point of view. Your durable power of attorney, however, can include specific instructions on what you would choose in the way of life-sustaining treatments including dialysis, surgery, chemotherapy, resuscitation orders (CPR), the use of a ventilator, or intravenous feedings.

DIFFERENCES BETWEEN THE LIVING WILL AND THE MEDICAL DURABLE POWER OF ATTORNEY

The living will simply states your wishes and preferences about life-sustaining treatment in the event of terminal illness or other conditions in which you are unable to communicate. It does not name an agent to speak for you, although in some states that information can be included in the living will.

The medical durable power of attorney is more flexible than the living will and can include more details about the types of instructions you wish to give. It can

1. Designate a person to act as your agent in the event that you are unable to communicate your wishes. Such an agent can

participate in discussions with health personnel and make decisions based on his or her best judgment in accordance with your wishes.

2. Apply to all kinds of medical decisions, not only those pertaining to terminal illness. You may specify limitations, however, according to your preferences.

3. Include instructions regarding specific types of treatment that you want to include or exclude.

Treatments that you may choose to restrict include

- Artificial respiration
- Artificial hydration and nutrition (food and water given through tubes)
- Cardiac resuscitation (CPR)
- Antipsychotic medications
- Psychosurgery
- Antibiotics
- Organ transplantation
- Dialysis
- Blood transfusions
- Abortion
- Sterilization

You should review this list with your physician before you sign it to be sure your decision is based on correct information. It is important that the decision be a cooperative one between you and your doctor.

It is advisable to have both a medical power of attorney and a living will, provided that both documents are in accordance with the laws of our state and in agreement with each other.

Because each state has special laws and regulations regarding the medical (or health care) power of attorney, it is necessary for you to check which forms are legal in your state. If you are in doubt, get legal advice or check with Choice in Dying, Inc., which has published a chart on the durable power of attorney and the living-will laws (see Appendixes A and C).[1]

HOW TO NAME A PROXY

Another way of being sure that someone will make appropriate medical decisions for you when you are unable to make them is to appoint a proxy within your living will. The person you choose as your proxy should be someone you trust, such as your spouse, a relative, or a close friend.

In some states, you can appoint a proxy directly on the living-will form; in other states, you may have to complete an additional form. Check the map in Appendixes A and C for specific information concerning your state.[2]

THE QUESTION OF ORGAN AND TISSUE DONATION

The personal decision about donating organs in case of brain death is another one that you should make along with your decisions about advance directives.

Federal law mandates that hospitals inform the family of a deceased person about organ donation.[3] Families, however, have the right to refuse organ or tissue donation even if the deceased meets all the criteria. This means that without family consent, organ or tissue donation will not be permitted. The family's wish prevails even if the individual has expressed a wish to donate or carries a card approving the removal of organs. A Gallup poll commissioned by the Dow Chemical Company in 1987 showed that 53 percent of Americans who were aware of transplantation did not know that the family's consent was essential before organs and tissues could be removed. Therefore, it is crucial that family members discuss their intentions about transplantation at death in advance of a crisis. Families who carry out a relative's wish to donate often find some meaning in what otherwise might seem a senseless death.[4]

There are several fears about donating organs or tissues. I

shall clarify several misconceptions that exist among the public today:

1. Donating organs will not interfere with receiving medical treatment in the hospital. Doctors are not more interested in obtaining organs than in providing their patients with proper treatment.

2. Organ donation is considered only after all attempts to save a life have been made.

3. Organ donation will not take place until the heart has stopped beating or brain death has been established. As discussed earlier, the techniques for establishing brain death are precise, and the criteria are strictly defined. The physician who establishes the diagnosis of brain death has no role in the procurement or transplantation of tissues or organs.

4. For viable organs, such as the heart, the lungs, the liver, the pancreas, and the kidneys, to be obtained, brain-dead individuals must be maintained on a respirator. However, the donation of eyes, bone, skin, and other tissues does not require maintenance on a respirator. These tissues can be obtained from six to twelve or twenty-four hours after breathing and heartbeat have stopped (see Appendix G for specific criteria for each organ).

5. The body will not be disfigured by organ donation. After the removal of the donated organs, the surgical team will leave the body intact for proper funeral or burial arrangements.

6. The family does not receive any compensation or fee for the donation. It is illegal to buy or sell organs or tissues.

7. There is no charge or fee connected with the removal of organs or tissues.

8. All major religions support the concept of organ and tissue donation as well as the concept of brain death.

Whether organ and tissue donation should remain a personal decision is being debated among ethicists. The problem today, which will continue over the coming decades, is how to cope with the increasing demand for organ transplants. The need for organs has risen steadily, and 1,878 people died in 1989 while waiting for organ transplantation, according to the United Network for Organ Sharing (UNOS).[5] Despite the rising need, the supply of donated organs has remained constant at a rate of 4,000 per year.

Currently, organ donation is governed by a voluntary system. However, health-care institutions are being asked to reexamine their policies and to consider a new policy of so-called presumed consent, which is already in effect in several European countries, including France and Belgium. This policy assumes that it is permissible to obtain organs unless objections are raised ahead of time by the potential donor or by the family. A modified version of this policy is already law in several states. Up to now, the policy in the United States has been to ask the family for permission to obtain organs if the deceased did not indicate a preference before death. In practice, however, this policy has not worked well, and therefore it has not answered the increasing need for organs.

Part of the problem is that physicians often feel awkward asking for organ donations from families stricken with grief, even though the opportunity to save another life may give families a sense of relief and a sense of some meaning to their loved one's death.[6] In the midst of the acute crisis following a death, the family may not think of the opportunity to donate organs but may later be grateful to the physician for having brought up the question.[7] In fact, the public seems to favor the idea of organ donation. A 1990 Gallup poll showed that 85 percent of a sample of Americans were in favor of organ donation by a loved one, and 60 percent said they would donate their own organs.[8]

Despite this receptive attitude of the public, Thomas G. Peters of the Jacksonville (Florida) Transplant Center maintains that relying on altruism will not solve the critical organ shortage.[9] He is suggesting a $1,000 benefit that would encourage families to grant permission for the donation of a relative's organs. As one would expect, this suggestion remains controversial, but it will stimulate more debate on the shortage of organs for transplant in the years to come.

You should be aware that jurisdictions have their own laws regarding organ donation. These laws are set in specific anatomical gift acts, so you should check on those of your own state so that your wishes can be carried out properly. In some states, for example, your wishes are indicated on your driver's license.

Here are a few more facts regarding organ donation that may be of interest to you:

1. Organ donation does not interfere with funeral arrangements. Funeral directors can direct embalmers to prepare the body appropriately.

2. The most common organ and tissue transplants are skin, lungs, heart, liver, kidneys, corneas, certain bones, pancreas, and middle ear.

3. Time is of the essence in most organ transplants except for skin and corneas, so the removal of most organs is likely to occur in the acute hospital.

4. Even if you have indicated your wish to donate organs, the medical transplant team may not accept the donation. Many variables must be considered, such as the health of the donor (See Appendix G).

5. Generally speaking, organs are more suitable if they come from people under seventy years old. Also, the organs of cancer patients (except in some cases of brain cancer) or of patients with infections or other serious diseases are not suitable for donation (see Appendix G).

6. Transportation and other incurred costs are usually covered by the organizations procuring the organs for transplant. There are many organizations that coordinate organ donation, and there is probably one in your area.

7. Whether or not you decide to donate your organs, there is already a federal law in the country to enact laws of "required request" that will require hospitals to inform the families of deceased patients of the option of organ donation. This is one more reason for having a prior discussion with your family to let them know of your preferences on this issue.

8. Organ donation does not interfere with a living will, which refers to your wishes while you are still alive, even if you are in a coma or persistent vegetative state. Organ donation can take place only when the donor is brain dead. In other words, if

your living will states that you wish to stop life-sustaining treatments, it does not imply that you are making an organ donation. Organ donations can occur only when a person's whole brain has ceased to function and she or he has been diagnosed as brain dead.[10]

If you wish to donate your organs, you can obtain a card from the Division of Organ Transplantation, a branch of the Public Health Service of the U.S. Department of Health and Human Services (see Appendix F). That card becomes a legal document when signed and witnessed by two adult persons, since it is in accord with the federal Uniform Anatomical Gift Act. There is also an international organization called "Living Bank" that deals with organ donation (see Appendix F).[11]

In summary, it is best to avoid all last-minute problems by indicating your wishes in advance. If you have not yet expressed your preferences in writing, at the very least you should have a discussion with your family as soon as possible. Such a discussion will prevent your family, or strangers, from later having to make decisions under pressure.

DECISIONS TO MAKE IN THE HOSPITAL AND INFORMED CONSENT

If you have completed the advance directives, you will not have to make any decisions regarding life-support measures unless you change your mind while you are in the hospital. No matter what you have decided in the past, you can always change your mind either orally or in writing.

You may still have to decide whether you wish to have surgery or any other procedure if it is suggested by your doctor. Remember that your doctor remains your main source of information, so do not hesitate to ask questions. As I have pointed out earlier, if you do not understand something, ask again until the explanation is clear. Your doctor may not always sense whether you have clearly understood. If you still have questions about whether to undergo a major procedure, you should ask for a second opinion, or even a third. Remember that these decisions often occur once in a lifetime. You want to have as much information as possible to make an intelligent and informed decision. Doctors usually welcome their patients' participation in taking responsibility. Their suggestions and recommendations are based on professional knowledge and experience, but the final decision must remain in your hands. Should you have any questions about the living will as it relates to your religious beliefs, you should resolve them with your clergyman.

Before you receive any medical treatment or procedure, you will be asked to sign an "informed consent." Before you sign, you should know the answers to the following questions:

1. Why is the procedure, surgery, or medical treatment necessary?

2. What are the risks involved?

3. What are the expected outcomes of the treatment or procedures?

4. What alternative interventions would be reasonable, given the risks and burdens of the treatment?

If you cannot answer the above questions, you need further discussion with your doctor. In the event of a serious illness, or a condition that might require artificial life support, you should also discuss the issue with your spouse, your family, and others closest to you.

As we discussed in Chapter 6, the question of emergency resuscitation procedures may have to be decided between you and your doctor. Cardiopulmonary resuscitation or CPR or "code," also known as *code 500*, is a set of emergency procedures carried out on a person whose heart and/or lungs have stopped suddenly. The resuscitation may involve external chest compression (pushing down on your chest) to restore circulation, electric shock to stimulate the heart, a breathing tube inserted in the windpipe, or medication. The patient is usually transferred to the intensive care unit as soon as feasible.

There are situations in which resuscitation may not be desirable. For example, in the case of terminal illness, patients and families may not wish to undergo these procedures if they will only prolong suffering in the dying process. In such situations, the main concern is to provide comfort and dignity.

But unless you and your physician decide otherwise, a code 500 will be carried out.

WHEN AND HOW TO DECIDE ON GUARDIANSHIP

The question of guardianship arises when the physician or the family believes that the patient is unable to make proper decisions about her or his health care, that is, is incompetent. A careful assessment must be made by the physician, but an official declaration of incompetence is a legal decision, not a medical or a psychiatric one.

The question of competency usually arises when the physician, the family, or someone else involved in the medical treatment disagrees with the course of action for the patient. This is often the case for elderly or terminally ill patients. Usually, the physician assesses the clinical situation before resorting to the legal route. When a substitute decision maker must be appointed, guardianship must be instituted.

Different states have different methods of appointing guardians, with different limitations. Most states, however, give the guardian the power to consent to medical care or treatment. At a court hearing, the patient, if able, is allowed to be present with legal counsel and can present further evidence by presenting witnesses. The judge then decides on the basis of the evidence whether the patient meets the legal criteria for incompetency and whether a guardian should be appointed. The decision on the choice of a guardian varies from state to state, but it generally includes the patient's spouse, parents, or grown children.

If documents such as a durable power of attorney for health care or the appointment of a proxy have been prepared, there should be no problem in the event that incompetency develops while a person is in the hospital. Otherwise, guardianship may have to be established by court order. If there is no family, a guardian *ad litem* will be appointed by the court.

The guardianship process can be expensive, complex, and restrictive. That is why some states, like Maryland, have adopted a system in which a substitute decision maker can be appointed without court involvement. In those cases, two physicians can decide whether the patient "lacks sufficient understanding or capacity to make or communicate a responsible decision on health care."[12] Then the next of kin is usually designated as guardian.

In summary, whenever the question of guardianship arises, it is best to work closely with the attending physician and with an attorney.

WHERE TO LOCATE YOUR DOCUMENTS

Once you have completed your advance directives, it is very important that they be safely stored and that copies be distributed to the appropriate parties. Many people who complete the documents file them in a drawer at home. Unfortunately, if your doctor, lawyer, or family does not have it, it will not be useful. Such documents should be filed with all other important family documents, such as ownership papers, account statements, insurance policies, will, and trusts.

A copy of the living will should also be filed in your medical and hospital charts. Extra copies should be given to your spouse, your next of kin or other designated individual, and your attorney. Durable-power-of-attorney copies should be filed with other family documents and should be easily accessible to the person(s) entrusted with making your health care decisions. Many people use safety deposit boxes or safe files at home. What is important consideration is that the proper person have either copies of these documents or access to them when the time comes for their use.

SUMMARY OF STEPS FOR ADVANCE DIRECTIVES

1. Check the laws in your state regarding living wills and the durable power of attorney for health care.

2. Put your wishes in writing, and be specific concerning resuscitation orders, organ donation, tube-feeding, and other medical procedures.

3. Sign and date your advance directives, and have them witnessed, in the presence of a notary, by two adult witnesses not related to you.

4. Keep a card in your purse or wallet that indicates what advance directives you have and where to find them.

5. Be sure to give your physician copies to be kept in your medical record.

6. Don't forget to discuss your advance directives and wishes with your family or close friends, giving a copy to whoever is likely to be notified in an emergency.

7. Review your advance directives from time to time, especially in the event of a serious illness, and inform your family, friends, and physician of any changes you make. You can always revise or cancel advance directives orally or in writing.

8. If you need more information, you can consult your physician, an attorney, or Choice in Dying, Inc.

As we have discussed at some length in this book so far, decisions concerning life and death are always difficult. I hope that you have reached a more informed point of view as you have read this book and before you enter a hospital. If you have delayed taking the steps outlined above, you still have a chance to express your feelings and make your decisions, but it is in your interest to accomplish the task as soon as possible.

YOUR PEACE OF MIND

Once you have completed the documents listed above, you can relax and enjoy your peace of mind. In the next chapter, I discuss some issues that will emerge over the next few decades to command our thoughtful attention.

NOTES

1. Society for the Right to Die, "What You Should Know about Medical Durable Power of Attorney, Proxy Appointments, Health Care Agents" (New York: Author, 1991).
2. Ibid.
3. Omnibus Budget Reconciliation Act of 1986, Section 9318. Hospital Protocols for Organ Procurement.
4. L. G. Hunsicker, "Families Must Know of Organ-Donation Plans," *New York Times*, 2 October 1987, 2.
5. American Health Consultants, "Proposals to Increase Supply of Organs Cause Concern," *Medical Ethics Advisor* 7 (1991): 97–99.
6. T. Gonda, "Organ Transplantation and the Psychosocial Aspects of Terminal Care," in *Psychosocial Aspects of Terminal Care*, ed. B. Schoenberg, A. C. Carr, D. Peretz, and A. H. Kutscher (New York: Columbia University Press, 1972).
7. George M. Burnell and Adrienne L. Burnell, *Clinical Management of Bereavement: Handbook for Healthcare Professionals* (New York: Human Sciences Press, 1989), 157.
8. American Health Consultants, 99.
9. T. G. Peters, "Life or Death: The Issue of Payment in Cadaveric Organ Donation," *Journal of the American Medical Association* 265 (1991): 1302–1305.
10. Society for the Right to Die, "Organ Donation and The Living Will" (New York: Author, 1991).
11. Harry van Bommel, *Choices: For People Who Have a Terminal Illness, Their Families and Their Caregivers*, 2nd rev. ed. (Toronto: NC Press, 1987), 139.
12. J. S. Janofsky, "Assessing Competency in the Elderly," *Geriatrics* 45 (1990): 45–48.

CHAPTER 11

Blueprint for the Future

Our society seems to be constantly evolving. As tested by public polls, concepts and attitudes are continually changing. What was once considered unimaginable is becoming acceptable or even desirable. As our life span is increasing in each decade, new issues arise about the subject of aging. After all, aging is another way of prolonging life.

Do we have a strategy for coping with the new problems of aging in an era of technology? How can an individual prepare to meet the challenges of a longer life? What will society do to help the individual adjust to the last decades of life? Will the laws adapt to the new demands of an older society? What role will economics play in shaping the elderly's adjustment to the coming century?

Although no definite answers can be given at this time, we must start the discussion that will eventually lead to answers, just as it has over the past few decades. Now is the time to draw a blueprint for the future.

In this chapter, I will examine other ways of prolonging life that will force us to think of new solutions.

AGING IN THE TWENTY-FIRST CENTURY

By the time we enter the next century, more than a quarter of the population in the United States will be sixty-five or older.

During this century, there has been a rapid rise in the number of aged and aging individuals. In 1900, 3.1 million people were elderly. Now the number is over 20 million. By the year 2000, the estimate is that there will be 41 million people aged sixty-five or older.

In 1984, the U.S. Census Bureau projected an "ultimate life expectancy" for the year 2080 in the range of 77.4 to 85.9 years, with an average figure of 81 years.[1] That is a gigantic leap forward in average life expectancy.

The group of seventy-five to eighty-four-year-olds is now eleven times greater than it was in 1900. By the year 2050, the ratio of young (below 56) to old (over 65) is expected to be 38 to 100. Undoubtedly, this ratio will have major repercussions in all aspects of our lives.

Take the problem of transplant surgery, for example. Transplant operations are becoming more sophisticated, but considering the shortage of organs, should we make them available to the elderly? And will the government want to continue subsidizing such expensive procedures?

In England, for example, transplant operations are not available to the elderly. The same thing may happen in the United States, where "the old will cost more and more," according to Milton Greenblatt, chief of psychiatry at Los Angeles, County-Olive View Medical Center, Sylmar, California.[2] In the late 1980s, health care costs for the aged soared to over 33 percent of the American health care budget; by 2040 it will be 45 percent. Does this mean that care for the aged should be restricted? Such a restriction would raise a host of ethical problems. Daniel Callahan, a prominent ethicist, writes in his book *Setting Limits*, "Are the aged a biologically surplus and financially burdensome group?"[3]

If the aged will not be allowed to prolong their lives by procuring rejuvenating operations, will they then be allowed to choose to die? One of the greatest fears of the elderly is becoming a burden to their children. This fear is reinforced by an increasing awareness of the impact on families of such chronic diseases as

Alzheimer's, Parkinson's, and Lou Gehrig's (amyotrophic lateral sclerosis), to name just a few. In fact, Alzheimer's disease has become the most dreaded disease of the aged. At a conference entitled "The Sandwich Generation: Intergenerational Partnership on Long Term Care," a group of women were polled on their attitudes toward aging. Over 50 percent admitted that, although they had fears of old age, they were unsure about their plans for long-term care.[4]

Anne R. Somers, an expert on health care policies in the United States, stresses that we must address the problems of the aging population in the next century with a set of brand-new policies. She says that it is ironic that, at a time when we are achieving the greatest medical advances, the presumed beneficiaries of such historic progress, the aged population, are focusing on the right to die.[5]

To counteract the problems of aging, several writers have made important suggestions for policymakers. Robert Butler, former director of the National Institute on Aging, now chairman of the Department of Geriatrics and Adult Development at Mount Sinai School of Medicine in New York, proposes that we focus on what he calls "productive aging."[6] This concept was explored further at a Salzburg international seminar in 1983, where experts stressed the value of mobilizing the productive potential of society's elders. The implication was that, if we continue to be active and productive, we will have a better chance of staying healthy as we age, that is, if we don't develop a chronic illness in the meantime.

Another writer, Walter Bortz, a former president of the American Geriatrics Society, also stresses the importance of remaining active and productive, coining the term "disuse syndrome," which reflects the old cliché of "use it or lose it."[7]

Others still, rather than emphasize productivity, have focused on health promotion and disease prevention in the aged. J.W. Rowe and R.L. Kahn wrote in a 1987 article in *Science Magazine*, "A major component of many age-associated declines can be explained in terms of life style, habits, diet, and an array of psychosocial factors extrinsic to the aging process."[8] Yet there is a prevailing feeling among the general population that medicine will eventually take care of all our aging problems. Arthur Barsky, an associate professor of psychiatry at Harvard Medical School, says, "Most people believe that medical science will develop cures for all of our most lethal diseases before they themselves are afflicted .... Disease seems to us a technical problem, like landing a man on the moon, that can be solved if only we bring enough resources and effort and skill into it."[9]

Others are also offering optimistic comments. Erik Erikson, Joan Erikson, and Helen Kivnick, in their book *Vital Involvement in Old Age*, emphasize the responsibility of society to take care of their elders and wonder what steps can be taken now to insure that the elderly in the future will remain an integral part of the social fabric. They conclude that "society owes its citizens encouragement and opportunity to develop their well-being and should provide as many avenues as possible for the maintenance of stamina in old age."[10] Bortz went even further by suggesting that we adopt an Age Constitution that addresses particularly the rights and responsibilities of our older selves, especially the responsibilities.[11]

Somers makes the following recommendation to the policymakers of tomorrow: "In our large, complex, heterogeneous, and highly organized democracy the relationship between rights and responsibilities often becomes attenuated and at times almost disappears from view. In the last analysis, however, we ignore the relationship at our own peril. U.S. aging policy, as in other ones, must reflect the balance of rights and responsibilities on the part of both the individual and society."[12]

How the government allocates funds is one indication of how the policymakers interpret recommendations on aging. In 1982, the federal government spent $191 billion on problems related to aging. Most of this went to support social services for the elderly.[13] Research on the aging process itself received only a fraction of the budget allocated to the Institute of Aging. Perhaps the government is not as interested as we are in prolonging life.

IS THERE A NURSING HOME IN YOUR FUTURE?

There are still other ways of prolonging life that may have less than desirable outcomes. Most of us who have gone to visit an elderly relative or friend who has been lying in a fetal position, in a semivegetative state for years, fed by nasogastric tubes, are familiar with the scene. Many of us have said, "I'll make sure that doesn't happen to me."

In all likelihood, long-term care will be a major concern for aging Americans. According to one study published in the *New England Journal of Medicine*, 43 percent of those who turned sixty-five in 1990 will spend some time in a nursing home before they die. Of those who will enter a nursing home, 55 percent will stay there at least one year, and 21 percent will stay five or more years. Among those who will reside in a nursing home, women will outnumber men at a ratio of 52 to 33 percent. As expected, these trends have major medical, social, and financial implications for the growing elderly population.[14]

The cost implications are tremendous, because most people will not be able to afford long-term care, except the poor who are covered by Medicaid. Elderly people who rely on Medicare are already finding out that coverage extends to only 100 days. Yet the average length of stay is 2.5 years. For the average middle-class family, funds will be exhausted within thirteen weeks at the rates currently charged by nursing homes for twenty-four-hour-a-day custodial care ($2,000 to $3,000 per month).[15]

In a presentation to the American Association of University Women in Honolulu, Jeanette Takamura estimated that, by the year 2020, the stay in a nursing home for one year will cost $220,000, and for two and a half years over $500,000![16] In her talk, entitled "Plan for Your Future," she recommended the following three steps: (1) make a careful review of your support system; (2) make sure that you have friends who are younger than you; and (3) look into insurance for long-term care with a great deal of caution.

Planning for nursing-home care will be a problem for at least the next few decades. Americans are clearly ambivalent about planning for such care. On the one hand, insurance companies are beginning to offer long-term care insurance; on the other hand, a study done by the Brookings Institution shows that most people will not be able to afford it.[17] Others have offered alternative solutions, saying that most people really do not need around-the-clock personal nursing care; they need only a few hours per day. These experts would separate the financing of personal care from the financing of the housing and hotel functions. They would recommend universal coverage for the personal care portion and coverage for the housing portion that will be based on the person's ability to pay.[18] Such different questions will concern all of us who are on the aging ladder as prolonging life becomes technologically easier.

DYING IN THE TWENTY-FIRST CENTURY

If aging is not a disease, some say, then what do people die of? Is there such a thing as "dying of old age"? We know of many people who die between the ages of 90 and 100. Yet the concept of death as a natural event still remains controversial among certain groups. Greek philosophers raised the question, "Why is it that man must die?" Since then, the quest for immortality has occupied writers, artists, and poets for centuries, and it will probably continue to do so.

But the question most of us ask today is not "Must we die?" but "When we die, can we die with dignity?" As we have seen in earlier chapters, modern medical technology has transformed the process of dying into a potential ordeal rather than a natural and gentle happening. Many people say they are not as afraid of death as they are of the process of dying.

Because we know how to prolong life by so many technological means, the debate will swing the pendulum from prolonging life at all costs to letting people die a natural death. The right to die a natural death will become an expectation, but part of that expectation will be that biomedical interventions will help ease the burdens of dying. The physician will have "to give permission to die."[19] The irony is that people will expect technology to help them die, when in fact it will often complicate the dying process. It is as though the "health consumer" has been taught that dying can occur only in the intensive-care unit.[20]

Advancing the argument a bit further, Robert Veatch says that "natural death may have a rather different future over the next decade or two .... We may discover that 'natural death' was nothing more than an accident in human history, arriving in the fifteenth century as humans began to discard the accretions of supernaturalism and departing in about 1984 when we realized that no death is a natural death."[21]

As the pathologist would say today, something always causes death; it never just happens. This view was echoed by Edward Schneider, deputy director of the National Institute on Aging, who said, "Natural death or dying from natural aging has gone down drastically as we actually found out what they were dying from. Now any diagnosis of natural death is because the physician is too lazy to find out what the person really died from. You don't die from old age; you die from disease."[22]

So the concern with death will become primarily a concern about dying with dignity, a painless and honorable death. Over the next two decades, many jurisdictions will pass natural-death acts, granting people the right to execute advance directives requesting that they be allowed to die without having to endure life-prolonging procedures or "heroic measures." Medical ethics courses will finally become compulsory in medical schools and will revise the doctrine that the main duty of the physician is to prolong life, teaching instead that each case is unique and that no general rules apply. A new goal for physicians and nurses will be to sharpen their skills in reducing patients' fears of dying and in providing them with adequate pain relief and comfort.

Patrick F. Sheehy, a cancer specialist, has offered yet another view of dying in the future. In his book *Dying with Dignity*, he writes, "With the current advanced art of medical science, physicians can tell us in the late stages of a disease that it is only a matter of weeks or months before a vital organ will cease functioning. We can also predict what the quality of the remaining time will be for the patient. If death is imminent, and if there are only the throes of physical pain and struggle left, I believe that a doctor should be allowed to give you a drug that will painlessly release you to death. As society matures, I foresee a time when this will be possible."[23]

No matter how radical those views seem now, the hope is that, in the near future, there will be individual choices about dying, whether it be through the use of a hospice, intensive treatment with life-sustaining measures, or the performance of euthanasia. Then it will no longer be necessary to view death as an enemy that needs to be conquered. Finally, death can be welcomed after a full and productive life.

ORGAN TRANSPLANTATION AND MEDICAL TECHNOLOGY

Medical technology in the 1990s has had an impact not only on the way we die but also on the aftermath of dying. We have seen in earlier chapters how modern medical technology can save lives or complicate the process of dying. Now we are being asked to plan ahead for the use of our organs and tissues as a potential benefit to other human beings.

Yet, despite considerable publicity and media coverage, people are still ambivalent about donating organs upon death. A recent public-television program announced that there were 24,000 persons awaiting the donation of a heart, a kidney, a liver, or a pancreas. For these people, the wait is filled with fear and anxiety because they must stay alive until someone's organ is delivered to the hospital. Despite the public's awareness of the need, recent surveys show that only 60 percent of families are willing to donate their loved ones' organs.

The shortage of organs poses serious problems for thousands of people in the country. The scarcity of organs raises the difficult question of who should receive the few available organs. Who should select the donees as organs become available? What criteria should be used for this selection? All of these questions will be the subject of debate, research, and legislation. John F. Kilner, an associate professor of social and medical ethics at Asbury Theological Seminary and a professor of medical ethics at the University of Kentucky, has proposed sophisticated criteria for patient selection in his book *Who Lives? Who Dies?*[24]

Some doctors speculate that in the future, donors will carry donor cards similar to credit cards. These cards will have a magnetic tape that contains the donor's biological data, such as blood and tissue types, age, and medical history. The information will be relayed to a central data bank accessible to physicians, who will be able to quickly locate and match recipients with available tissues or organs.

As we discussed in Chapter 10, legislation for so-called required request has already been enacted in 1986 in response to the increasing demand by a population eligible for organ transplantation. Meanwhile, donor centers must educate the public to overcome fears and prejudices. As one potential donor said to *Newsweek* magazine, "It is simple, logical, scientifically useful—and it is one foolproof way of beating the undertaker."[25] George Schreiner, past president of the National Kidney Foundation, put it another way: "When living, generosity has to do with financial means. This, however, is really the most democratic and essential charity man can give."[26]

In the coming years, as the world becomes even more accessible and barriers tumble, organs will be flown from one country to another to save lives across the globe. At that point, when one person willingly offers the gift of life to another, the world will truly have become a better place.

THE PROBLEM OF AIDS

Prolonging life and hastening death have become daily questions for people struggling with the deadly virus of AIDS. In the next few years, millions of people afflicted with this disease will be asking for life-sustaining treatments or for aid in dying, and the health and legal systems will have to come up with criteria for meeting patients' requests. I believe that planning should start now, despite the government's tendency to postpone the inevitable.

Although the prognosis for AIDS has greatly improved, the number of cases is still rising worldwide. According to a World Health Organization report, the number of reported cases in the world was 418,403 in 1991, the United States accounting for 191,600 cases.[27] Other countries that are severely affected include Tanzania and Uganda, followed by Brazil and France. The report also said that nine to eleven million people are infected with the HIV virus worldwide.

Because of such awesome statistics and an increasing demand for medical research and supportive services, health personnel will have to develop better criteria for care and the allocation of resources. Individuals will be expected to take increasing responsibility for home care. Many people will need emotional support to cope with terminal illness. New drugs are already beginning to appear, and new forms of therapy will undoubtedly emerge from the research on arresting and curing the dreadful disease.[28]

THE PROBLEM OF ALZHEIMER'S DISEASE

Prolonging the life of someone suffering from Alzheimer's disease is dreaded by many of us. There are no easy answers for the best way to cope. My own mother, once a vibrant and intelligent businesswoman, spent the last few years of her life not knowing where she was or what was going on around her. It was not an ending she would have wanted for herself. But as I chronicled in Chapter 4, her death was complicated by an unforeseen series of events. Almost every month, I see relatives of patients with Alzheimer's disease who are seeking ways to cope with a loved one they describe as "not the person I used to know."

In the 1960s, I spent several years in academic research studying the possible causes and the effects of Alzheimer's disease. Thirty years later, we still don't know what causes this disease, although some recent research points to a genetic predisposition. It may take another decade or more for us to gain control of the condition, but in the meantime, how do we cope with it? The disease itself is not fatal, but it makes the individual vulnerable to other illnesses that will attack the weakened body. Nevertheless, the person may live for several years in a state of "mind death" or "partial brain death," as some people have called it.

There is perhaps no better argument for having advance directives and a durable power of attorney for health care than the possibility of Alzheimer's disease. The argument is even more persuasive if you have a family history of the disease, as is true in my own case. Executing advance directives may turn out to be the most important decision for yourself and your family that you will make in your lifetime. Until a cure is found sometime in the future, planning ahead is the best that you can do.

FUTURE LEGISLATION

Because we are likely to see all states enact some version of the natural-death act, one of the most advanced at this time is a proposal for a new Death with Dignity Act in California. A draft has been prepared by the group called Americans against Human Suffering, spearheaded by Robert Risley, an attorney who is the president of that organization.

The California Death with Dignity Act would permit an adult to request and receive a physician's aid in dying in carefully defined circumstances. It would provide physicians and

health-care professionals with immunity from civil and criminal
liability in carrying out their patients' wishes. In order to qualify for
such aid, a competent terminally ill adult would have to sign a
Death with Dignity Act directive, as specified in the statute.[29] Along
with California, Oregon and Colorado are considering similar
legislation involving death with dignity, including aid in dying.*

CHANGING ROLES FOR
PHYSICIANS AND FAMILIES

Physicians rarely initiate discussions of advance directives
with their patients, even if their patients are elderly.[30] This is true
even when patients are eager to discuss the issues.[31] But public
awareness and proposed legislation will force physicians to take
a more active role in counseling patients about life-sustaining
measures and advance directives.

Anticipating this need, a group of researchers have developed a questionnaire called the Values History. It will help health
professionals develop a dialogue with patients once the questionnaire is completed.[32] The structured instrument inquires about
the individual's attitudes toward illness, dying, and death, and it
also leads to answers to the two crucial questions of who should
be empowered to make decisions about one's health care (e.g., a
family member, a friend, or a nursing-home administrator) and
what information the decision should be based on. This question–answer format will encourage the dialogue that must take
place between doctor and patient. It will stimulate the kind of
conversation that is often lacking in the doctor's office, and that
will respect the patient's autonomy and wishes.[33] It will also
afford an opportunity to review advance directives from time to
time in your lifetime. Although we cannot predict our future, it

---

*The California Death and Dignity initiative, known as Proposition 161, was
defeated on the November 3, 1992 ballot by a 46% yes vote (4,562,110) against a
54% no vote (5,348,947).

will at least let the doctor know the person we are and hope to be in the very end.

The same questionnaire can be used to initiate and carry on a discussion with your family. Most people have not been able to find the words to discuss these difficult questions, and more often than not, family members are quick to brush the subject aside. The irony is that most people, especially when they are seriously ill, would welcome a frank discussion.

Unfortunately, the topic is often misinterpreted as meaning that the patient expects to die soon. That expectation is mistakenly viewed as a negative thought that is demoralizing to the person who is ill. This is one more reason for bringing up the subject when a person is well. In the next few decades, I suspect that such taboos will relax and people will feel free to talk about death and dying openly and frankly.

CONCLUSION

It has been said that "to make death no longer a source of dread is one of the great challenges of the age."[34] The 1990s will continue to be a decade of major social change. The rights of the individual will be discussed in all phases of life, and vigorous efforts will be made to preserve self-respect and autonomy. Exercising the right to die may well be our ultimate right in the modern world of technological choices. It should be permitted under the law because self-determination is the most basic of freedoms and is constitutionally protected. Self-determination includes the absolute right to control our destiny, our goals, and our values as long as we do not infringe on the rights of others. This right ought to include our right to choose the kind of treatment we wish to have at life's end. It should also provide individuals with the freedom to decide with their physicians about the kind of ending they wish to have for themselves.

This notion goes along with the maturing of a democratic society. Such a freedom will be very encouraging for future generations. No longer will we have to live with hidden agendas, unspoken truths, and undeclared feelings.

Perhaps we will even reach a point where we will no longer have to lie to anyone, not even to ourselves, until death do us part.

NOTES

1. U.S. Department of Health and Human Services, *Health, United States,* ed. National Center for Health Statistics Public Health Service, DHHS Pub. No. (PHS)87-1232, (Washington, DC: U.S Government Printing Office, 1986).
2. "An Aging America May Necessitate New Attention to Ethical Issues," *Clinical Psychiatry News* 16 (April 1988): 21.
3. D. Callahan, *Setting Limits: Medical Goals in an Aging Society* (New York: Simon & Schuster, 1987), 197.
4. Ann Clark, "The Sandwich Generation: Intergenerational Partnership on Long Term Care," Special meeting of the American Association of University Women, Honolulu, September 10, 1991.
5. Anne R. Somers, "Aging in the 21st century: Projections, Personal Preferences, Public Policies—A Consumer View," *Health Policy* 9 (1988): 49–58.
6. R. N. Butler and H. P. Gleason, eds., *Productive Aging: Enhancing Vitality in Later Life* (New York: Springer, 1985).
7. Walter M. Bortz II, *We Live Too Short and Die Too Long: How to Achieve and Enjoy Your Natural 100-Year Plus Life Span* (New York: Bantam Books, 1991), 135–136, 263.
8. J. W. Rowe and R. L. Kahn, "Human Aging: Useful and Successful," *Science* 237 (1987): 194.
9. Arthur Barsky, *Worried Sick: Our Troubled Quest for Wellness* (Boston: Little, Brown & Co., 1988).
10. Erik Erikson, Joan Erikson, and Helen Kivnick, *Vital Involvement in Old Age* (New York: Norton, 1986).
11. Bortz, 263.
12. Somers, 49–58.
13. R. Bayer and D. Callahan, "Medicare Reform: Social and Ethical Perspectives," *Journal of Health Politics, Policy and Law* 10 (1985): 534.
14. P. Kemper and C. M. Murtaugh, "Lifetime Use of Nursing Home Care," *New England Journal of Medicine* 324 (1991): 595–600.

15. P. Hunter, "Insurance Covers Long-Term Care in Nursing Homes," *The Sunday Star-Bulletin and Advertiser*, 21 September 1986, B-3.

16. Jeanette Takamura, "Plan for Your Future," presentation for the Special Community Program of the American Association of University Women, Honolulu, September 10, 1991.

17. A. M. Rivlin and J. M. Wiener, *Caring for the Disabled Elderly: Who Will Pay?* (Washington, D.C.: Brookings Institution, 1988).

18. R. L. Kane and R. A. Kane, "A Nursing Home in Your Future?" *New England Journal of Medicine* 324 (1991): 627–629.

19. Eric Casssel, "Permission to Die," *BioScience* 23 (1973): 475–478.

20. Robert M. Veatch, *Death, Dying and the Biological Revolution: Our Last Quest for Responsibility* (New Haven: CN: Yale University Press, 1989), 224–244.

21. Ibid., 229.

22. L. Thompson, "Age Won't Kill You," *The Washington Post*, 9 July 1986, 13.

23. Patrick F. Sheehy, *Dying with Dignity* (New York: Pinnacle Books, 1981), 236.

24. John F. Kilner, *Who Lives? Who Dies? Ethical Criteria in Patient Selection* (New Haven, CN: Yale University Press, 1990).

25. David Hendin, *Death as a Fact of Life* (New York: W. W. Norton, 1974), 255.

27. "AIDS Cases Increase to 418,403 Worldwide," *Honolulu Advertiser*, 5 October 1991, B-1.

28. Terry R. Bard, *Medical Ethics in Practice* (New York: Hemisphere, 1990), 95.

29. Robert L. Risley, *Death with Dignity: A New Law Permitting Physician Aid-in-Dying* (Eugene, OR: Hemlock Society, 1989), 81–102.

30. E. R. Gamble, P. J. McDonald, and P. R. Lichstein, "Knowledge, Attitudes, and Behavior of Elderly Persons Regarding Living Wills," *Archive of Internal Medicine* 151 (Feb. 1991): 277–280.

31. E. Diamond, J. A. Jernigan, R. A. Moseley, V. Messina, and R. McKeown, "Decision-Making Ability and Advance Directive Preferences in Nursing Home Patients and Proxies," *The Gerontologist* 29 (1989): 622–626.

32. Pam Lambert, Joan McIver Gibson, and Paul Nathanson, "The Values History: An Innovation in Surrogate Medical Decision-Making," *Law, Medicine and Health Care* 18 (1990): 202–212.

33. Jay Katz, *The Silent World of Doctor and Patient* (New York: Free Press, 1984).

34. "How to Civilize Death," *World Press Review* (October 1991): 60.

Glossary

Advance directives (also known as *Advance medical directives*) Refers to a set of documents including a living will, a durable power of attorney, and a proxy statement (see below for individual definitions) instructing the physician to provide, continue, withhold, or withdraw life-sustaining procedures in the event of a terminal condition.

AIDS (acquired immune deficiency syndrome) A disease in which normal defense mechanisms against infections and cancer are reduced.

Alzheimer's disease A condition first identified in 1907 by a German physician named Alois Alzheimer. The disease usually appears after age sixty-five and results from brain atrophy. The cause is still unknown. The main symptoms are loss of memory (mostly recent memory), disorientation, and a deterioration in social habits.

Amyotrophic lateral sclerosis (ALS) A disease causing a deterioration of the spinal cord resulting in the wasting away of muscles. Also known as *Lou Gehrig's disease.*

Analgesic Pain-relieving drug.

Anoxia The absence of oxygen supply to the tissues.

Apnea The absence of the reflex of breathing, which leads to an inability to breathe spontaneously.

Artificial feeding The feeding of food and water by means of tubes inserted into the body (e.g., a nasogastric tube or a G-tube).

Autonomy (also see *principle of autonomy*) Independence; self-containment; self-government.

Barbiturate A type of sleeping pill.

Beneficence The quality of charity or kindness; a charitable act or gift. This term is often used by doctors in the phrase "principle of beneficence" when a treatment is weighed in terms of its beneficial outcome versus its burdensome effects.

Best interest This term is used in the context of right-to-die court decisions; it is a standard for making health care decisions based on what others believe to be "best" for a patient. It is sometimes referred to as an *objective standard* (for contrast, see *substitutive judgment,* below).

Biomedical ethics (also known as *bioethics*) The rules and standards governing the conduct of professionals involved in the medical care of individuals.

Biopsy The microscopic examination of a portion of body tissue that helps in the diagnosis of a disease. The tissue is usually removed by surgery or by insertion of a needle into the tissue to be examined.

Bone marrow test The introduction of a needle into the bone (usually a hipbone or the breastbone) in order to remove a sample of bone marrow for diagnostic purposes, such as the diagnosis of leukemia or certain types of anemia.

Brain death A condition in which there is a complete cessation of all electrical brain activity. A person is considered brain dead if he or she (1) is unresponsive to external stimuli including pain; (2) shows no spontaneous movements or breathing; (3) has no reflexes; and (4) has a flat EEG.

Cardiac arrest Stoppage of the heart.

Catheter A hollow tube inserted into various organs (e.g., the stomach, the intestines, or the bladder) to introduce or remove fluids or to perform certain measurements.

CAT scan (computerized axial tomography) A powerful, complex diagnostic X-ray approach that provides views of various organ systems in the body.

CCU (coronary care unit) A separate unit in the hospital for patients who have had or are suspected of having had heart attacks.

Chemotherapy Drug therapy against infection or malignancy aimed at destroying bacteria or cancer cells.

Coma A deep, prolonged state of unconsciousness.

Consent form A form signed by a patient to agree to participate in a given study or treatment. It is related to *informed consent* (see below). The form lists the risks and benefits of a given treatment proposal.

CPR (cardiopulmonary resuscitation) A method used to restore stopped breathing and/or heartbeat.

Defibrillator An electrical device used to restart the heart after it has stopped.

Dementia (also see *Alzheimer's disease*) A deterioration of a person's mental capacity due to changes in the brain.

Dialysis See *kidney dialysis.*

DNR orders (Do-not-resuscitate orders) Orders not to resuscitate the patient that are recorded in the medical chart by the physician. These orders reflect the patient's or the family's wishes for the patient not to be resuscitated in the hospital in case of cardiac arrest or sudden or imminent death.

Donee Any person authorized to accept gifts of bodies or body parts, such as a hospital, a surgeon or other physician, an accredited medical or dental school, or a bank or storage facility for organs and tissues.

Donor (organ donor) An individual who makes a gift of all or part of her or his body (organs or tissues).

DPA (durable power of attorney) A written document authorizing someone you name (your "agent" or "attorney-in-fact") to make decisions for the disposition of your assets and property. A DPA for health care is a document authorizing someone to make health care decisions for you if you are unable to speak for yourself. The document specifies the instructions and guidelines you want your agent to follow in making these decisions. It is one of several advance directives (along with the living will and the proxy).

EEG (electroencephalogram) A recording of the electrical currents produced by the brain.

EKG (electrocardiogram) A recording of electrical activity of the heart.

Ethic A principle of right or good conduct.

Ethical conflict Occurs when one or more ethical principles are incompatible, antagonistic, or contradictory in ethical decision making, for example, the doctor's duty to save life and the need to relieve the suffering of the dying.

Ethical principle A higher standard used to establish the correctness of a value judgment.

Ethics (used with a singular verb) (1) A body of ethical principles; a system of moral principles or values; (2) the study of the general nature of morals and of specific moral choices; (3) the rules or standards governing the conduct of the members of a profession.

Euthanasia, active   Active steps taken to end a life. You cannot legally be assisted by anyone to die, as this assistance would constitute assisting suicide, which is a felony. So far, only one country—the Netherlands, since 1984—has permitted doctors to help suffering patients speed up their end. Initiatives for aid in dying by a physician have been presented on the ballot in Washington State and California in 1991 and 1992.

Euthanasia, passive   The act of discontinuing all life-support measures, such as ventilators, kidney dialysis machines, tube-feeding, intravenous fluids, and antibiotics in cases of terminal illness.

G-tube   See *Gastrostomy*.

Gastrostomy   A small opening made through the abdomen so that a tube can be inserted into the stomach. A gastrostomy tube (also known as a *G-tube*) is used instead of a nasogastric tube in long-term artificial feeding.

Guardian ad litem   Someone who is appointed by the court to protect the interests of a ward in a legal proceeding.

Hospice   An institution or home care, where symptomatic treatment is given to people with terminal illness. Hospice programs often emphasize home care or treatment in a hospital setting.

ICU (intensive care unit)   Unit in a hospital where seriously ill or postoperative patients receive intensive care.

Incompetent   Describes patients who are unable to make decisions because (1) they are no longer able to understand information about their medical condition and its implications, or (2) they are able to understand but are unable to communicate their decisions. A patient's ability to understand other unrelated concepts is not relevant.

Informed consent   The common-law doctrine of informed consent states that, before accepting medical treatment and any touching of one's body, one must be given information about the proposed treatment and touching.

Informed refusal   The process by which a patient, having been fully informed about the risks and benefits of a given management proposal, decides not to receive the proposed treatment or procedure.

Intravenous (IV) therapy   A method of providing food, water, and/or medication through a tube placed in a vein, when patients can no longer eat or drink normally.

Irreversible coma   A term sometimes used as a synonym for *persistent vegetative state, brain death,* or *locked-in state* (conscious without movement). Although a person who is without brain function and is maintained on a respirator may still appear to be in a deep sleep, by medical criteria such a person may not be regarded as in a coma or other living state.

Kidney dialysis   A treatment for kidney failure that consists of removing the toxic substances from the blood.

Leukemia   Cancer of the white blood cells, which multiply abnormally and interfere with red cell formation.

Life-sustaining procedure   Any medical procedure or intervention that will serve only to prolong dying. In some states, the definition includes the provision of fluids, nourishment, and medication (such as antibiotics).

Living will   Also referred to as an *advance directive* or *declaration.* This is a document, executed while the person is able to make health care decisions, that expresses the person's wishes and preferences about certain types of medical treatment in the event of a terminal illness or injury. It instructs the physician to provide, withhold, or withdraw life-sustaining treatments in the event of a terminal condition. It applies especially when the person is incompetent, that is, unable to make decisions about medical treatment. Its validity and interpretation, however, vary from state to state.

Living-will legislation   Legislation also called *natural-death, death-with-dignity,* and *right-to-die legislation.* This legislation applies to statutes providing for patients to execute advance directives about health care decisions.

Maleficence   The characteristic of being harmful, hurtful, or evil. In contrast to beneficence, it implies that a given treatment may have burdensome effects that outweigh its beneficial effects.

Mercy killing.   Killing another person without her or his consent, usually by strangulation or shooting. It is definitely not endorsed by proponents of euthanasia, which refers to the injection of a lethal drug only with the patient's consent.

Metastasis   The spreading of cancer cells from their original site to other parts of the body.

Nasogastric tube   A pliable tube inserted through the nose and guided into the stomach, so that food or liquid can be given through the other end of the tube.

Oncologist   A physician who specializes in the treatment of tumors and cancer.

Palliative care   A treatment that relieves symptoms rather than cures the disease. The term is used in conjunction with hospice care, which provides the patient with physical, emotional, and spiritual care.

Persistent vegetative state (or *persistent noncognitive state*)   This term describes various states resulting from damage to the higher brain or the midbrain. Patients in this condition are often described as awake but not aware: they often can breathe, chew, swallow, and even groan but show no signs of consciousness, perception, cognition, or other higher brain functions.

Principle of autonomy   Our moral right to decide what we wish to do with our lives; includes the right to refuse treatment.

Principle of proportionality   In applying this principle, doctors must take into account not only the benefits the patient may derive from treatment but also the patient's personal values, religious convictions, and ability to cope with the treatment psychologically.

Principle of self-determination   A fundamental legal right to determine what shall be done to one's own body. It sets the standards of informed consent for medical procedures.

Prognosis   Prediction of the future course of a disease or illness based on previous scientific studies. It is only a prediction and should not be accepted as fact.

Proxy   A method by which one can designate someone else to make medical decisions on one's behalf if one is unable to make these decisions. The designation can be made in a living will (in some states) or it can be made on a separate form (in other states). See Appendix A.

Respirator (or *ventilator*)   Machines used to keep patients breathing when they are unable to breathe spontaneously.

Right to privacy   The right to be let alone, recognized by the U.S. Supreme Court. This right is not conferred directly by the U.S. Constitution, but the Supreme Court has interpreted the First, Fourth, and Fifth Amendments of the Bill of Rights as creating this right.

Self-determination   A principle that states that all individuals are masters of their own bodies and, if of sound mind, have the right to decide what shall be done with their bodies and what medical treatment to authorize or refuse.

State interests A term applied in right-to-die decisions, in which the state opposes the right to refuse life-sustaining treatment, based on four interests of the state: (1) the preservation of life; (2) the prevention of suicide (this is usually irrelevant, as the removal of life support results in death due to natural causes and not due to the patient's intention or actions); (3) the protection of innocent third parties; and (4) the safeguarding of the integrity of the medical profession.

Substitutive judgment A doctrine that permits another person to make a choice for the patient when the patient is unable to make a choice. The decision maker must stand "in the patient's shoes" and make the same decision that the patient would have made in similar circumstances. Decision makers are not allowed to make decisions according to their own thinking about what is best for the patient but must make decisions based on what they think the patient would have chosen. This is sometimes referred to as a *subjective standard.*

Terminal illness (also *terminal condition*) Any incurable or irreversible disease, illness, injury, or condition that, without life-sustaining procedures, would result in death in a relatively short time. The term is sometimes used in a legal sense, but the courts have not defined the term. Most living-will statutes do refer to terminal illness or conditions, but definitions vary widely by state. Some courts focus on the patient's life expectancy, and others on the possibility that the patient may return to a cognitive life. Specific statutes should be consulted for local definitions. From the medical viewpoint, hospices sometimes refer to terminal illness when death is expected within a period of six months. The U.S. Uniform Rights of the Terminally Ill Act defines a terminal condition as "an incurable or irreversible condition that, without the administration of life-sustaining treatment, will, in the opinion of the attending physician, result in death within a relatively short time."

Thanatology The study of death and dying.

Tracheotomy An operation in which an opening is made in the windpipe.

Transplantation The process of implanting a donor organ in the body of recipient.

Uniform Anatomical Gift Act Legislation, revised in 1990, now enacted in all fifty states, which makes provision for donor cards, pledging the donation of organs or tissues upon death.

Uniform Rights of the Terminally Ill Act   A new act amended by the National Conference of Commissioners on Uniform State Laws since the 1985 version of the act. The new act combines the three basic statutory provisions preserving the rights of dying patients by authorizing the refusal of life-sustaining treatment by means of surrogate decision-making provisions, namely, a living will, a health care agent, or a durable power of attorney.

Ventilator   Another term for a respirator.

Appendixes

APPENDIX A

State Law Governing Living Wills/Declarations and
Appointment of a Health Care Agent

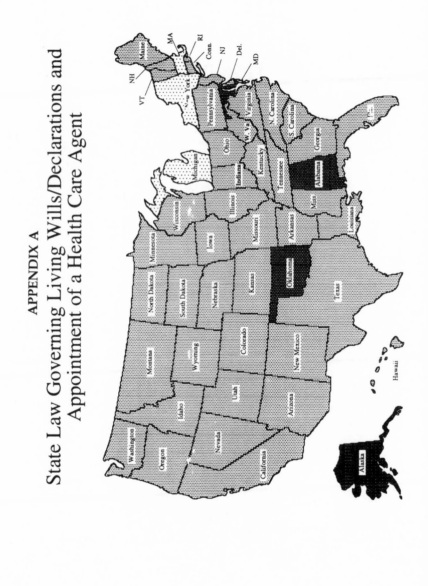

Appropriate documents for each state are available from Choice In Dying.

Jurisdictions with legislation that authorizes both living wills/declarations and the appointment of a health care agent (**the District of Columbia and 43 states: Arizona, Arkansas, California, Colorado, Connecticut, Delaware, Florida, Georgia, Hawaii, Idaho, Illinois, Indiana, Iowa, Kansas, Kentucky, Louisiana, Maine, Minnesota, Mississippi, Missouri, Montana, Nebraska, Nevada, New Hampshire, New Jersey, New Mexico, North Carolina, North Dakota, Ohio, Oregon, Pennsylvania, Rhode Island, South Carolina, South Dakota, Tennessee, Texas, Utah, Vermont, Virginia, Washington, West Virginia, Wisconsin and Wyoming).**

States with legislation that authorizes only living wills/declarations (**4 states: Alabama, Alaska, Maryland and Oklahoma.**)

States with legislation that authorizes only the appointment of a health care agent (**3 states: Massachusetts, Michigan and New York**).

Note: The specifics of living will and health care agent legislation vary greatly from state to state. In addition, many states also have court-made law that affects residents' rights. For information about specific state laws, please contact Choice In Dying.

Reprinted by permission of Choice In Dying (fomerly Concern for Dying/Society for the Right to Die), 200 Varick Street, New York, NY 10014.

APPENDIX B

ADVANCE DIRECTIVE
Living Will and Health Care Proxy

D *eath is a part of life. It is a reality like birth, growth and aging. I am using this advance directive to convey my wishes about medical care to my doctors and other people looking after me at the end of my life. It is called an advance directive because it gives instructions in advance about what I want to happen to me in the future. It expresses my wishes about medical treatment that might keep me alive. I want this to be legally binding.*

If I cannot make or communicate decisions about my medical care, those around me should rely on this document for instructions about measures that could keep me alive.

I do not want medical treatment (including feeding and water by tube) that will keep me alive if:

- I am unconscious and there is no reasonable prospect that I will ever be conscious again (even if I am not going to die soon in my medical condition), or
- I am near death from an illness or injury with no reasonable prospect of recovery.

I do want medicine and other care to make me more comfortable and to take care of pain and suffering. I want this even if the pain medicine makes me die sooner.

I want to give some extra instructions: [*Here list any special instructions, e.g., some people fear being kept alive after a debilitating stroke. If you have wishes about this, or any other conditions, please write them here.*]

The legal language in the box that follows is a health care proxy.
It gives another person the power to make medical decisions for me.

I name _____ , who lives at

_____ , phone number _____ ,

to make medical decisions for me if I cannot make them myself. This person is called a health care "surrogate," "agent," "proxy," or "attorney in fact." This power of attorney shall become effective when I become incapable of making or communicating decisions about my medical care. This means that this document stays legal when and if I lose the power to speak for myself, for instance, if I am in a coma or have Alzheimer's disease.

My health care proxy has power to tell others what my advance directive means. This person also has power to make decisions for me, based either on what I would have wanted, or, if this is not known, on what he or she thinks is best for me.

If my first choice health care proxy cannot or decides not to act for me, I name _____

_____ , address _____ ,

_____ , as my second choice.

phone number _____ .

APPENDIX B (continued)

I have discussed my wishes with my health care proxy, and with my second choice if I have chosen to appoint a second person. My proxy(ies) has(have) agreed to act for me.

I have thought about this advance directive carefully. I know what it means and want to sign it. I have chosen two witnesses, neither of whom is a member of my family, nor will inherit from me when I die. My witnesses are not the same people as those I named as my health care proxies. I understand that this form should be notarized if I use the box to name (a) health care proxy(ies).

Signature _____

Date _____

Address _____

Witness' signature _____

Witness' printed name _____

Address _____

Witness' signature _____

Witness' printed name _____

Address _____

Notary [to be used if proxy is appointed] _____

Drafted and distributed by Choice In Dying, Inc.—the national council for the right to die. Choice In Dying is a national not-for-profit organization which works for the rights of patients at the end of life. In addition to this generic advance directive, Choice In Dying distributes advance directives that conform to each state's specific legal requirements and maintains a national Living Will Registry for completed documents.

Reprinted by permission.

APPENDIX C

Information About the Health Care Proxy

This is an important legal document. Before signing this document, it is vital for you to understand the following facts:

This document gives the person you name as your agent the authority to make all health care decision for you, except to the extent you indicate otherwise in this document. "Health care" includes any treatment, service, or procedure to diagnose or treat your physical or mental condition. Unless you say otherwise, your agent will have the authority to make all health care decisions for you, including decisions about withdrawing or withholding life sustaining treatment. Unless your agent knows your wishes about artificial nutrition and hydration, he or she will not be allowed to refuse those measures on your behalf. Your agent's authority will begin when physicians determine that you lack the capacity to make health care decisions.

You may specify in this document any treatment that you do not desire and/or those that you want to make sure you receive. Your agent will be obligated to follow your instructions when making decisions for you.

Examples of medical treatments about which you may wish to give your agent special instructions are listed below. This is not a

your agent or as your attending physician; the law does not permit a physician to do both at the same time. Also, if you are a patient or resident of a hospital, nursing home or mental hygiene facility, there are special restrictions about appointing someone who works for that facility as your agent. You should ask personnel at the facility to explain those restrictions.

You should inform the person you appoint that he or she will be your health care agent. You should discuss your health care wishes with your agent and give him or her a signed copy. Your agent will not be liable for health care decisions made in good faith.

Even after you have signed this document, you have the right to make health care decisions for yourself as long as you are able to do so, and treatment cannot be given to you or stopped over your objection. You have the right to revoke the authority granted to your agent by informing him or her or your health care provider orally or in writing.

Instructions for Completing the Health Care Proxy

Item (1): Insert your name (i.e., the name of person who is appointing a health care complete list of the treatments about which you may leave instructions.

- artificial respiration
- artificial nutrition and hydration (nourishment and water provided by feeding tube)
- cardiopulmonary resuscitation (CPR)
- antipsychotic medication
- electroconvulsive therapy
- antibiotics
- psychosurgery
- dialysis
- transplantation
- blood transfusions
- abortion
- sterilization

It is important that you discuss this document with a physician or another health care professional before you sign it to make sure that you understand the types of decisions that may be made for you. You may also wish to give your physician a signed copy. You do not need a lawyer's assistance to complete this document.

The person you appoint as agent must be over eighteen years old, the parent of a child, or married. If you appoint a physician as your agent, he or she may have to choose between acting as

agent) and the name, home address and telephone number of the agent.

Item (2): If you have special instructions for your agent, you should write them here. Also, if you wish to limit your agent's authority in any way, you should say so here. If you do not state any limitation, your agent will have authority to make all health care decisions that you could have made, including the authority to consent to or refuse life-sustaining treatment.

Item (3): You may, if you wish, insert the name, home address and telephone number of an alternate agent.

Item (4): The proxy will remain in effect indefinitely unless you specify an expiration date or condition for its expiration. This section is optional and should be filled in only if you want the proxy to expire.

Item (5): You must date and sign the proxy. If you are unable to sign yourself, you may direct someone else to sign in your presence. Be sure to include your address.

Item (6): Two persons 18 years of age or older must sign your proxy as witnesses. The person who is appointed agent or alternate agent cannot sign as a witness.

APPENDIX C (*continued*)
Health Care Proxy

(1) I, _____

hereby appoint (name, home address, and telephone number), as my health care agent to make any and all health care decisions for me, except to the extent I state otherwise.

This health care proxy shall take effect in the event I become unable to make my own health care decisions.

(2) NOTE: Although not necessary, and neither encouraged nor discouraged, you may wish to state instructions or wishes, and limit your agent's authority. Unless your agent knows your wishes about artificial nutrition and hydration, your agent will not have authority to decide about artificial nutrition and hydration.

If you choose to state instructions, wishes, or limitations, please do so below (attach additional pages if more space is needed):

_____
_____
_____
_____
_____
_____

I direct my agent to make health care decisions in accordance with my wishes and instructions as stated above or as otherwise known to him or her. I also direct my agent to abide by any limitations on his or her authority as stated above or as otherwise known to him or her.

(3) In the event the person I appoint above is unable, unwilling or unavailable to act as my health care agent, I hereby appoint (name, home address and telephone of alternate agent)

_____
_____

(4) I understand that, unless I revoke it, this proxy will remain in effect indefinitely or until the date or occurrence of the condition I have stated below. (Please complete the following if you do not want this health care proxy to be in effect indefinitely):

This proxy shall expire: (specify the date or condition)

_____

_____

_____

(5) Signature: _____

      Address: _____

      Date: _____

(6) I declare that the person who signed or asked another to sign this document is personally known to me and appears to be of sound mind and acting willingly and free from duress. He or she signed (or asked another to sign for him or her) this document in my presence and that person signed in my presence. I am not the person appointed as agent by this document.

Witness: _____

Address: _____

Witness: _____

Address: _____

From *Medical Ethics Advisor* 6(8):100–101, 1990.
Reprinted by permission.

The Hippocratic Oath

I swear by Apollo Physician and Asclepius and Hygeia and Pana-cea and all the gods and goddesses, making them my witness, that I will fulfill according to my ability and judgment this oath and this covenant:

To hold him who has taught me this art as equal to my parents and to live my life in partnership with him, and if he is in need of money to give him a share of mine, and to regard his offspring as equal to my brothers in male lineage and to teach them this art—if they desire to learn it—without fee and covenant; to give a share of precepts and oral instruction and all the other learning to my sons and to the sons of him who has instructed me and to pupils who have signed the cove-nant and have taken an oath according to the medical law, but to no one else.

I will apply dietetic measures for the benefit of the sick according to my ability and judgment; I will keep them from harm and injustice.

I will neither give a deadly drug to anybody if asked for it, nor will I make a suggestion to this effect. Similarly I will not give to a woman an abortive remedy. In purity and holiness I will guard my life and my art.

I will not use the knife, not even on sufferers from stone, but will withdraw in favor of such men as are engaged in this work.

Whatever house I may visit, I will come for the benefit of the sick, remaining free of all intentional injustice, of all mischief and in particular sexual relations with both female and male persons, be they free or slaves.

Whatever I may see or hear in the course of treatment in regard to the life of men, which on no account one must spread abroad, I will keep to myself holding such things shameful to be spoken about.

If I fulfill this oath and do not violate it, may it be granted to me to enjoy life and art, being honored with fame among all men for all time to come; if I transgress it and swear falsely, may the opposite of all this be my lot.*

* L. Edelstein, "The Hippocratic Oath: Text, Translation and Interpretation." *Ancient Medicine*, edited by O. Temkin and C. Lillian Temkin (Baltimore: Johns Hopkins University Press, 1967), 3–63. Copyright 1967 Johns Hopkins University Press. Reprinted by permission.

The Death with Dignity Act and What It Does

- Permits a competent terminally ill adult the right to request and receive physician aid-in-dying under carefully defined circumstances.
- Protects physicians from liability in carrying out a patient's request.
- Combines the concepts of Natural Death Acts and Durable Power of Attorney for Health Care laws, and makes them more usable.
- Permits a patient to appoint an attorney-in-fact to make health care decisions, including withholding and withdrawing life-support systems, and can empower the attorney-in-fact to decide about requesting aid-in-dying if the patient becomes incompetent.
- Requires decision of the attorney-in-fact to be reviewed by a hospital ethics or other committee before the decision is acted upon by the physician.
- To take advantage of the law, a competent adult person must sign a Death with Dignity (DA) directive.
- Permits revocation of a directive at any time by any means.
- Requires hospitals and other health-care facilities to keep records and report to the Department of Health Services after the death of the patient and then anonymously.
- Permits a treating physician to order a psychiatric consultation, with the patient's consent, if there is any question about the patient's competence to make the request for aid-in-dying.
- Forbids aid-in-dying to any patient solely because he/she is a burden to anyone, or because the patient is incompetent or terminal and has not made out an informed and proper (DDA) directive.
- Forbids aiding, abetting, and encouraging a suicide which remains a crime under the Act.
- Does not permit aid-in-dying to be administered by a loved one, family member, or stranger.

- Forbids aid-in-dying for children, incompetents, or anyone who has not voluntarily and intentionally completed and signed the properly witnessed (DDA) directive.
- Attempts to keep the decision-making process with the patient and health-care provider, and out of court.
- Makes special protective provisions for patients in skilled nursing facilities.
- Provides for amendment by a two-thirds vote of the legislature and signature of the Governor.
- Permits doctors, nurses, and privately owned hospitals the right to decline a dying patient's request for aid-in-dying if they are morally or ethically opposed to such action.

Prepared by Robert L. Risley, author of the Death with Dignity Act, formerly the Humane and Dignified Death Act Initiative, and president of Americans against Human Suffering. Reprinted by permission of the National Hemlock Society.

Directory of Organizations

RIGHT TO DIE ORGANIZATIONS

In Canada

Dying with Dignity (East)
175 St. Clair Ave.
W. Toronto, ON M4V 1P7, Canada
Tel. (416) 921-2329

Dying with Dignity (West)
865 W. 10th St., Ste. 7
Vancouver, BC V5Z 1L1 Canada
Tel. (604) 873-5696

In The Netherlands

Nederlandse Veregniging Voor Vrijwillige Euthanasie
(Dutch Voluntary Euthanasia Society)
Postbus 5331, 1007 AH
Amsterdam, The Netherlands
Tel. 020-793561

In the United Kingdom

Voluntary Euthanasia Society (formerly EXIT)
13 Prince of Wales Terrace
London W8 5PG, England
Tel. 01-937-7770

In the United States

Choice In Dying, Inc. (formerly Society for the Right to Die)
200 Varick St.
New York, NY 10014
Tel. (212) 366-5540

The Hemlock Society
P.O. Box 11830
Eugene, OR 97440
Tel. (503) 342-5748

Americans against Human Suffering (AAHS)
P.O. Box 11001
Glendale, CA 91226
Tel. (818) 240-1986

RIGHT-TO-LIFE ORGANIZATIONS

Alliance for Life
B1-90 Garry St.
Winnipeg, MB R3C 4H1, Canada
Tel. (204) 942-4772

National Right to Life Committee
419 Seventh St. N.W., Ste. 402
Washington, DC 20004
Tel. (202) 942-4772

ORGAN DONATION ORGANIZATIONS

Division of Organ Transplantation
Bureau of Health Resources Development
Health Resources & Services Administration
5600 Fishers Lane, Room 11A-22
Rockville, MD 20857
Tel. (301) 443-7577

Living Bank
Box 6725
Houston, TX 77265
Tel. (713) 528-2971 or toll-free (800) 528-2971

Organ Donors Canada
5326 Ada Blvd.
Edmonton, AB T5W 4N7, Canada
Tel. (403) 474-9363

British Organ Donation Society
Balsham
Cambridge, England CB1 6DL
Tel. 02 23893636

United Network for Organ Sharing (UNOS)
P.O. Box 13770
Richmond, VA 23225
Tel. (800) 243-6667

Donor Criteria Chart

Organs	Age	Brain death by	Contraindications	Tissue	Age	Cause of death	Contraindications
Kidneys/ pancreas	6–60 years	Acute neurological or neurosurgical trauma	Sepsis	Bone	15–65 years	Brain death or cardiac death	Same as organs, plus: No tissue radiation No chronic steroid therapy
		Intracranial hemorrhage	Death of unknown etiology	Eye	2–70 years		Same as organs, plus: No viral encephalitis No Creutzfelt–Jakob disease No rabies Note: Extracranial malignancy acceptable
		Gunshot wound to the head Primary brain tumor Metabolic disorder	Transmissible disease IV drug use Extracranial malignancy	Heart valves	3 months– 55 years		Same as organs
Heart	Term newborn– 45 years	Cerebral anoxia (e.g., drowning, smoke inhalation)					
Lung Liver	12–55 years Term newborn– 55 years						

Reprinted by permission of the Organ Donor Center of Hawaii.

APPENDIX H

State Law Governing
Surrogate or Family Decisionmaking
For Patients Without Advance Directives

June 23, 1992

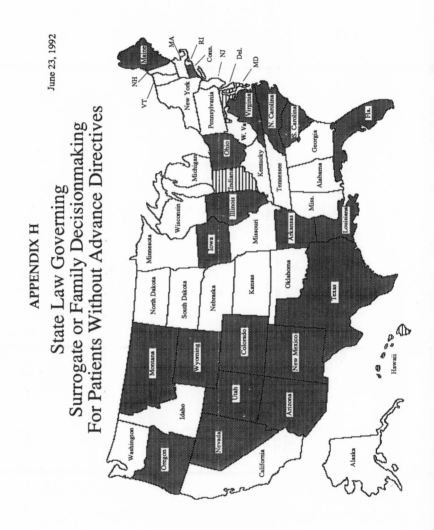

■ Jurisdictions with statutes that authorize surrogate decisionmaking on behalf of incapacitated patients who do not have advance directives (the District of Columbia and 20 states: Arizona, Arkansas**, Colorado, Connecticut, Florida, Illinois**, Iowa, Louisiana**, Maine, Montana, Nevada, New Mexico**, North Carolina, Ohio, Oregon, South Carolina, Texas**, Utah, Virginia and Wyoming).

▤ States with statutes interpreted by Attorney General Opinions or court decisions to authorize surrogate decisionmaking (3 states: Hawaii, Indiana* and Maryland*).

☐ States with no statutes governing surrogate decisionmaking (27 states: Alabama, Alaska, California, Delaware, Georgia, Idaho, Kansas, Kentucky, Massachusetts, Michigan, Minnesota, Mississippi, Missouri, Nebraska, New Hampshire, New Jersey, New York, North Dakota, Oklahoma, Pennsylvania, Rhode Island, South Dakota, Tennessee, Vermont, Washington, West Virginia and Wisconsin).

* The surrogacy laws in these states may not allow for the withdrawal of artificial nutrition and hydration.

** The surrogacy laws in these states allow for medical decisions to be made on behalf of a minor.

Reprinted by permission of Choice In Dying.

Suggested Reading

GENERAL INTEREST

P. Ariés, *Western Attitudes toward Death: From the Middle Ages to the Present.* (Baltimore: Johns Hopkins University Press, 1974).

A. Stedeford, *Facing Death: Patients, Families, and Professionals.* (London: William Heinemann Medical Books, 1984).

Norman Cousins, *Head First: The Biology of Hope.* (New York: E. P. Dutton, 1989).

David Sobel, *The People's Book of Medical Tests.* (New York: Summit Books, 1985).

Hannelore Wass, Felix M. Barardo, and Robert A. Neimeyer. *Dying: Facing the Facts,* 2nd ed. (Bristol: Hemisphere, 1991).

PHILOSOPHY OF DEATH AND DYING

Victor Frankl, *Man's Search for Meaning.* (New York: Pocket Books, 1980).

Robert Kastenbaum, *The Psychology of Death.* (New York: Springer, 1976).

Elisabeth Kübler-Ross, *Death: The Final Stage of Growth.* (Englewood Cliffs, NJ: Prentice-Hall, 1975).

H. S. Kushner, *When Bad Things Happen to Good People.* (New York: Schocken Books, 1981).

R. Lonetto and D. I. Templer, *Death Anxiety.* (Bristol: Hemisphere, 1986).

Arnold Toynbee et al., *Man's Concern with Death.* (London: Hodder & Stoughton, 1968).

Avery D. Weisman, *The Coping Capacity: On the Nature of Being Mortal.* (New York: Human Sciences Press, 1984).

RELIGIOUS VIEWPOINT ON EUTHANASIA AND PROLONGING LIFE

Catholic Tradition

D. McCarthy and A. Maraczewski, eds., *Moral Responsibility in Prolonging Life*. (St. Louis: Pope John XXIII Center, 1981).
C. J. McFadden, *Medical Ethics*. (Philadelphia: Davis, 1967).

Jewish Tradition

D. Gribetz and M. Tendler, ed., "Medical Ethics: The Jewish Point of View." *Mt. Sinai Journal of Medicine 51 (1984): 1.*
F. Rosner and B. Bleich, *Jewish Bioethics*. (New York: Sanhedrin Press, 1979).

Religions and Euthanasia

Gerald A. Larue, *Euthanasia and Religion*. (Los Angeles: Hemlock Society, 1985).

ETHICAL PROBLEMS IN TERMINAL ILLNESS

Lesley F. Degner and Janet I. Beaton, *Life-Death Decisions in Health Care*. (Washington, DC: Hemisphere, 1987).
Al Jonsen et al., *Clinical Ethics: A Practical Approach to Ethical Decisions in Clinical Medicine*. (New York: MacMillan, 1986).
Shannon M. Jordan, *Decision Making for Incompetent Persons: The Law and Morality of Who Shall Decide*. (Springfield, IL: Charles C. Thomas, 1985).
Ruth Macklin, *Mortal Choices*. (New York: Pantheon Books, 1987).
Society for the Right to Die, *The Physician and the Hopelessly Ill Patient: Legal, Medical and Ethical Guidelines*. (New York: Author, 1985).
Robert M. Veatch, *Death, Dying and the Biological Revolution: Our Last Quest for Responsibility*. (New Haven, CT: Yale University Press, 1989).

CARE OF TERMINAL ILLNESS

Deborah Duda, *A Guide to Dying at Home.* (Santa Fe: John Muir, 1982).

Deborah Whiting Little, *Home Care for the Dying: A Reassuring Comprehensive Guide to Physical and Emotional Care.* (New York: Dial Press, Doubleday, 1985).

Ernest Rosenbaum and Isadora R. Rosenbaum, *A Comprehensive Guide for Cancer Patients and Their Families.* (Palo Alto, CA: Bull, 1980).

Cicely M. Saunders, ed., *The Management of Terminal Disease,* 2nd ed. (London: Edward Arnold, 1984).

Bernie Siegel, *Love, Medicine and Miracles.* (New York: Harper & Row, 1986).

Richard Turnbull, ed., *Terminal Care.* (Washington, DC.: Hemisphere, 1986).

Harry van Bommel, *Choices: For People Who Have a Terminal Illness, Their Families and Their Caregivers,* 2nd rev. ed. (Toronto: NC Press, 1987).

CHOOSING TO FORGO
LIFE-SUSTAINING TREATMENTS

Hastings Center, *Guidelines on the Termination of Life-Sustaining Treatment and the Care of the Dying.* (Briarcliff Manor, NY: Author, 1987).

Joanne Lynn, ed., *By No Extraordinary Means: The Choice to Forgo Life-Sustaining Food and Water.* Medical Ethics Series. (Bloomington: Indiana University Press, 1989).

President's Commission for the Sutdy of Ethical Problems in Medicine and Biomedical and Behavioral Research, *Deciding to Forgo Life-Sustaining Treatment.* (Washington, DC: U.S. Government Printing Office, 1983).

HOSPICE CARE

Robert W. Buckingham, *The Complete Hospice Guide.* (New York: Harper & Row, 1983).

Paul M. DuBois, *The Hospice Way of Death.* (New York: Human Sciences Press, 1980).

Sandol Stoddard, *The Hospice Movement: A Better Way of Caring for the Dying.* (New York: Vintage Books, 1978).

J. M. Zimmerman, *Hospice: Complete Care for the Terminally Ill.* (Baltimore: Urban & Schwarzenburg, 1981).

RIGHT TO DIE AND EUTHANASIA

Arthur S. Berger and Joyce Berger, eds., *To Die or Not to Die: Cross-Disciplinary, Cultural and Legal Perspectives on the Right to Choose Death,* 1st ed. (New York: Praeger, 1990).

Derek Humphry, *Euthanasia.* (Eugene, OR: Hemlock Society, 1991).

Derek Humphry, *Final Exit.* (Eugene, OR: Hemlock Society, 1991).

D. Humphry and A. Wickett, *The Right to Die: Understanding Euthanasia* (New York: Harper & Row, 1986).

Society for the Right to Die, "The Right to Die . . . The Choice Is Yours." 14-minute video. Available from Choice in Dying, Inc. (See Appendix H.)

David D. Thomasma and Glenn C. Graber, *Euthanasia: Toward an Ethical Social Policy.* (New York: Continuum, 1990).

PAIN CONTROL

Bruce Smoller and Brian Schulman, *Pain Control: The Bethesda Program.* (New York: Doubleday, 1982).

Wen-Hsien Wu, ed., *Pain Management: Assessment and Treatment of Chronic and Acute Symptoms.* (New York: Human Sciences Press, 1985).

PERSONAL STORIES

Simone de Beauvoir, *A Very Easy Death.* (Harmondsworth, UK: Penguin Books, 1969).

Arnold R. Beisser, *A Graceful Passage: Notes on the Freedom to Live or Die.* (New York: Doubleday, 1990).

Betty Rollin, *Last Wish.* (New York: Signet, 1985).

Philip Roth, *Patrimony: A True Story.* (New York: Simon & Shuster, 1991).

Martha Weinman-Lear, *Heartsounds.* (New York: Pocket Books, 1980).

TALKING WITH FAMILIES AND FRIENDS

David Carroll, *Living with Dying*. (New York: McGraw-Hill, 1985).
W. Winslade and R. Ross, *Choosing Life or Death: A Guide for Patients, Families, and Professionals*. (New York: Free Press, 1986).

ORGAN DONATION AND TRANSPLANTATION

James Shanteau and R. J. Harris, eds., *Organ Donation and Transplantation: Psychological and Behavioral Factors*. (Washington, DC: American Psychological Association, 1990).
Task Force on Organ Transplantation, *Organ Transplantation: Issues and Recommendations*. (Washington, DC: U.S. Department of Health and Human Services, 1986).

LEGISLATION

Law Reform Commission of Canada, *Report on Euthanasia, Aiding Suicide and Cessation of Treatment*. (Ottawa: Ministry of Supply and Services, 1983).
Robert L. Risley, *Death with Dignity: A New Law Permitting Physician Aid-In-Dying*. (Eugene, OR: Hemlock Society, 1989).
John A. Robertson, *The Rights of the Critically Ill*. (New York: Bantam, 1983).

Index